THE NATIONAL CURRICULUM OUTDOORS

YEAR 5

A complete scheme of work

Deborah Lambert,
Michelle Roberts and Sue Waite

BLOOMSBURY

BLOOMSBURY EDUCATION

Bloomsbury Publishing Plc

50 Bedford Square, London, WC1B 3DP, UK

BLOOMSBURY, BLOOMSBURY EDUCATION and the Diana logo are trademarks of
Bloomsbury Publishing Plc

First published in Great Britain, 2020 by Bloomsbury Publishing Plc

A catalogue record for this book is available from the British Library

ISBN: PB: 978-1-4729-7621-5; ePDF 978-1-4729-8438-8

2 4 6 8 10 9 7 5 3 1

Printed and bound in the UK by Ashford Colour Press

Dedication

We dedicate this book to all teachers who are willing to take their teaching outside the classroom
and offer exciting learning opportunities, foster positive health and wellbeing outcomes and connect
children with their natural environment. They are our hope for an education for excellence
and sustainability.

We also dedicate it to Deborah's mum Jennifer Lilley for her support and guidance, her brother
Jason Lilley for his shared passion for Art and her partner; Andy Rimmer for his patience and support
throughout the writing process; to Michelle's partner Andy Mitchell for his continued support and
excellent photographs and to her nephew and niece Robbie and Alice, who have inspired many of
the KS2 ideas, alongside Coads Green Primary School; and to Sue's family,
fellow committed nature and learning lovers.

Contents

Photos and further resources

Illustrative photos and further resources are available online at
www.bloomsbury.com/NC-Outdoors.

Acknowledgements

This book has been inspired by the children who have shown us their wonder and excitement at discovering and learning in the outdoors. We would like to acknowledge the many writers and organisations that have shared ideas to promote experiential activities for children, and the policymakers that are making changes that support this movement.

Michelle and Deborah were encouraged to write this book having worked for the last five years on the development and delivery of the Wild Tribe outdoor learning programme. This is an outdoor learning programme developed in South East Cornwall and is now part of The West Country Schools Trust, with the intention of engaging teachers and children in learning through the outdoors. Through this programme, more than 250 teachers have now been trained in outdoor learning, with many thousands of children now receiving outdoor learning on a weekly basis. This programme is being extended nationally in partnership with other schools across the country. Wild Tribe was a pivotal partner in the Natural Connections Demonstration project, and we are grateful to Natural England, the Department for the Environment, Food and Rural Affairs, and Historic England for funding that project. Sue led Natural Connections, working with over 125 schools across the South West to embed curricular learning in local natural environments. Learning from the project has influenced the development of the 'nature friendly schools' initiative, part of DEFRA's 25-year plan (DEFRA, 2018).

We are especially indebted to Kayleigh Halifax from the West Country Schools Trust for providing some inspirational ideas for the KS2 music chapter.

Foreword

As adults, when we reflect upon our education and the value of what we learned during our years at school, a variety of memories and associated emotions surface. We tend to recall with more clarity the outdoor experiences we had compared with our time inside. This may have been school trips, residentials or what our playtimes were like. The practical subjects, such as woodwork, home economics and art, and what you learned in these classes have probably stuck in your mind more than which aspect of maths you were working on in January of Year 5.

Thus, integrating practical, creative and outdoor experiences into our ordinary, everyday school lives is a route to profoundly changing children's memories and perceptions of the learning that happens. The evidence is growing year on year for the benefits of learning and playing outside, particularly when this happens in a natural space. It is no longer simply a 'jolly good thing' to do. There is a fundamental shift happening in education as we recognise that our mainstream schools need to be more responsive to children and the complex world in which they live. This is part of a wider understanding of how children learn and what they need in their lives to help them gain the emotional resilience and flexibility to adapt and cope with what life will throw at them.

One of the key challenges facing primary teachers is knowing what to teach outside and how. These books positively address both matters. The authors take a systematic approach that enables teachers to plan and deliver a series of lessons in many different subject areas. The lessons are designed to be undertaken in a range of different contexts, so you are not relying on a beautiful beach or perfect school grounds or to find a willing volunteer to dress up as a Roman soldier to ensure success.

The authors have incorporated the use of tools and techniques that deepen the learning beyond the core skills, knowledge and understanding within the National Curriculum. As part of the array of lessons presented, children are learning how to be outside, to take in what is happening and to develop a sensitivity and positive regard for the natural and built world in which we live.

This book is a timely and welcome addition to help primary teachers grow their confidence and competence to undertake great teaching – outdoors!

Juliet Robertson

Creative STAR learning (www.creativestarlearning.co.uk)

Why teach outdoors in Year 5?

Research has shown that from the Early Years Foundation Stage to Key Stage 1 (KS1) there is a marked decline in opportunities for children to learn outside the classroom (Waite, 2010). These opportunities are even further reduced when children enter Key Stage 2 (KS2) and yet children still value outdoor learning. By continuing outdoor teaching and learning, KS2 teachers can capitalise on earlier learning practice while gradually introducing more challenge. There is a wealth of research that shows how beneficial learning outside the classroom is for making knowledge, understanding and skills stick.

Embedding teaching outdoors into your practice

It is increasingly recognised that creative and challenging outdoor learning activities develop personal, social and thinking skills, communication, problem-solving and teamwork, breadth of understanding and an introduction to the essential knowledge that children need to develop into confident and responsible citizens who value and appreciate the natural environment around them.

But this raises questions such as: Should 'outdoor learning' be treated as a separate subject or can it rather be a valuable teaching method that enables teachers and children to meet National Curriculum requirements across different disciplines? Is it possible to integrate curriculum learning with an outdoor learning pedagogic approach that enables teachers and children to meet National Curriculum requirements through the medium of the outdoors? Structured outdoor activities linked to the curriculum provide a depth and relevance that can be difficult to achieve indoors. Ofsted recognises that well-informed teachers can plan outdoor learning programmes that enable pupils to take part in a range of exciting curriculum-linked activities that not only develop self-confidence and self-esteem, but also enable them to manage risk and contribute to developing spiritual, moral, social and cultural understanding. (See, for example, the 2018 Ofsted report for Holsworthy Primary School in Devon.)

Benefits

There has been a long history of children learning through playful engagement with the environment outside the classroom in the Foundation Stage (age three to five years), following in the footsteps of early childhood education pioneers such as Susan Isaacs, Margaret McMillan and Friedrich Froebel (Garrick, 2004). Evidence also points to hands-on experiential learning in natural environments contributing to other key learning factors (Waite et al., 2016), promoting improved creativity, engagement and understanding (Rowe and Humphries, 2012).

The need to continue promoting these fundamental learning building blocks does not suddenly cease at age five, or indeed at seven years of age; they underpin successful learning at any age. A 2019 study showed that children and young people, particularly those from lower socioeconomic backgrounds, would prefer to have more practical hands-on subject teaching in their schooling (Araneda, Guzmán and Nussbaum, 2019).

The pedagogies that encourage these building blocks require chances to grapple with questions that don't necessarily have one correct answer, better reflecting the complexity of the world that faces us all outside the classroom. Asking not just 'what' but 'how' and 'why' and 'what might be done about it' encourages critical thinking and problem-solving skills; while teamwork and collaboration acknowledge that others may think differently and that we need to be able to take diverse views and strengths into account.

The value of outdoor learning on children's health and wellbeing, as well as in stimulating their natural curiosity about the world, has been recognised by researchers (Wood et al., 2016; Morgan and Waite, 2017) and policy-makers here and abroad (DEFRA, 2018; Ho, 2014). As the Institute for Outdoor Learning (2018) states:

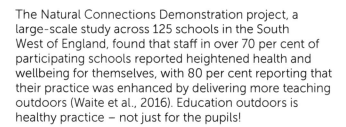

At a time when we are increasingly concerned about the physical and emotional wellbeing of our children and young people, and question whether they will leave education with the skills and competencies they will need for the future, outdoor learning brings with it a range of benefits which are now widely evidenced, acknowledged and accepted.

The Natural Connections Demonstration project, a large-scale study across 125 schools in the South West of England, found that staff in over 70 per cent of participating schools reported heightened health and wellbeing for themselves, with 80 per cent reporting that their practice was enhanced by delivering more teaching outdoors (Waite et al., 2016). Education outdoors is healthy practice – not just for the pupils!

Moreover, Public Health England has recommended green exercise and nature experiences as preventive strategies to counteract many contemporary physical and mental health challenges that children and young people face (PHE, 2014a; DHSC, 2018), with the school context being identified as a universal access point to deliver these key learning benefits to those who might otherwise miss out (Natural England, 2013). There is an evidenced link between whole-school approaches that transform schools' ethos and environment for outdoor learning and improvements in pupils' social and emotional skills and their physical health (PHE, 2014b). These benefits can be achieved via a recognised pathway to impact on pupil attainment through increasing the regularity and quality of outdoor learning (Waite et al., 2016).

Figure 1: The pathway to raised attainment through outdoor learning (Waite et al., 2016, p. 10)

Figure 1 illustrates that by enabling children to engage with different learning contexts and methods, teaching outdoors can bring improvement in attainment and other key desirable outcomes, broadly identified as falling into the following categories:

- healthy bodies and lifestyles
- social, confident and connected people
- self-directed learning skills
- effective contributors and collaborators
- concerned active citizens.

(Malone and Waite, 2016)

Yet despite this wealth of positive evidence, there is a substantial waning of opportunities to benefit from learning outdoors as children move through primary school.

Challenges

Perhaps the greatest perceived barrier to teaching outdoors is the weather. However, the prevalence and success of outdoor play and learning in colder and wetter climes, such as Scandinavia, suggests that the real challenge is to be properly dressed. Getting parents informed and on board and providing waterproof kit and wellies can help to overcome this. Teachers also need to be well prepared, so that they are comfortable whatever the weather. Surprisingly, weather was not found to be a major barrier in the Natural Connections Demonstration project. The main challenges (and solutions) to outdoor learning that the project identified fell into three main themes:

- **People-related**, with issues often centred around staff confidence to teach outdoors; these were overcome by the use of whole-school approaches, supported by positive leadership and by demonstrating and sharing clearly what had been done, why (the intent) and what had been learned.

- **Place-related**, with the provision of easily accessible and suitable outdoor learning areas within a setting; for example, including ground works in school improvement plans played a key part in embedding outdoor curricular learning.

- **Policy-related**, with schools reporting difficulties in balancing outdoor learning with other dominant performance measures, such as a dependence on written records for assessment, especially if outdoor learning was perceived as an additional activity rather than an enriching one (see also the chapter 'Assessment outdoors').

Over the course of the Natural Connections Demonstration project, the majority of teachers overcame a variety of barriers to taking learning outdoors, as they strongly appreciated its value for children's:

- enjoyment of lessons
- engagement with and understanding of nature
- social skills
- engagement with learning
- health and wellbeing
- behaviour
- attainment.

Teachers wanted support in linking outdoor activities to the National Curriculum in order to maximise the time available to teach outdoors (Edwards-Jones, Waite & Passy, 2017). Our response to this has been the creation of *The National Curriculum Outdoors* series of books, showcasing how outdoor learning can be delivered as an integral part of the school curriculum delivery with the provision of a clear set of lesson plans explaining not only the 'what' but 'how' they can be delivered. This provides children with the opportunity to experience outdoor learning, while their teachers grow in knowledge and confidence.

As outdoor learning becomes established throughout your primary school, it is worth remembering that not all outdoor learning needs to happen in the school grounds. Identifying other local green spaces can extend the possibilities for learning, provide opportunities for progression in experience of different natural environments and help to make use by all classes of outdoor learning areas more sustainable. A mix of familiar and new places offer complementary support for health and wellbeing and environmental awareness.

How to use this book

This book offers support to KS2 practitioners in terms of how to take the National Curriculum outdoors, by providing well-structured, motivating, relevant and accessible progressions especially planned for children as they move through KS2, using local outdoor spaces to enhance teaching and learning and help make it memorable. The progressions include detailed teacher-directed activities to build confidence in teaching outdoors, linking this to National Curriculum content. The content throughout the progressions gradually builds on knowledge, concepts and understanding to enable all pupils to make progress from their individual starting points; activities are repeated in different contexts to provide opportunities for pupils to practise what they know in order to deepen their understanding. However, the intention is to use pedagogical approaches that will offer chances for children to initiate and follow their own lines of enquiry. These 'squirrel moments', when something unanticipated happens in the natural environment and captures the children's imagination, form a valuable element in teaching and learning outside and are well worth capitalising upon (Waite et al., 2006).

The progressions provide six structured sessions for each of the core subjects of English, mathematics and science and the foundation subjects of art and design, design and technology, geography and history, along with religious education and a language (French). Music is covered in a whole KS2 set of progressions.

Set in the autumn term, to provide a consistent point in the academic year from which to reinforce and build on previous learning experiences, the progressions enable schools and teachers to deliver activities that have been carefully planned to support progression across a single year group in Key Stage 2, aligning with the content of prescribed programmes of study and attainment targets of the 2014 National Curriculum. The context for the outdoor learning is also generally assumed to be the school grounds or natural environments within easy walking distance to maximise learning time. However, as we advised earlier, progression in terms of the places in which children learn should also be considered. At KS2, it would be valuable to include more varied and distant locations for field trips and residential visits, contributing to children's development and understanding of their place in the world (Waite, 2013; York Consulting, 2015).

Questions posed throughout the progressions provide continuous 'assessment for learning' opportunities, promoting a deeper level of understanding in line with Ofsted expectations.

Is anything missing?

Progressions for physical education and computing are not included in this book. However, all progressions offer opportunities for increased physical activity and lowered levels of sedentary behaviour (Aronsson et al., 2015) and for satisfying physical education objectives in part. There are also many opportunities to apply computing objectives back in the classroom, following outdoor sessions, using 'technology purposefully to create, organise, store, manipulate and retrieve digital content' (DfE, 2014) within many of the subjects (Opie, Ansell & Goto, 2017).

Personal, social, health and economic education (PSHE) is a non-statutory subject on the school curriculum. However, Section 2.5 of the National Curriculum (DfE, 2014) states that all state schools 'should make provision for personal, social, health and economic education, drawing on good practice', and this has been strengthened in line with recommendations about mental health and wellbeing (National Health Service (England), 2018), with trailblazer schools in the Link Programme testing methods during 2019. Activities within the progressions that encourage effective social interaction and independent, creative and critical thinking provide coverage of key PSHE objectives, with many of these opportunities highlighted under the 'health and wellbeing' section in the introduction of each unit.

The 'natural connections' sections, also in the introduction to each unit, show how children's attention can be focused on the natural world, increasing awareness, care and understanding to develop feelings of being a 'part of nature' and engendering responsibility for environmental stewardship, alongside the curricular-based learning. Further opportunities to follow up children's interests in, or draw attention to, their environment will naturally emerge when teaching outside the classroom. Together with changes in pedagogical approach, the overarching themes of health and wellbeing and natural connections will help to form a thread of education for sustainability throughout the curriculum (Green and Somerville, 2015; Bourn et al., 2016).

Conclusion

The expectation is that teachers will still wish to adapt these plans to their own contexts, but much of the time-consuming work of thinking through rationales, curricular links, health and safety, assessment and resources has been taken care of, so that more time is available to extend and develop personal or school-wide ideas and practice. One important aspect to bear in mind is the centrality of stimulating curious minds and offering choice and autonomy when teaching outside the classroom so that children accept responsibility for and want to drive their learning. Developing self-regulated learning habits and intrinsic motivation will provide strong foundations for success at secondary and higher education stages.

There are many superb additional resources online linked to curriculum subjects from organisations such as the Wildlife Trusts, Woodland Trust, Council for Learning Outside the Classroom and Field Studies Council. With careful planning and experience, these and ideas in books such as Juliet Robertson's *Dirty Teaching*, Jo Schofield and Fiona Danks' *The Stick Book* and Marina Robb, Victoria Mew and Anna Richardson's *Learning with Nature* are great sources of other activity ideas that, with experience, can be linked effectively to the curriculum. *Educating Outside* by Helen Porter also has some great curriculum-linked ideas to expand your repertoire over time.

Our aim with this book has been to provide progressions over six sessions with clearly identified curriculum content. We hope that using this book and its companions for Key Stage 2 will be only the start of some really exciting teaching outdoors for you, your pupils and your school.

Assessment outdoors

Part of our impetus for writing this book was the acknowledgement that, with changes to curriculum policy and the emphasis being placed on recording learning, schools need to provide evidence that they know *why* key curriculum content is included, *whether* the curriculum is being implemented effectively and *what* impact their outdoor curriculum is having on pupils' knowledge and understanding. A 2018 report that informed the greater concentration in the new Ofsted inspection framework on curriculum intent, implementation and impact noted:

> ... the main focus was on putting a plan together, but not checking the implementation of that plan effectively enough. This was linked to an onus on delivering the content of the national curriculum for foundation subjects, but without careful thought given to the progression of knowledge and skill that would make this useful learning for pupils. (Ofsted, 2018, p. 15)

Ofsted inspectors reported that the most telling indicators of curriculum quality were a coherent rationale, knowledge of curriculum concepts and an ambitious curriculum. Subject leadership knowledge, a progression model and robust assessment of the curriculum were also vital (Ofsted, 2018). As far as we know, this is the first book to support teachers in meeting all these criteria when teaching the curriculum outside.

Assessment has two main functions: first as a guide to planning the next steps for the children, i.e. assessment *for* learning, and second to summarise what a pupil has learned, i.e. assessment *of* learning. The latter, summative assessment, such as end-of-unit or key stage tests, provides evidence of levels of understanding and secure knowledge of content. As Waite et al. (2015) note, there are two aspects to robust tracking of a child's learning journey:

1. children's achievement of lesson objectives

2. an evaluation of the impact of lesson activities.

This enables teaching and learning to build productively on what has gone before, with awareness of what has worked well and which concepts or skills may need other approaches. We address both these aspects in the carefully structured progressions in this book, providing clear learning objectives linked to the National Curriculum content, together with evaluation prompts through open questioning about the activities. Linking to the National

Curriculum content provides each session with subject-specific criteria against which the success of taking the learning outside may be measured, reassuring Ofsted and school leadership that teaching outdoors offers valuable curricular learning opportunities.

Throughout each progression, pupils are encouraged to consider and explain their own successes or failures to themselves and to take responsibility for their own learning (Hawe and Parr, 2014). They are guided towards the recognition that some factors that lead to success or failure are controllable, such as the tools and materials suiting the task, how much they are interested in the task or how much effort they put into making it a success. Other factors may not be so controllable, such as the weather or the need for adult support and supervision. Children are encouraged to learn to attribute successes and failures to controllable factors, and to develop a clear idea of what good work looks like and what they need to do to reach this standard (Weiner, 1986; Dweck, 2008). These curricular learning opportunities are underpinned by a range of pedagogical strategies (Paniagua and Istance, 2018), such as experiential learning, encouraging pupil autonomy, independent and group working, and self-regulation of learning (Educational Endowment Foundation, 2018).

The adult role

The adults supporting learning are encouraged to model the activity themselves, acknowledging the tricky parts, recognising difficulty and being positive about the management of any difficulties. If the adult presents mistakes as an opportunity for learning, the children will start to see that it is possible to learn from failure, to keep trying, to try different or creative approaches or to tackle the problem from a different perspective. This develops children's resilience and perseverance in the face of problems. Allowing such experimentation and creativity, coupled with teachers' use and repetition of questions, encourages the use of new vocabulary to clarify meaning in context, and adds depth and breadth to children's learning experiences. The adult has overall responsibility for safety, but it is equally important that they know when to step back and encourage children to think for themselves, solve problems and be creative. Outdoor spaces have been shown to facilitate more autonomy in and self-regulation of learning (Bølling et al., 2018).

Across the units, activities are repeated in different contexts, providing reinforcement and deepening or layering of knowledge so the children can build upon previous knowledge and experiences, and offering the chance to gauge improvement over time. The sections on prior learning in the session plans aid progression and provide opportunities for mastery. Teachers can thus make judgements about whether pupils are 'exploring', 'meeting' or 'exceeding', 'emerging – expected – exceeding' or 'working towards', 'working at' or 'working beyond' targeted levels of knowledge and understanding.

Supporting special educational needs and disability

An important part of assessment is to enable school staff to tailor teaching and support effectively so that all pupils can access and achieve across the curriculum. Every unit in this book includes advice on how to adapt practices to make them more inclusive and extend learning. The space, task, equipment and people (STEP) approach can be adopted throughout the book. By changing the space, task, equipment or people, the activity can be made more challenging or easier to understand, enabling all pupils to take part. For example:

1. Consider the **space** the children will be working in: is it well-resourced and accessible, with distractions minimised?

2. Does the **task** need to be simplified or scaffolded or need adult support, or should it be extended to stretch the most able and talented children?

3. Consider the **resources**: are they accessible and suitable for the purpose, or do they need to be simplified or made more challenging in some way? Does equipment need to be smaller, lighter or adapted in some way?

4. Think about the **people** that could support better adaptations. Consult the pupil about the kind and level of support they need, e.g. by buddying up or working independently. Seek advice from the special educational needs and/or disability coordinator if in doubt. Consider how adult roles might be shaped to facilitate experiences of autonomy and challenge.

The STEP approach was developed by the Training and Development Agency for Schools (TDA, 2009, Appendix A, pp. 29–31).

Gathering the evidence

Maynard et al. (2013, p. 295) found that some teachers struggled 'with documenting children's learning particularly given the perceived need to meet statutory curriculum requirements'. However, many techniques used by colleagues in Early Years in outdoor contexts can be used at later stages of children's education.

Examples can include taking photos of the learning process, including children measuring, collecting specimens or creating pictograms using natural materials. Selecting and annotating photos back in the classroom provides the opportunity for written records or to apply computing objectives, using 'technology purposefully to create, organise, store, manipulate and retrieve digital content' (DfE, 2014). It can also serve as a visual summative record, evidencing which parts of the curriculum have been experienced and mastered.

Opportunities to address children's connection to the natural environment and health and wellbeing outcomes have been included under 'Natural connections' and 'Health and wellbeing' in the introductions to each set of progressions in this book. Other methods that can help to assess improvements in pupils' health and wellbeing include, for example, resources in Wright et al.'s (2016) *Creating Happy and Healthy Schools through Outdoor Learning*. Teachers and children can report physical activity and happiness levels using simple questionnaires developed through research, enabling schools to monitor the contributions of lessons to pupils' health and wellbeing. Assessment of children's connection to nature can also be used to explore the effects of increasing outdoor teaching and learning on children's environmental values; see, for example, Hunt et al.'s (2017, p. 60) 'Nature Connectedness Scale'.

End-of-unit or key stage summative assessment tests can provide evidence of children's levels of understanding and secure subject knowledge. However, assessing learning through the provision of carefully planned activities, through the use of open questioning for self-assessment and by providing positive and constructive task-focused adult and peer feedback can help shape student understanding across their learning, thus encouraging children to become more involved in their learning processes and gain in confidence as they acquire a deeper awareness of where they are and where they want to be in their learning and achievement. It can also provide clearer insight into the skills and processes that children are using in their learning within subject disciplines, which will form the basis of later development and progress in that subject.

Integrated and progressive assessment

Evidence of learning can thus be gathered wherever it occurs, together with an appreciation of all that can be achieved in outdoor contexts. In many units, we have included classroom extensions such as compiling interactive displays, which will demonstrate learning over the course of progressions. Joining up learning inside and outside the classroom also helps to ensure that assessment happens in a variety of contexts, reinforcing and consolidating knowledge, skills and understanding. Assessment reflecting pupil achievement resulting from teaching and learning outdoors will help schools to recognise that learning can and does take place anywhere – that outdoor learning is not an 'extra' but can be integral to the delivery of the National Curriculum and can contribute to school priorities, including attainment and progression (Waite, Passy and Gilchrist, 2014).

Health and safety outdoors

Children are spending more and more time inside, with a 2018 survey of 2,000 parents reporting that children aged six to 16 only spent about seven hours outside each week in total, but more than twice that time just playing video games indoors (OnePoll, 2018). One of the reasons for writing this book was to inspire and encourage teachers and teaching assistants to take learning outdoors, thus offering and promoting children's experiences of natural environments. Teaching curriculum subjects outdoors not only offers children a range of different ways of learning but also enables them to experience success in different contexts, offering the opportunity to raise the confidence and aspirations of all children, but particularly those who may struggle inside the classroom.

One of the biggest perceived barriers to teaching outdoors is often identified as concerns over health and safety. In this chapter, we provide advice and guidance about safe practice for lead practitioners, aiming to promote the safe delivery of outdoor learning in order to meet current health and safety guidance. In a primary school setting, it is ultimately the responsibility of the headteacher to ensure that activities delivered on the school site are safe and follow best practice, but everyone, including the children, should take some responsibility for assessing risks and managing them appropriately.

The law

In simple terms, the law requires those responsible to take reasonable steps to ensure that the risks are at an acceptable level. As stated by the Department for Education, health and safety law requires the school to assess risks and put in place proportionate control measures (DfE, 2018a). The key task is to carry out a 'suitable and sufficient risk assessment' and to act on its findings. What counts as 'suitable and sufficient' – for instance, the type of risk assessment, the level of detail and whether or not it is written down – depends on the circumstances. However, what is expected is a *proportionate* approach. The Health and Safety Executive (HSE, 2018) makes it clear that health and safety is not about generating excessive paperwork (Gill, 2016). The DfE (2018a) also states that schools must have a health and safety policy. Health and safety outdoors should form part of your outdoor learning policy, and also include the implications of teaching outdoors for your behaviour management and safeguarding policies. There are many online resources that support schools in developing an outdoor learning policy. An example template with associated guidance can be found on the Council for Learning Outside the Classroom site (www.lotc.org.uk/plan-deliver-lotc/policy-and-curriculum-planning).

Assessing risks and benefits

A risk assessment is a key prerequisite for planning teaching outdoors that should be included in the outdoor learning policy. It will be something that most teachers are familiar with from planning school trips, and it does not mean that all risks need to be eliminated. The outdoor learning policy should set out the roles and responsibilities within the risk-management processes, the mechanisms to control risk and specific control measures that need to be put in place. However, risk assessments should always balance benefits against potential hazards (Waite, Wickett and Huggins, 2014).

> *Risk-benefit management is a fundamental part of life and is a skill needed for young people's safety and wellbeing. Staff have a duty of care towards young people. However, this certainly does not mean 'wrapping them in cotton wool'. Therefore, we have responsibility not only to keep young people safe, but also to enable them to learn to manage risks for themselves.*
> (LOTC, 2018)

There are three things that should be considered when deciding whether a risk is acceptable: (Ball et al., 2008, p. 114)

1. likelihood of children coming to harm

2. severity of that harm

3. benefits, rewards or outcomes of that activity for the children.

Some risk assessment considerations

In the following sections, we gather together specific advice about how to manage some common risks when teaching outdoors.

Behaviour and safeguarding

The outdoor learning policy should reflect the school health and safety and behaviour policies. Whilst the outdoors can provide an exciting and stimulating environment, it is always important to provide clear expectations of behaviour, with consistent consequence systems to ensure safe practice. Positive reinforcement through effective communication and engagement should always be demonstrated. Children should be encouraged to understand what unacceptable behaviour is, with incidents recorded in line with school policy where appropriate.

Where unacceptable behaviour occurs and an oral reprimand has been given, the more informal atmosphere outside the classroom often provides time and opportunity to discuss possible consequences of such behaviour, such as the potential harm caused and loss of privileges, e.g. use of tools or lighting fires. It may also provide space to discuss feelings and emotions underlying the inappropriate behaviour (Hopper, 2017). However, where the child is at serious risk of hurting themselves or others and likely to suffer or inflict significant harm, the child should be removed from the context, following school procedures in line with the school's safeguarding policy (DfE, 2018b).

First aid

Injuries are not very common when safe practices are adopted and children have been involved in discussions about what needs to be done to keep everyone safe in the outdoor area and why. When delivering outdoor activities, it is important to adhere to your setting practice and policy. With reference to first aid, it is often recommended that the lead practitioner holds an up-to-date recognised first aid qualification. If not, they must have a working knowledge of first aid appropriate to the activities that they are leading and the location in which they are working. They must also have immediate access to a qualified first aider in the event of needing further support. The general school policy about administering or securing first aid should always be followed (Hammett, 2016; DfE, 2018b). When working in areas where there is a risk of ticks, long-sleeved tops and trousers tucked into socks should be worn and parents alerted to check their children for ticks after school.

If working away from site, or more than ten minutes from immediate help, we strongly recommend attending a two-day emergency first aid in the outdoors course (such as one offered by BASP UK), which covers remote first aid practices and procedures and will give additional confidence in managing potential hazards.

Fire-lighting, cooking and use of tools

To support you with the activities in this book, we have put together some step-by-step principles for the safe use of tools, the teaching of fire-lighting and cooking in the outdoors, and the use of a storm kettle. The step-by-step principle has been used to support children in developing key skills and breaking these skills down into key components, which they can then apply to the task. These have been adapted from the Wild Tribe Outdoor Learning programme (2019).

Fire-lighting and safe practice

Fire can be hazardous and dangerous when not managed effectively. It can have a devastating impact on the environment and natural landscapes if it gets out of control. However, children find fire exciting and, if the skills of fire-lighting are taught with safety as a prerequisite, lessons that include fire will ignite children's imaginations.

Fire safety advice

* Provide adequate supervision for young people when using fires and ensure that they have been taught the appropriate skills to make a fire.

* Avoid making fires on stones or near tree roots.

* Monitor weather conditions and changes in wind direction. A strong wind could contribute to a fire becoming out of control.

* Do not light fires in excessively dry conditions.

* Place all equipment, including fuel, in safe boxes.

* Never leave a fire unattended.

* Keep wood and other fuel sources away from fire.

* Have a supply of water available to extinguish the fire and to remedy burns.

* Do not underestimate the power of fire.

* Thoroughly extinguish all fires.

* Leave no trace (for more information, see: lnt.org/why/7-principles/minimize-campfire-impacts).

Lighting fires: safe preparation, lighting and management

Equipment:

* matches or fire strikers

* water

* wood of various thicknesses: about 15–20 cm (6–8 inches) long

* tinder, such as dried leaves, birch bark or cotton wool balls

* petroleum jelly, e.g. Vaseline®.

Preparation:

1. Identify the area to be used as a group fire-lighting area (the main area) and surround this with well-defined markers such as large branches or tree stump seats.

2. Place four sticks of wrist-thickness in a square in the middle to denote a safety area, about 45 cm (18 inches) square.

3. Collect fuel for the fire. If the weather has been wet, collect sticks for the fire a few days prior to the session and allow them to dry out. You can then scatter these dry twigs in the area for the children to 'find'. As an alternative, a bag of bought kindling can also be used.

4. Keep a selection of dried sticks of varying widths – pencil, finger, thumb and wrist width – in a bag near the fire circle for teacher use.

5. Seated around the prepared area, talk to children about safety aspects of fires, emphasising safe practice around a fire.

   a. Hair needs to be tied back. Hair contains high levels of oil, which is highly flammable.

   b. Appropriate clothing (long sleeves and long trousers) should be worn.

   c. Responsible behaviour will negate risk to self or others.

   d. No one to enter the inner fire square unless invited to do so.

   e. If invited, adopt the safe stance: kneeling on one knee and one foot on the ground.

   f. Point out the container of water placed near the fire area used to extinguish the flames.

Step-by-step method

Introduce the 'fire triangle theory', i.e. that fires need three things – heat, fuel and oxygen.

Show children how to light a fire using a step-by-step method:

1. Choose a suitable site. This could be a flat or sloped area, grass covered or bare ground.

2. Clear the area of loose vegetation and stones. **See A**

3. Show the children how to make a platform of about four or five sticks on which to build a fire to keep it off the damp floor and provide oxygen (draught). **See B**

4. In groups, ask the children to:
   a. Find a good area for the fire.
   b. Clear the area from vegetation and stones.
   c. Find four sticks to mark a safe area in which to build the fire.
   d. Find four or five sticks to put as a platform on which to build the fire.

5. Once groups have achieved this, bring them back to the main area and explain that now they need fuel for the fire.

6. Show the children the prepared selection of sticks and group them according to width – pencil, finger and thumb. **See C**

7. Ask the children to suggest why this has been done. Explain that when the fire is lit, the smallest sticks will be used as fuel first, before gradually adding the larger sticks.

8. Ask the children to collect a selection of sticks with different widths. Explain that they need to be able to 'snap', as this shows that they are dry and able to burn.

9. The children now order their sticks by thickness.

10. Explain that the next step is how a fire should be laid – would just throwing the sticks in a pile work or would they suggest arranging them in some way? Do we need anything that will light easily to put on first?

11. Demonstrate how to place pulled cotton wool and petroleum jelly or a straw sphere on the prepared platform.

12. Show how to add the tinder, building the fire base up using the thinnest pencil sticks first, ensuring that there is enough air between the sticks. **See D**

13. What else do we need for our fire in case we need to stop it? Ensure that there is a container of water next to the demonstration fire.

14. Revise talk of safety around the fire: the safety stance.

15. Demonstrate how to ignite the kindling using a long match or fire strikers, reinforcing the safety stance.

16. Children return to their prepared bases to lay their fires, each group checking that they have a bottle of water to place next to their prepared areas.

17. Once the adult with the group is happy with the laying of the fire, they should supervise the lighting of it.

18. The children must sit down once the fire is lit and be supervised at all times.

19. Children can put more wood on, one piece at a time, when needed, but must not lean across the fire to do so.

NEVER LEAVE THE FIRE UNATTENDED.

Key steps for using a storm kettle

The storm kettle looks hollow (which acts as a chimney) but has an internal chamber for water, which is not

obvious. Take the time to show the storm kettle to the children and ask them how they think it works.

The main differences to consider when using a storm kettle compared to lighting a fire are:

1. Clearing a base – this needs to be a very level site so that the storm kettle doesn't fall over.

2. The fire is built in the storm kettle base, so although pencil, finger and thumb sticks still need collecting, the length of them needs to be quite short to fit into the base, like this: **See A**

3. When putting the storm kettle on and taking it off the base, keep the handle horizontal so that fingers are not over the hot chimney, to avoid burns. The safe method looks like this: **See B**

Your setting may also recommend the use of heat-resistant gloves.

4. Once the kettle is on the base, the fire is fed through the chimney.

   a. Short sticks should be put onto the rim and tipped into the chimney.

   b. At no point should fingers go across the chimney.

5. When the water is boiled and the kettle lifted off, the water should be poured into cups using the handle and the cork. **See C**

6. Cups should be put onto a flat surface or held by an adult when the water is being poured. The children must not hold them until they have cooled.

7. Once the storm kettle is cool, you should remove any remaining water and then empty any remaining embers from the base of the kettle.

8. You should then follow the principles below for

extinguishing fires to deal with the remaining embers. **See D**

9. Once the storm kettle is cool, it can be safely stored by turning the base upside down and inserting it inside the bottom of the storm kettle, before placing the kettle in its bag.

Extinguishing fires – leaving minimal trace

1. Once all the cooking has been completed and it is time for the fire to be put out, choose a responsible child to slowly pour a bottle of water over the fire.

2. Make sure they demonstrate the safe stance, kneeling with one knee up.

3. Check that the white ash from the wood, which is the hottest part, has been covered with water, and that the fire is properly out.

4. With a stick that has not been used on the fire, ask the children to scrape the embers around so that no remains of the fire can be seen, and that the area is left as it was found.

If it is a permanent fire area on the site, the remaining charcoal can be left.

As the children become more experienced and proficient and are able to demonstrate safe practice, they can become more independent; however, strict adult vigilance should be observed at all times.

Using tools – principles and practices

Children should be taught how to use tools safely and with respect. We recommend the following general safe practice under close adult supervision (Outdoor and Woodland Learning, 2017):

- Ensure that the tools are appropriate and suit the purpose.
- Keep tools in a safe place (e.g. a locked cabinet) and ensure they are well maintained.
- Ensure that tools are counted out at the beginning and counted back in at the end of a session.
- Mark tools with coloured tape so they are easy to spot, especially if they are green or black.

- During a session tools should be kept in a marked-off area and children should only access them when they are given permission, with adult supervision.
- Ratios for tool use should initially be one to one and no more than six to eight per adult once children have been trained and are confident in using them safely.
- Children should position themselves in a safe space prior to using any tools. They should not be able to make contact with another child when they stretch out their arms.

Using a bow saw

1. Show the children the parts of the saw: handle, blade, and cover.
2. Remove the cover and show the cutting edge.
3. Show how to hold the saw using the handle with the blade pointing down.
4. Working in pairs, one child or adult should hold the piece of wood to stop it from moving. The other places their hand through the handle of the bow saw so that their sawing hand is well away from the cutting edge, as shown.
5. When the saw is not in use, it should be placed with the blade facing in and down.

Using a folding saw to cut small pieces of wood

1. Show the children the parts of the saw: handle, button to release the blade and cutting edge.
2. Show how to use the button to release the cutting edge.
3. Show how to hold the saw. The free hand goes over the saw and holds the material.
4. Work in pairs. Push forwards and pull backwards with the blade pointing downwards.
5. After using the saw, show how to press and pinch to close the blade. When passing the saw, it should be face downward with the blade closed.

Using a bill hook to split wood (under close supervision)

1. Show the children the parts of the bill hook: handle, blade and cutting edge.
2. Show them that their free hand should be placed behind their back when they are using the bill hook.
3. Demonstrate using the blade away from the body, hook facing downwards, keeping the blade parallel and close to the wood.
4. Always carry the tool by the handle with the blade facing downwards.
5. Adults should replace the cover on the blade after use.

Using a sheath knife

1. Show the children the parts of the knife: handle, sheath (cover), blade and cutting edge.
2. Show how to remove the sheath safely.
3. Demonstrate how to assume a bent knee position with the knife away from the body and move the knife downwards and away.
4. When not in use, the knife should be placed in its sheath.
5. Show how to pass the knife with the sheath pointing downwards.

Using secateurs to cut twigs (diameter smaller than 1p coin)

1. Show the children the parts of the secateurs: handle and blades.
2. Show how to release the blades and show the cutting edge.
3. Explain that your free hand holds the item you are cutting, like when using a big pair of scissors.
4. To pass the secateurs, children must close the blades and pass them using the handle with the blades pointing downwards.
5. When not in use the blades should be securely closed.

Using loppers to cut branches (diameter smaller than 2p coin)

1. Show the children the parts of the lopper: handle, blade and cutting edge.
2. Show them how to hold the loppers with two hands.
3. Demonstrate how to pass the loppers, with blades pointing down.
4. Show the children how to cut the wood in pairs, like this:
5. When not in use, the loppers should be placed down with the blades facing towards the back of the child.
6. Show how to carry them pointing downwards.

Drilling

Drilling stumps are useful: they help children keep the wood still and provide a safe space.

Using a palm drill to make small holes in wood and remove pith

1. Show the children the parts of a drill: handle and drill bit.
2. Use the drill with one hand and twist and push down.
3. When removing the drill bit pull it up and out.
4. Show how to point the drill bit down and pass with the handle to another person.
5. Replace the drill in the toolbox after use.

Using a hand drill to make larger holes in wood

1. Show the children the parts of the drill: handle, bit holder and drill bit.
2. Show how to turn the bit holder to open it to insert the drill bit.
3. Turn the bit holder the opposite way to close the bit holder.
4. The children will need to use two hands, one hand holding the drill and one hand turning the drill bit.
5. Children should pass the drill by holding the handle with the drill bit facing down or removed.
6. Replace the drill in the toolbox after use.

Accepting challenge and staying safe

Practitioners are advised to attend training courses and practise before delivering a session with children. Attending a training course will advance your own skills, and ensure you are delivering high quality safe sessions. Health and safety considerations are positive aspects of teaching outdoors rather than barriers since they enable children to take risks in a safe and secure risk-assessed environment. Through experiencing challenges, children develop the capability to weigh up situations and take appropriate action. This is a vital life skill that schools can foster by providing proportionate responses to any identified health and safety issues.

English

In this unit, children will be focusing on the development of their writing and reading skills, based on the Key Stage 2 English objectives identified in the 2014 National Curriculum for England. It encourages the children to question what is important to them about a place: how would they describe their favourite place? What would be in an imaginary place? This unit also aims to evoke the children's thoughts and feelings about places that matter to them. They will gain an understanding of how, as authors, they can use figurative and other forms of language to create an impact on their readers. They will also understand the importance of identifying the audience and the purpose of their writing, and selecting the appropriate form of writing.

To support inclusive practice or to extend learning, the space, task, equipment and people (STEP) approach can be adopted throughout this unit. By changing the space, task, equipment or people, the activity can be made more challenging or easier to understand, enabling all pupils to take part in the activity, as explained in the assessment chapter in this book. The children will be expected to work as a whole class directed by the teacher, in pairs or small groups with support from adults, and independently.

The role of the adult is to lead the sessions safely and model the activities, allowing experimentation and independence whilst providing direct support and resilience.

You may wish to record the activities using a camera.

Natural connections

- Enhanced awareness of the local natural environment
- Understanding of physical processes of change within the natural environment
- Using observation skills to look at how things affect and impact on the natural environment.

Health and wellbeing

- Physical activity
- Being focused and attentive
- Teambuilding
- Emotional resilience
- Reflection
- Mindfulness
- Independent learning.

Word bank

My place

- sense of place
- emotions
- feelings
- imagination
- reflection
- sounds
- senses

English

- figurative language
- personification
- metaphors
- similes
- audience
- purpose
- concrete poetry
- impact
- performance
- intonation
- volume
- presentation and meaning

Summary overview

Progression	Curriculum content	Learning experiences/activities
Lesson 1	Discuss and evaluate how authors use language, including figurative language, considering the impact on the reader.	Children are introduced to figurative language and the idea of a sense of place. They explore and take images of important places to them in the outside space. They write a descriptive piece about the place and create natural frames from wood using a range of tools and knots.
Lesson 2	Prepare poems to read aloud and to perform, showing understanding through intonation, tone and volume so that the meaning is clear to an audience.	Children study *A poem to be spoken silently...* by Pie Corbett. They perform the poem and answer a range of questions to show understanding of the text. They find a secret place to reflect, listen and observe sounds. They create their own soundbites of sounds from the outdoor area and perform their own sound poetry.
Lesson 3	Pupils should be taught to perform their own compositions, using appropriate intonation, volume, and movements so meaning is clear. Explain and discuss their understanding of what they have read, including through formal presentations and debates, maintaining a focus on the topic and using notes where necessary.	Children consider the audience they are writing for. They listen to and perform a pollution rap. They consider the impact of pollution in the ocean and develop their own pollution raps. They use tools to make their own rhythm sticks.
Lesson 4	Discuss and evaluate how authors use language, including figurative language, considering the impact on the reader.	Children read a range of autumn poems. They create a concrete fireworks poem using leaves. They look at figurative language used by the author in the poem and develop their own poems using personification. These are performed around a fire, with some tastes of autumn.
Lesson 5	Explain and discuss their understanding of what they have read, including through formal presentations and debates, maintaining a focus on the topic and using notes where necessary.	Children create an imaginary place. They receive a letter from a developer who wishes to buy part of the school field. They do some research on the impact of this development to prepare for a debate.
Lesson 6	Explain and discuss their understanding of what they have read, including through formal presentations and debates, maintaining a focus on the topic and using notes where necessary.	Children take part in a great debate about their school field. They celebrate the outdoor space and present their work to an audience of their choice.

PREPARATION

Ensure that there is a safe outdoor space in which the children can observe, reflect and think about the importance of the outdoor space to them.

Copy a descriptive extract from *Peter's Place*, enough for one per pair.

Review https://members.scouts.org.uk/supportresources/3661/scout-skills-simple-knots.

Resources

- *Peter's Place* by Sally Grindley (illustrated by Michael Foreman). Alternatively, you could use a different book about a place that suffers due to an environmental disaster (in *Peter's Place*, an oil tanker spills oil along the coastline)
- Question cards about the outdoor place
- Tablets, paper and pencils
- Descriptive extracts from *Peter's Place*
- Hazel sticks
- String
- Folding saw, secateurs and/or bow saw

CONSIDER

Health & Safety

Assess and evaluate hazards and risks in your setting. See the health and safety chapter.

LESSON OBJECTIVES

We are developing a descriptive piece of writing about a favourite place in the outdoors.

National Curriculum Content

- Discuss and evaluate how authors use language, including figurative language, considering the impact on the reader.

ADULT ROLES

- Model the use of figurative language in describing a place.
- Support the children in collecting and describing images of their favourite places.

WARM UP IDEAS

Talk to the children about the outdoor learning area of the school. Have a range of questions written on cards and give each child a different question. Questions could include the following:

- What is their favourite part of the area and why? Do they have a favourite tree or plant in the area?
- Where do they go to reflect? Where do they go when they want to be alone?
- Where do they enjoy being with their friends? Where would they hide?
- Which part of the area do they not like? How would they feel if someone dropped litter everywhere or vandalised the area?
- What action would they take if they saw someone deliberately vandalising a part of the area?

Ask the children to move around a defined part of the outdoor space. Every time they meet someone, they ask their question and then they swap questions and move on to talk to someone else.

Introductory activity

Review some of the answers to the questions with the children and discuss how important the outside area is to them.

Read *Peter's Place*, or an alternative book about a beautiful place that suffers due to an environmental disaster. Ask the children questions about the text. What part of the story did the children like in particular? Ask the children about the way language is used in the book to describe a beautiful place. Which words and phrases particularly stood out for the children?

MAIN ACTIVITIES

My place

Refer to the questions asked in the warm up activity. Explain that in this unit, children will focus on places that matter to them. They will be exploring texts where authors have used figurative language to strengthen their impact on the reader. Revise the meaning of 'figurative language' – for example, using metaphors, similes or personification to add interest and meaning to literal text.

Today the focus is on the outdoor spaces at the school.

Challenge 1 (in pairs)

Collect images of favourite places

Pairs explore all outdoor spaces of the school, taking images using a tablet or making drawings. These could link to the questions answered in the introductory activity. The children could collect images in answer to the questions, or they may develop questions of their own with images to answer them.

When the children have taken some images, encourage them to develop some descriptive phrases about the images.

- Can they use any metaphors or similes within their descriptions?
- Can they start to draft a description about their favourite place at the school?

Look at an extract from *Peter's Place* or another book you have used for this progression. How has the author used descriptive language? Talk to the children about key words and phrases they can use to describe their favourite place at the school.

Challenge 2 (individual)

Make picture frames for their favourite place in the outdoor space

- Explain that children need to collect and cut four sticks to the same length to make a picture frame. Use a folding saw, secateurs and/or bow saw to cut four lengths of hazel. Put the frame together, using clove hitch knots and square lashing on each of the four corners. Look at the preparation section.
- Children collect leaves, which will be laminated onto paper later – see the Back in the classroom section below.

PLENARY

What descriptive language could the children use to describe their favourite place? They share their ideas in pairs. Ensure that they give each other feedback on what is effective about their description and what they could do to improve it.

Back in the classroom

- Ask the children to bring or send in photos of their favourite place and to write a description of it using descriptive and figurative language.
- Create a display of 'My place' in the classroom, using the pictures and descriptive writing that the children have developed.

EVALUATION/FOLLOW ON

- What went well today?
- Which children understood the concepts?
- Which children needed more help?
- Are there other resources you can use?
- Can you use the images and descriptions to continue work in the classroom?

PREPARATION

Ensure that there are spaces where the children can go to reflect and listen to sounds.

Source Pie Corbett's poem online.

Resources

- *A poem to be spoken silently* by Pie Corbett
- Postcards, pens and whiteboards
- Tablets
- Fire-making kit and water to extinguish fires

Previous learning

Talk to the children about their previous session and where they collected images in the outdoor space. How did they describe their favourite place?

CONSIDER

Health & Safety

Assess and evaluate hazards and risks in your setting. See the health and safety chapter.

LESSON OBJECTIVES

We are developing an understanding of *A poem to be spoken silently...* by Pie Corbett and creating a sound poem.

National Curriculum Content

- Prepare poems to read aloud and to perform, showing understanding through intonation, tone and volume so that the meaning is clear to an audience.

ADULT ROLES

- Model the use of a reflective space to record sounds and observations.
- Support the children in developing their own sound poems.

WARM UP IDEAS

Encourage the children to find a space where they can reflect and think quietly about the sounds around them. Encourage them to listen to the sounds and observe the space around their reflective place. What type of music would they play to describe their place?

Introductory activity

Read *A poem to be spoken silently...* by Pie Corbett. Ask the children questions about the poem and encourage them to think of questions themselves.

- Why did the writer use the word 'rustle' to describe the sound of his thoughts?
- Why would paving stones groan as if they were muscling for space?
- How do objects act like people in this poem? Can you give two examples?
- Are there any other words that mean a similar thing to 'silent' in this poem?
- Which part of the poem makes you feel the most peaceful and calm?
- If the author came to our school, what would you ask him about this poem?
- Focus on the line 'I heard the trees ease off their coats of bark.' What sounds does this line remind you of?
- Can you come up with some lines that are like the ones Pie Corbett has used to describe the soundscape in the outdoor learning area? Share a few.

Ask the children to read the poem out loud to a partner. Less confident children could alternate reading each stanza with their partner.

MAIN ACTIVITIES

A silent place

Challenge 1 (individual and in pairs)
Describing sounds in words

- Ask the children to return to their reflective space with a postcard and pen, with a copy of the poem and some of the adjectives highlighted from the poem.

- Can they use the poem as inspiration to describe some of the sounds they can hear in their own reflective space?

- Ask the children to consider whether their space is peaceful or not. Is there anything disturbing the peace – and if so, what is it?

- Once the children have had some time in their own reflective space to record and describe their sounds, ask them to discuss their sounds with a partner.

- Can they start to draft a poem about sound?

Challenge 2 (in pairs and groups of four, whole class)
Create soundbites of outdoor spaces

Using a tablet, can children find different spaces with different sounds to record? Ask the children to record six to eight different sounds and make a note of where they recorded the sounds.

- Once they have recorded their sounds, the children join with another pair.

- The pairs then take it in turns to identify where in the outside space they think that the soundbites were recorded.

- How easy are they to identify? What sounds are more difficult to distinguish?

- How would they describe the soundbites they have recorded? Can they use the soundbites to inspire them to develop their sound poems further?

Share their sound poems with the class. How have they used descriptive language in their poems? Have they used figurative language? How does the language used impact on the reader? What do they now need to do to improve their poems?

Challenge 3 (groups of four or whole class)
Extension – poem performance

If there is time, using the step-by-step principles for fire-making in the health and safety chapter, groups or the class make a fire. Once the fire is lit, encourage children to perform their poems about sound around the fire. Ask the children to listen to and consider the sounds of the fire. Could they include some descriptive language about fire sounds in their poems?

PLENARY

Talk to the children about the poems they have developed. What have they learned about the sounds in the outdoor area? How have these sounds influenced their writing?

Back in the classroom

- Children use the soundbites of the outdoor space to stimulate figurative language in their writing.

- They develop their sound poems and create a book of sound poetry about special places.

- Continue to develop a 'My place' display in the classroom using the sound poems.

EVALUATION/FOLLOW ON

- What went well today?

- Which children understood the concepts?

- Which children needed more help?

- Are there other resources you can use?

- Can the soundbites be used to further extend this work?

PREPARATION

Look at *The Pollution Rap* on www.writing.com/main/view_item/item_id/574420-The-Pollution-Rap and *Forest Craft* by Richard Irvine.

You will also need to prepare some clean-up resources.

Resources

- Hoops and a range of items that do or do not belong in the ocean e.g. string, plastic bags, pictures of wildlife, etc.
- Copies of *The Pollution Rap*
- Plastic sea animal toys, natural shells and pebbles
- Cocoa powder mixed with vegetable oil, shredded plastic and coffee granules
- Empty tanks/containers
- Toothbrushes, water containers, tongs, tweezers, water filtration tablets and clean-up items
- Newspaper articles on pollution
- Campaign resources and posters about ocean pollution
- Folding saw, knives, gloves, mallet and hazel wood

Previous learning

Talk to the children about what they learned in Progression 1 and what is important to them about the outside space. How has it changed in autumn?

CONSIDER

Health & Safety

Assess and evaluate hazards and risks in your setting. See the health and safety chapter.

LESSON OBJECTIVES

We are looking at the effects of pollution in the ocean and developing a pollution rap to perform to other members of the class.

National Curriculum Content

- Pupils should be taught to perform their own compositions, using appropriate intonation, volume, and movements so meaning is clear.
- Explain and discuss their understanding of what they have read, including through formal presentations and debates, maintaining a focus on the topic and using notes where necessary.

ADULT ROLES

- Model the use of words to create a rhythm.
- Support the children in developing their own pollution rap.

WARM UP IDEAS

(Whole class)

Talk to the children about sea pollution (if you used the book *Peter's Place* in Progression 1, you could refer this book again here). Ask the children what happens when there is an oil spillage in an ocean. Can they give other examples of sea pollution? What are the long-term effects of sea pollution and what can be done to reduce it?

Oil is only one form of pollution that affects our oceans. Talk to the children about other items that end up in our oceans and which can cause damage. Show the children a range of pictures and campaigns related to sea pollution.

Introductory activity (groups of about six)

In teams, the children do an ocean pollution race. Each team has one hoop. Inside each hoop are a range of items – some that belong in the ocean (e.g. a shell) and some that do not (e.g. a piece of string).

The children must take it in turns to collect an item from the hoop and place it in one of two piles: a pile for items that belong in the ocean and a pile for items that do not.

Which team can sort the items the quickest?

MAIN ACTIVITIES

A polluted place

Challenge 1 (whole class and groups of four)

Problem of pollution

Model how children can use the resources to make a miniature ocean by adding water and sea animals, shells and pebbles etc. into a tank or container:

- Groups can add coffee granules or cocoa and oil to the water to simulate a pollution incident in the ocean.

- They might also add shredded plastic to their mini ocean.

- Once they have added the pollutants, they can try to clean some of the shells, plastic sea animals, etc. To do this, they need to put on gloves.

- They can use fairy liquid, cloths, toothbrushes, a sieve, etc. One group could use a water filtration tablet to try to clean up the pollution and see whether that is more effective.

- Discuss the findings with the children.

- How quickly did the pollution spread? How easy was it to clean up? Which parts of the mini ocean were most affected?

Discuss with the children large-scale pollution and look at its impact. Use newspaper articles of recent cases to show the impact.

Challenge 2 (whole class and groups of four)

Anti-pollution persuasion

Read a copy of The Pollution Rap aloud and ask:

- How does the writer use words and phrases to appeal to the audience?

- How are the words used to create a rhythm?

- Can groups start to develop their own pollution rap?

- What key words and phrases can they use? How will they engage their audience? Who is the rap intended for?

- Can they develop a rhythm that works with the words in their group?

Groups perform their raps to each other.

Challenge 3 (in pairs)

Extension – rhythm sticks

Encourage the children to develop a musical instrument to create a rhythm. Following the guidance in the health and safety chapter, encourage pairs to saw a series of notches along the length of the middle section of a stick. The notches should be about 2 cm apart. A rubber mallet can be used to help create the notches. Once this 'rhythm stick' has been created, the children can use a smaller stick to rub up and down the rhythm stick, creating different sounds.

PLENARY

Talk to the children about the pollution raps they have created. How have they developed a rhythm with the words they have used? How can they improve their performance of the rap?

Back in the classroom

- Develop a campaign to reduce plastic waste at your school.

- Create a video of the children's pollution raps and perform some in an assembly.

- Design a superhero to engage children in Key Stage 1 with the need to reduce plastic waste and pollution. What superpowers would they need to have? Present the ideas to Year 1 or 2.

- Start to monitor the prevalence of single-use plastics in the class and see whether it can be reduced.

EVALUATION/FOLLOW ON

- What went well today?

- Which children understood the concepts?

- Which children needed more help?

- Are there other resources you can use?

PREPARATION

Review the following for copies of poems and recipes:

https://www.familyfriendpoems.com/poems/nature/fall

www.bbcgoodfood.com/recipes/13599/homemade-toffee-apples.

Resources

- Pens (to write on leaves)
- Autumn-themed poetry, including at least one poem which uses metaphors, similes and / or personification
- Toffee apples, lolly sticks and toppings
- Blackberries
- Fire-making kit and water to extinguish fire
- Cooking utensils

Previous learning

Talk to the children about what they learned in Progression 1 and what is important to them about the outside space. How has it changed in autumn?

CONSIDER

Health & Safety

Assess and evaluate hazards and risks in your setting. See the health and safety chapter.

LESSON OBJECTIVES

We are developing concrete poetry and a poem about autumn that includes personification.

National Curriculum Content

- Discuss and evaluate how authors use language, including figurative language, considering the impact on the reader.

ADULT ROLES

- Model the use of personification in a poem.
- Support the children in the development of concrete poetry and autumn poems.

WARM UP IDEAS

(Individual and whole class)

Ask the children to look at and reflect on the outdoor spaces around the school in autumn. Can they identify any of the leaves that have fallen? Can they identify any of the fruit on the trees?

Children collect some leaves and think of some powerful adjectives to describe the colours, smells, sounds and sights of autumn, writing them on their leaves. Together, can the class create an autumn leaves descriptive tree on the ground? Pick out and share some of the unusual imagery and words used.

Introductory activity

Read your chosen poem containing metaphors, similes and / or personification.

Remind the children that personification is like a metaphor. It gives non-living objects or ideas human characteristics, e.g. 'the leaves danced in the autumn breeze'.

Can the children identify any metaphors, similes or use of personification within the poem?

MAIN ACTIVITIES

Autumn place

Challenge 1 (groups of four)
Concrete poetry

Remind the children that a concrete poem is sometimes described as a shape poem. It is therefore a poem that matches the visual appearance of the topic of the poem. Can they work in a group to create a concrete poem about fireworks, using leaves and other natural objects to create a firework? They can write the words of the poem on the leaves. Where will the poem start? Where will it end? Take photos or ask them to draw the shape they have produced.

Challenge 2 (pairs or groups of four)
Autumn poetry with personification

Give pairs or groups copies of a selection of autumn poems using personification. Possible examples could include *Sing to Me, Autumn* by Patricia L. Cisco or *The Last Leaf on the Tree* by David A. Berwick, both available on www.familyfriendpoems.com.

- Can the children identify the personification in each poem?

- Can they underline key words and phrases used?

- Discuss what they notice and what they find is effective for conveying meaning.

- Pairs or groups then develop their own autumn poem using the examples as inspiration, together with words they used in their concrete poetry, as autumn is when fireworks are seen.

- Encourage the children to use personification within their poetry.

Challenge 3 (whole class)
Extension – a celebration of autumn poetry around the fire

If there is time, discuss the season of autumn and the changes that take place in autumn. Would children associate any particular tastes with autumn? For example, many apple dishes are eaten in autumn due to the apple harvest, and blackberries are in the hedgerows. Using the step-by-step principles for making a fire, make a fire to cook toffee apples, apples with blackberries, or an item of the children's choice.

Can they describe the smells and tastes of autumn? Can they include this sense of taste in their poetry? When their poems are finalised, they perform them to each other while sitting around the fire.

PLENARY

Talk to the children about the concrete poem and autumn personification poems they have created. How have they developed a rhythm with the words they have used? How have they included personification? How effective is this in creating an image in their poem? Can they perform their poem to a peer or the rest of the class?

Back in the classroom

- Develop further autumn poems and perform them to different audiences.

- Create a display of the concrete poems about fireworks.

- Develop autumn recipe cards and recipe books.

- Write a restaurant review of the autumn tastes.

EVALUATION/FOLLOW ON

- What went well today?
- Which children understood the concepts?
- Which children needed more help?
- Are there other resources you can use?
- Can you use some of the concrete poetry to extend further work?

PREPARATION

Write an imaginary letter from a housing developer (see Challenge 2).

Review www. reducereuserecycle.co.uk and www.recycling-guide.org.uk/schools.html.

Resources

• A range of natural objects

• Imaginary letter from a housing developer

Previous learning

Talk to the children about what they have learned about places and what is important to them about a place. What would their imaginary place look like?

CONSIDER

Health & Safety

Assess and evaluate hazards and risks in your setting. See the health and safety chapter.

LESSON OBJECTIVES

We are developing and describing an imaginary place. We are preparing for a pollution/development debate.

National Curriculum Content

• Explain and discuss their understanding of what they have read, including through formal presentations and debates, maintaining a focus on the topic and using notes where necessary.

ADULT ROLES

• Model creating an imaginary place with the children, using natural resources.

• Support children in collecting notes in preparation for the debate.

WARM UP IDEAS

Talk to the children about what is important to them in a place or space. What do they like to see in a place? What do they dislike about places?

Many people do not like to see littering. Why do they think this offends people? What does litter do to places? What can be done with litter? Explain the 'reduce, reuse, recycle' campaign. How could they promote this campaign in school?

Introductory activity

(Groups of four)

Using natural and man-made objects, groups plan ways of promoting a reduce, reuse, recycle campaign for the school.

This could be in the form of a 'litter bug' character that promotes the campaign and informs children about what they need to do to reduce their use of materials or how they can reuse and recycle. The litter bug could be made from recyclable waste. Or they could create a poster with a tree on it to promote recycling, using objects, words and recyclable materials.

MAIN ACTIVITIES

Imaginary place

Challenge 1 (whole class, individual, in pairs)

Develop an imaginary place

Explain that children are going to develop an imaginary place that they would like to visit or live in. Prompt ideas:

- What would be in this special place? What physical features would it have, e.g. lakes, mountains, beaches?

- Model some ideas with the children about how you can use natural resources to replicate a miniature version of a place, e.g. large stones could be used as mountains.

- Who would live in this place?

- Would there be houses or would the residents of this place live in something else?

Once children have developed ideas about what their imaginary place looks like, they mark out an area using sticks or stones, then build a model of it using natural resources.

Once their model is completed, they describe their imaginary place to a partner. They explain why they have chosen particular features. Why would they like to live in or visit this place? Why is this place important to them? How would they feel if it was destroyed or polluted, or someone tried to develop it?

Challenge 2 (whole class and groups of four)

Destruction and pollution debate

Show the children an imaginary letter from a housing developer. In the letter, the developer says that they would like to purchase some of the school field and put up a large phone mast in the field next door to the school. In return, the school will be given a small adventure playground area to replace the loss of nearly half of their field and some of the outdoor learning area.

Talk to the children about the letter. Explain that groups will need to do some research first about the proposal before they decide whether this is a good idea or not. They may wish to consider the following:

- Different viewpoints: how might the council feel about it? Or the school staff or their parents?

- How important is this space to them?

- What will happen to existing wildlife?

- Will there be any pollution?

- Is the remaining space big enough?

- What about the phone mast? Should this be near a school?

Encourage the children to discuss and plan how they will do the research, make notes and start to work towards forming an opinion about who is for and who is against the proposal. Explain that they will have the chance to take part in a debate in the next lesson, so they need to collaborate beforehand.

PLENARY

Talk to the children about the imaginary place they developed. How did they describe their imaginary place? What language did they use? Did their partner understand how important it was to them and why? How will they prepare for the debate? What do they need to do to prepare?

Back in the classroom

- The children could make 3D models of their imaginary place.

- Can the imaginary place be used as a setting for a story?

- Children continue to prepare their notes and arguments for the debate.

- Give the children further opportunities to take part in debates about pollution issues.

EVALUATION/FOLLOW ON

- What went well today?

- Which children understood the concepts?

- Which children needed more help?

- Are there other resources you can use?

- Can you develop a display or introduce follow-up work on imaginary places?

PREPARATION

Ensure that there is a space where seating can be placed in the outdoor area, e.g. log seating, so that children can take part in a debate.

You will need to prepare some role-play cards for the debate in advance of the session.

Resources

- A collection of poems and items the children have made and images taken during the progressions
- Tablets
- Log seating
- Example role-play cards for the debate for each of the groups

Previous learning

Talk to the children about the notes they have made in preparing for the debate about the school field.

Get children to select their favourite pieces of work from the unit to share.

CONSIDER

Health & Safety

Assess and evaluate hazards and risks in your setting. See the health and safety chapter.

LESSON OBJECTIVES

We are taking part in a debate about the school field and performing poems and presentations about 'Our place'.

National Curriculum Content

- Explain and discuss their understanding of what they have read, including through formal presentations and debates, maintaining a focus on the topic and using notes where necessary.

ADULT ROLES

- Model the way in which issues can be debated with arguments for and against.
- Support the children in their debate and celebration of their work.

WARM UP IDEAS

Talk to the children about the previous lessons and the pieces of work that they particularly like or are proud of.

Introductory activity

(Whole class and groups of four)

Think about places and spaces children have looked at in this unit. Explain that they will make some presentations to an invited audience at a future point. They will be celebrating 'their favourite places and spaces' and debating a special place.

- How can they present their work to others in the local community?
- How can they use what they have written to influence others?
- Who are the decision-makers in the school and in the local community?
- Who would they like to talk to about what they have found out about places that matter to them?
- How can they continue to improve the spaces and places that are important to them?

Give the children the opportunity to discuss this in groups and then feed back to make a decision about their audience and plans.

MAIN ACTIVITIES

Places and spaces

Challenge 1 (groups of four to six)

'The Great Debate' about the school field development

The children will be split into various groups, which they can choose, e.g. some will form a group from the housing developers, some from the school staff, some from the pupils' perspective, some from the council and some from the local community.

- These groups need to discuss and prepare an argument from that viewpoint to take part in a debate about the school field.

- Children can be given the role play cards to provide them with examples of possible arguments these groups may have, but should also add their own arguments based on the group they are in.

Once they have prepared their arguments, assemble the children into 'for' and 'against' groups on either side of you and chair the debate, letting each side take a turn. After every group has presented their case, discuss which arguments were most persuasive. Take a vote about whether the development should go ahead. This could be done by children dropping a leaf into one of two boxes to make a choice and then counting them.

Challenge 2 (groups of four to six)

Planning a celebration of spaces and places

Talk to the children about presenting their work to their intended audience. What sorts of demonstrations of their work will be appropriate?

- Choose some spaces in the outdoor areas of the school where groups can present and perform different pieces of their work, e.g. a soundbite area, a poetry area, a campaign area, etc.

- Give the groups the opportunity to select their work and practise for their performance.

Note: Children should be given the opportunity to celebrate, perform and display their work after this final lesson – for example, at a parents' evening. The celebration should take place in the outdoor spaces that matter to the children. They could select various venues around the site where they are going to perform or present the work they have completed in this unit, e.g. poetry, raps, descriptive writing, pollution campaigns, picture frames, a debate, etc.

PLENARY

Talk to the children about what they have learned from this unit.

- What have they learned about writing for different purposes and different audiences?

- How can they use figurative language to impact on readers?

- What do they need to continue to develop in their writing?

- How do they need to prepare for a debate?

- What piece of work are they most proud of? Why do places and spaces matter?

Back in the classroom

- Develop a guide to special places and spaces on the school site and in the local area.

- Give the children the opportunity to present their own ideas to the headteacher or governors about how they can continue to improve their outside space.

- Create a final display of work about 'Our place', including feedback from the audience that they invited.

EVALUATION/FOLLOW ON

- What went well today?

- Which children understood the concepts?

- Which children needed more help?

- Are there other resources you can use?

Maths

In this unit, children use and apply the Year 5 vocabulary linked to geometry from the 2014 National Curriculum for England, whilst exploring properties of angles and regular and irregular polygons in the outdoor learning area. They use problem-solving and team-building activities, including Raccoon Circles. You can find over 150 Raccoon Circle activities in *The Revised and Expanded Book of Raccoon Circles* by Jim Cain and Tom Smith, and you can download a free collection of Raccoon Circle activities at: www.teamworkandteamplay.com. The activities in this unit also provide opportunities for assessment for learning. Integral to the activities are vocabulary and objectives associated with calculation and estimation and measures.

To support inclusive practice or to extend learning, the space, task, equipment and people (STEP) approach can be adopted throughout this unit. By changing the space, task, equipment or people, the activity can be made more challenging or easier to understand, enabling all pupils to take part in the activity, as explained in the assessment chapter in this book. To support differentiation and individual needs, the Year 4 objectives are also referenced where appropriate.

The main activities offer opportunities for adult-directed whole class and smaller-group work, as well as opportunities for individual exploration and experimentation where appropriate.

You may wish to record the activities using a camera.

Natural connections

- Leaf and tree identification
- Using nature's clues to tell directions
- Care for the environment

Health and wellbeing

- Physical activity
- Teamwork
- Self-regulation and independence
- Risk management.

Word bank

Geometry – properties of shape

- regular and irregular polygons
- quadrilateral
- pentagon
- hexagon
- heptagon
- octagon
- nonagon
- decagon

Geometry – position and direction

- protractor
- vertex
- dimensions
- angles: right-angled, acute, reflex, obtuse
- degrees: 60°, 90°, 180°, 360°
- clockwise
- anticlockwise

Summary overview

Progression	Curriculum content	Learning experiences/activities
Lesson 1	Know that angles are measured in degrees. Estimate and compare acute, obtuse and reflex angles. Use the properties of rectangles to deduce related facts and find missing lengths and angles. Distinguish between regular and irregular polygons, based on reasoning about equal sides and angles.	Children use sticks to make and name as many geometric shapes as possible, also naming their properties. In team-building activities using a length of tubular webbing, they 'Shape up' and 'Step in' to explore the properties of a circle. Children revise and explore the properties of different regular polygons by creating them physically using specified criteria.
Lesson 2	Know that angles are measured in degrees. Use the properties of rectangles to deduce related facts and find missing lengths and angles. Distinguish between regular and irregular polygons, based on reasoning about equal sides and angles.	Children use 'Random pairing' and 'Walk and talk' to revise prior shape learning, before exploring irregular and regular polygons. They 'Step in' to describe properties. In smaller groups, they make polygon shapes, matching shape properties. They use 'Step in' to suggest ways of completing the task.
Lesson 3	Know that angles are measured in degrees. Estimate and compare acute, obtuse and reflex angles. Draw given angles and measure them in degrees (°).	Children explore the properties of acute, right-angled, obtuse and reflex angles using sticks. They create their names out of sticks and estimate and compare acute, obtuse and reflex angles. They create a tableau picture of stick people in a variety of activities, using acute, right-angled, obtuse and reflex angles.
Lesson 4	Know that angles are measured in degrees. Estimate and compare acute, obtuse and reflex angles. Draw given angles and measure them in degrees (°).	Following the introduction of a protractor in the classroom, the children use tubular webbing to estimate angles on a curve (e.g. on a netball semicircle). They use angles to create a picture in the style of Kandinsky, using found objects.
Lesson 5	Identify angles in one whole turn (total 360°), half turn (total 180°) and other multiples of 90°.	Children use the 'Pass the knot' activity to explore clockwise and anticlockwise turns. They identify angles in one whole turn (total 360°), half a turn (total 180°) and other multiples of 90°, following given instructions. They plot a course using turns across the outdoor learning area for another pair to follow.
Lesson 6	Identify 3D shapes, including cubes and other cuboids, from 2D representations.	Children build fires from 2D representations of 3D shapes. They decide which would best satisfy the fire triangle criteria and light a fire as modelled, understanding and managing the risks involved.

PREPARATION

Become familiar with the water knot used to join the lengths of tubular webbing (see www.bloomsbury.com/NC-Outdoors). This knot, also known as a tape knot, is strong under pressure but also easy to undo after use.

Prepare a set of 'properties of polygons' cards (see the examples on page 33).

Resources

- Collection of sticks
- 13 m length of tubular webbing or soft rope
- 6 m lengths of tubular webbing or soft rope
- 'Properties of polygons' cards

Previous learning

This progression builds on children's previous geometry learning.

CONSIDER

Health & Safety

Assess and evaluate hazards and risks in your setting. See the health and safety chapter.

LESSON OBJECTIVES

We are exploring, identifying and comparing the properties of regular polygons.

National Curriculum Content

- Know that angles are measured in degrees.
- Estimate and compare acute, obtuse and reflex angles.
- Use the properties of rectangles to deduce related facts and find missing lengths and angles.
- Distinguish between regular and irregular polygons, based on reasoning about equal sides and angles.
- Year 4: Compare geometric shapes based on their properties.
- Year 4: Identify acute and obtuse angles.
- Year 4: Identify lines of symmetry in 2D shapes presented in different orientations.

ADULT ROLES

- Support with making the shapes only when necessary, e.g. to control safety or to promote 'on task' behaviour, as a key element of the tasks is to work independently as a team.
- Allow experimentation but consider safety.
- Ask questions to encourage the use of mathematical vocabulary.

WARM UP IDEAS

Explain that over the next six weeks children will be exploring shape and angles in the outdoors.

Ask the children what maths they have done outdoors in the past.

Give a brief overview of the next few progressions and tell them that today's lesson will be about using named properties to create regular polygons. Can they define the term 'polygon'? Then give them the definition: a closed 2D shape with straight sides (which means it has at least three sides).

Introductory activity (groups of four)

Children identify trees from the area and collect 12 sticks no longer than their forearm to make as many polygons as possible.

Can they use mathematical vocabulary to describe the properties of the polygons they have made, e.g. number of sides, acute, right-angled and obtuse angles, lines of symmetry, what makes a polygon regular, etc.?

MAIN ACTIVITIES

Properties of regular polygons

Reintroduce the Raccoon Circles activities (see page 30 for more information on Raccoon Circles). The following activities require a long length of tubular webbing with its ends joined with a water knot.

Challenge 1 (whole class)

'Shape up' and 'Step in'

1. Holding the webbing at waist height, the class works together to make a perfect circle.
2. Carefully work together to place the webbing on the ground. This may take a few attempts. Just try again, remedying any problems as they occur.
3. When it is on the ground, the class walk around the outside of the circle, looking to see whether it matches the properties of a circle, in order to get a different perspective.
4. When they are back in their starting positions, revise vocabulary describing shapes by asking children one at a time to 'step in', stepping over the tape and into the circle, while stating one property of the circle, such as 'It has no corners or edges', 'It is a two-dimensional curved shape', etc.
5. Children may state that it has lines of symmetry, a diameter, radius and circumference. Actually walk along these lines to reinforce them and keep the session active.
6. Ask the children to 'step in' to name other polygon shapes that they know. Can they name the properties of these?
7. Ask the children what a regular polygon is. Give the definition: a shape whose sides are all the same length and whose angles are all equal.
8. Can they work out what an irregular polygon is? Give the definition: a shape whose sides are different lengths and whose angles are different sizes.

Challenge 2 (groups of four)

Make different regular polygons from a description of their properties

Introduce the 'properties of polygons' cards.

Groups choose a card, then work together to name and make a specific polygon from the given properties, using the tubular webbing as modelled above, e.g. a triangle, heptagon or decagon.

Properties of regular polygon cards

3 equal sides 3 equal angles	4 equal sides 4 equal angles
5 equal sides 5 equal angles	6 equal sides 6 equal angles
8 equal sides 8 equal angles	10 equal sides 10 equal angles

PLENARY

Encourage the children to explain what they have been doing in the session and state what they have found out about shapes.

EVALUATION/FOLLOW ON

- What went well and why?
- What didn't go as well as expected?
- What could be changed?
- Who stood out and why?

The National Curriculum Outdoors: Year 5   33

PREPARATION

Rehearse the water knot (see www.bloomsbury.com/NC-Outdoors).

Prepare cards in the format shown below for regular and irregular versions of all polygons between three and eight sides.

Resources

- 13 m length of tubular webbing or soft rope
- 6 m lengths of tubular webbing or soft rope
- 'Make your polygon' cards

Previous learning

Children may have experienced 'Random pairing' and 'Walk and talk' activities.

CONSIDER

Health & Safety

Assess and evaluate hazards and risks in your setting. See the health and safety chapter.

LESSON OBJECTIVES

We are working as a team to explore, describe and compare the properties of regular and irregular polygons.

National Curriculum Content

- Know that angles are measured in degrees.
- Use the properties of rectangles to deduce related facts and find missing lengths and angles.
- Distinguish between regular and irregular polygons based on reasoning about equal sides and angles.
- Year 4: Compare and classify geometric shapes, based on their properties and sizes.
- Year 4: Identify acute and obtuse angles and compare and order angles up to two right angles by size.
- Year 4: Identify lines of symmetry in 2D shapes presented in different orientations.

ADULT ROLES

- Encourage independence, working with a partner or as a team for support.
- Model the activities yourself, acknowledging the tricky parts and being positive about the management of any difficulties.
- Allow experimentation but consider safety.
- Ask questions to encourage the use of mathematical vocabulary.

Make your polygon cards

Irregular triangle	Regular octagon
3 sides of different lengths	8 equal sides
3 angles of different sizes	8 equal angles

WARM UP IDEAS

Explain that today children will be exploring the properties of regular and irregular polygons. Revise the terms 'polygon', 'regular' and 'irregular'.

Tell the children that they will be using the activities 'Random pairing' and 'Walk and talk' to revise prior shape learning before exploring 'regular' and 'irregular'.

This gives them the chance to interact with children outside of their immediate friendship group. It is also a way of assessing learning by listening to the conversations!

MAIN ACTIVITIES

Polygon properties

Challenge 1 (whole class)

'Random pairing' and 'Walk and talk'

Join the ends of the long length of tubular webbing with a water knot.

1. Holding the webbing at waist height, the class carefully work together to place it on the ground as a perfect circle. This may take a few attempts.

2. Revise the 'step in' activity from Progression 1 by asking for volunteers to 'step in' to name and describe properties of a variety of regular polygons.

3. Once this has been done, invite every other child to step into the circle so that an equal number of children are outside and inside the circle.

4. 'Insiders' turn to the right and 'outsiders' turn to the left and walk around the circle in opposite directions, i.e. the insiders walk anticlockwise and the outsiders clockwise.

5. Once the children have walked around the circle and a bit more, call out 'Stop!' and the children turn to face the person nearest to them – an outsider facing an insider.

6. This is now their talking and sharing partner to share ideas and talk through answers.

7. The children stand shoulder to shoulder in their relative positions (with tubular webbing between them on the ground) and all walk in the same direction, e.g. all walk clockwise.

8. As they walk, they talk (but not all at the same time!) The insider is the listener and the outsider is the talker. The children swap places and roles at the knot.

9. Ask the children to share with their partner what they have learned so far about the properties of shapes and what they know about regular and irregular polygons. What new vocabulary can they remember and use?

Challenge 2 (groups of four)

Make regular and irregular polygons with properties matching the named polygon shape.

Introduce the 'Make your polygon' cards. Groups choose a card, then work together to make the named polygon, using the tubular webbing.

1. Holding the tape at waist height, the group works together to make the named polygon, satisfying the properties described on the card.

2. To check that it matches the properties criteria, the group carefully works together to place it on the ground. This may take a few attempts.

3. When it is on the ground, the group walks around the outside of the shape, looking to see whether it matches the properties of the named polygon on the card, in order to get a different perspective.

4. Children 'step in' to suggest ideas to complete the task, for the team to listen to and apply if they agree, e.g. making possible changes to the length of a side or an angle.

5. What could they use to check? Use their ideas to carry out checks.

6. Share the polygons with the whole class, identifying their properties and discussing the elements of teamwork used to complete the task.

PLENARY

Using the 'Walk and talk' activity above, the children explain to their walk and talk partner what they have found out about regular and irregular shapes and about working together.

Back in the classroom

Children can draw the shapes they created, adding captions and speech bubbles to describe their properties.

EVALUATION/FOLLOW ON

- What went well and why?
- What didn't go as well as expected?
- What could be changed?
- Who stood out and why?

PREPARATION

Resources

- Selection of sticks and twigs
- Large protractors

Previous learning

This extends and applies previous learning about angles.

CONSIDER

Health & Safety

Assess and evaluate hazards and risks in your setting. See the health and safety chapter.

LESSON OBJECTIVES

We are exploring and estimating angles and naming them.

National Curriculum Content

- Know that angles are measured in degrees.
- Estimate and compare acute, obtuse and reflex angles.
- Draw given angles, and measure them in degrees (°).
- Year 4: Identify acute and obtuse angles and compare and order angles up to two right angles by size.

ADULT ROLES

- Encourage independence, working with a partner or as a team for support.
- Model the activities yourself, acknowledging the tricky parts and being positive about the management of difficulties.
- Allow experimentation but consider safety.
- Ask questions to encourage the use of mathematical vocabulary.

WARM UP IDEAS

Explain that this session is about angles. What angles can children name and describe?

Can they think of real objects in the setting with:

- Acute angles, such as a swing frame, a partially opened door or the angle for using a fire striker.
- Right angles (lots!).
- Obtuse angles, such as a wide-opened door, roof trusses, scissors, etc.

Introductory activity (in pairs)

Explore angles, using sticks to assess and reinforce understanding.

1. Children collect sticks no longer than their hand from the area. Can they remember the trees that are in the area? Can they use clues, such as fallen leaves, to identify them?
2. Join two sticks at one end and identify the 'vertex' and the 'arms' or straight sides, which open and close to increase and decrease the size of the angle.
3. Use the sticks to create different angles from specified criteria, e.g. show me an angle less than 90°, show me an angle more than 90°, show me an angle more than 90° but less than 180°, show me an angle greater than 180°, show me an angle of 180°, etc.
4. In pairs, they repeat the modelled activity, with one partner specifying the angle and the other making it using sticks. They then swap over.
5. Can they describe and name different categories of angles?

MAIN ACTIVITIES

Angle estimation

Explain to the children that now they can compare, describe and name acute, right, obtuse and reflex angles, they are going to use these to explore the angles in their names.

Challenge 1 (whole class and individual)

Identify the angles in your name

Demonstrate to the children how capital letters can be made using straight lines (sticks).

- Which letters have acute angles, e.g. A, M, W?
- Which letters have right angles, e.g. L, H, T?
- Which letters have obtuse angles, e.g. K, X, Y?

Children work individually to collect enough sticks to make their names using straight lines.

- Whose name has the most angles?
- Whose name has the most acute/right-angled/ obtuse angles?
- Did anyone find a reflex angle, such as over the top of the A?

Challenge 2 (whole class and individual)

Use different angles to make stick people

Demonstrate to the children how a simple stick person can be 'drawn' on the ground using straight lines (sticks).

Model how the sticks can be placed and added to, to show a stick person in different positions. Can they identify angles used in the figure? Children create a tableau or picture showing a group of stick people doing something, e.g. a stick person on a bike or playing football. They could also create stick animals if they want to.

They identify and describe the angles in their picture.

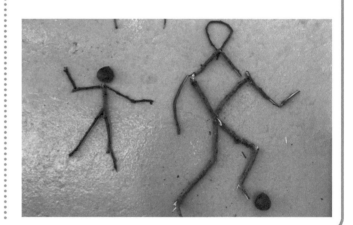

PLENARY

Encourage the children to explain what they have been doing in the session and state what they have found out about angles.

Back in the classroom

Children add captions or instructions to photos of their stick names and stick people, demonstrating their understanding of angles. For example, the children could label the different types of angles they can see in the photos. These photos could also be used as starting points for creative writing.

EVALUATION/FOLLOW ON

- What went well and why?
- What didn't go as well as expected?
- What could be changed?
- Who stood out and why?

PREPARATION

Source a collection of sticks and natural objects suitable for the pictures prior to the session. If the children are not going to use tools, cut the sticks to size.

Resources

- Netball court (the D part around the goal) or draw a semicircle in chalk

- 13 m length of tubular webbing

- Collection of sticks and natural objects

- Images of paintings by Kandinsky: www. wassilykandinsky.net

- Bow saws, loppers, secateurs and safety gloves

Previous learning

Practice with using a protractor in the classroom would be beneficial prior to this session.

CONSIDER

Health & Safety

Assess and evaluate hazards and risks in your setting. See the health and safety chapter.

LESSON OBJECTIVES

We are exploring angles and using these to create images based on the artist Kandinsky, using natural materials.

National Curriculum Content

- Know that angles are measured in degrees.

- Estimate and compare acute, obtuse and reflex angles.

- Draw given angles, and measure them in degrees (°).

- Year 4: Identify acute and obtuse angles and compare and order angles up to two right angles by size.

ADULT ROLES

- Encourage independence, working with a partner or as a team for support.

- Model the activities yourself, acknowledging the tricky parts and being positive about the management of difficulty.

- Ask questions to encourage the use of mathematical vocabulary.

WARM UP IDEAS

Following the introduction of how to use a protractor in the classroom, tell the children that this week they will be practising using a giant protractor to estimate angles, before using angles to create natural artwork.

Introductory activity

The children stand around the curved part of the semicircle facing inwards.

1. Tell the children that this represents the protractor 'curve'.
2. The goal line of the court represents the 'baseline' of the protractor.
3. The netball post represents the 'origin' of the protractor or 'vertex' of the angle. If the post is not in place, then the teacher or a child can stand at that point.
4. Ask the children what a protractor is used for, and then what angle it can measure up to.
5. Can they point to the person standing at 90°, 45°, 135°, etc.?
6. The person at the specified angle 'steps in', stepping over the line into the semicircle.

MAIN ACTIVITIES

Kandinsky angles

Continuing from the introductory activity, use the semicircle and 13 m length of tubular webbing (untied) to estimate and create angles.

Challenge 1 (whole class)

Explore angles on a curve using tubular webbing

Use the tubular webbing to provide a visual representation of the 'arms' forming an angle.

1. Give one end of the webbing to a child at the 0/180° point.
2. Pass the webbing around the pivot point (such as the netball post) and out to the semicircle of children to form two rays, arms or lines, forming an angle around the vertex formed by the netball post.
3. With the end of the webbing held at 0°, invite the children to pass the end of the webbing until it reaches an angle of 90°, 45°, 135°, etc.
4. Do they all agree? How did they work it out?
5. Can they describe and name the angles?
6. Can they make angles that are acute, right, obtuse, or reflex?

Challenge 2 (groups of four)

Use natural materials to create artwork and sticks to make angles

In the natural outdoor learning area, explain that children will use natural materials to create artwork and sticks to make angles, sharing the images of paintings by Kandinsky.

Can they identify the different angles used in Kandinsky's paintings?

Model how to make the angles using sticks, adding additional detail such as colour and texture using found objects from the area.

Groups use angles to create a picture in the style of Kandinsky, with natural materials and found objects providing an opportunity to identify trees and leaves in the learning area.

PLENARY

Evaluate the effectiveness of the children's pictures and discuss the angles they have used.

Back in the classroom

Print off some photos of the children's pictures and ask them to create a display that labels the angles and shapes present to demonstrate their understanding of vocabulary and concepts

EVALUATION/FOLLOW ON

- What went well and why?
- What didn't go as well as expected?
- What could be changed?
- Who stood out and why?

PREPARATION

Create the 'turn' cards (see the examples below).

Resources

- 13 m length of tubular webbing
- 'Turn' cards
- Whiteboards and a pen

Previous learning

Talk to the children about what they have learned about angles so far.

CONSIDER

Health & Safety

Assess and evaluate hazards and risks in your setting. See the health and safety chapter.

'Turn' cards

One whole turn (total 360°)	Half a turn (total 180°)
One quarter turn (90°)	Two quarter turns (total 180°)
Three quarter turns (270°)	Two half turns (total 360°)

LESSON OBJECTIVES

We are using turns to map a route in the outdoor learning area.

National Curriculum Content

- Identify angles in one whole turn (total 360°), half turn (total 180°) and other multiples of 90°.

ADULT ROLES

- Encourage independence, working with a partner or as a team for support.
- Model the activities yourself, acknowledging the tricky parts and being positive about the management of the difficulty.
- Allow experimentation but consider safety.
- Ask questions to encourage the use of mathematical vocabulary.

WARM UP IDEAS

Explain to the children that in this session they will be using angles to describe a 'turn' (such as a quarter turn or half turn) to plot a course around the outdoor learning area.

Introductory activity

Pass the knot

Join the ends of the 13 m webbing using a water knot. Explain that children are going to explore turns using the tubular webbing.

1. The class stands in a circle, holding the webbing 'overhand' (over the top of the tape, rather than grabbing it from below).
2. Note who is nearest the knot – name them the 'keeper of the knot'.
3. Working together, they pass the knot around the circle in an anticlockwise direction to acclimatise themselves to the feel and effect. Ensure that the overhand rule is kept.
4. As it returns to the keeper, everyone raises the tape above their heads and then back to waist height again. Add a cheer!
5. Repeat but in a clockwise direction, ensuring that the overhand rule is kept.
6. How quickly do they think they could pass the knot? Count as the knot is passed.
7. Could they pass it faster?
8. Does it make a difference which direction it goes in?

MAIN ACTIVITIES

Turns to map a route

Challenge 1 (whole class)

Explore turns in direction

1. All the children stand in the circle facing the same direction.

2. Four children are chosen to step out of the circle and to stand at twelve, three, six and nine o'clock to represent north, east, south and west positions as markers. They could hold whiteboards marked with N, E, S and W. These children can also be the 'callers'.

3. The 'callers' take it in turns to give instructions to the whole group to 'turn' a number of times – each turn being 90° to the right or left to revise and reinforce prior learning.

4. Do they know of another way of describing a turn, e.g. one whole turn (total 360°), half turn (total 180°) and quarter turn (90°) or even a three-quarter turn (270°) to the left or right?

5. Use these to give instructions to the class. Callers can refer to the 'turn' cards for help.

Challenge 2 (in pairs)

Give directions using turns (robots)

Children take it in turns to give instructions to a partner to turn and take so many steps forwards to move safely around the outdoor area, using the vocabulary of one whole turn (total 360°), half turn (total 180°) and other turns of multiples of 90°.

Challenge 3 (in pairs)

Use directions to plot a course using turns

Pairs decide on a start and finish position and then plot and describe a course, using angles to describe the turns, across the outdoor learning area. They then record their instructions on paper.

They give the route to another pair to try out from the given start position. They then try another pair's course.

PLENARY

Evaluate the effectiveness of the course directions and discuss the pros and cons of each one, giving reasons.

Does anyone know how to tell the direction from the sun or from asymmetry in trees, such as more moss growing on the damper north side of tree trunks (as the sun tends to dry out the south side), or denser tree growth and foliage on the southern (sunny) side?

EVALUATION/FOLLOW ON

- What went well and why?
- What didn't go as well as expected?
- What could be changed?
- Who stood out and why?

PREPARATION

Source images of 2D representations of 3D shapes, and make them into cards.

Identify the area to be used as a fire-lighting area. Surround this with well-defined markers to create the safety zone.

See the health and safety chapter for information about fire-lighting.

Resources

- '2D representations of 3D shapes' cards
- Additional adult support for fire-lighting
- Fire strikers
- Kindling
- Collection of fuel such as straw and dry sticks of varying lengths and widths
- Water to extinguish the fires
- Heat-resistant gloves

Previous learning

This links to fire-lighting in other progressions in this book.

It consolidates learning about 3D shapes.

CONSIDER

Health & Safety

Assess and evaluate hazards and risks in your setting. See the health and safety chapter.

LESSON OBJECTIVES

We are using our knowledge of 2D and 3D shape properties to light a fire, and to understand (and manage) the risks involved.

National Curriculum Content

- Identify 3D shapes, including cubes and other cuboids, from 2D representations.
- Year 4: Compare and classify geometric shapes, based on their properties.

ADULT ROLES

- Encourage independence, working with a partner or as a team for support.
- Model the activities yourself, acknowledging the tricky parts and being positive about the management of difficulty.
- Allow experimentation but consider safety.
- Ensure safe practice around the fire.

WARM UP IDEAS

Explain that today's lesson will be using fire-building to explore shapes. Which 2D shape would work best for a group so that the heat is fairly shared and safely accessible from any direction?

Introductory activity

Why do we need to create a safety zone around a fire? Revise key safety points outlined in the health and safety chapter.

MAIN ACTIVITIES

2D and 3D fire-building

Explain that the children are going to build 3D-shaped fires from 2D representations and show them the images of shapes. They are going to explore which 3D shape would best satisfy the 'fire triangle' criteria.

Can the children remember the fire triangle theory from prior learning, i.e. that fires need heat, fuel and oxygen?

Challenge 1 (whole class)

Collect fuel for the fire

Ask the children to collect snappy sticks.

Ensure that the children understand the sticks need to be able to 'snap' as this shows that they are dry and able to burn.

Challenge 2 (whole class)

How to use sticks to build 3D shapes from 2D images

Introduce the 2D images or drawings of the 3D shapes. Can the children identify and name the 3D shapes that the 2D drawings are showing?

Model how to use a 2D drawing of the 3D shape to make a 3D model using the sticks and straw. For example:

- Make a sphere by rolling the straw into a ball.

- Create a cuboid tower by placing two pieces of wood parallel to each other, with an air gap about the width of the wood between them. Place another two pieces of wood on top of the first two, at a 90° angle and with an air gap between them, and don't forget to leave a large gap through which to light the fire. Continue until you have at least eight pieces of wood.

- Show how to make a pyramid by leaning sticks together. It can have a triangular or square base.

Challenge 3 (whole class)

How to light a fire safely using 2D and 3D shapes

Demonstrate the key step-by-step fire-lighting principles, reinforcing safety and shape vocabulary.

1. Place a container of water near the fire circle.
2. Make a clear space.
3. Create the base (oxygen).
4. Place kindling in this gap (fuel).
5. Use all the thinner and very dry pieces first, as these will catch fire easiest.
6. Use the fire striker to light the kindling (heat).
7. Give the children fire strikers to practise making sparks, taking turns. Count five attempts before passing it to a partner to have a go. Adult tip: Check the acute angle of the striker.

Challenge 4 (groups of four to six)

Build 3D-shaped fire from 2D images

Give the children the '2D images of 3D shapes' cards.

Children explore which 3D shape works best for fire-lighting as modelled above, using mathematical vocabulary to describe shapes. They light their fire with adult supervision, once the decision has been made about the best shape for the fire and their bases have been suitably prepared.

PLENARY

Encourage the children to explain what they have been doing in the session and state what they have found out about 2D representations of 3D shapes. Which shape burnt best and why?

Back in the classroom

Photos of the children's fires can be used to record the learning, adding text boxes (using computing) or by writing descriptions using mathematical vocabulary.

EVALUATION/FOLLOW ON

- What went well and why?
- What didn't go as well as expected?
- What could be changed?
- Who stood out and why?

Science

In this unit, children will be focusing on scientific skills and observation. Based on the Key Stage 2 science objectives identified in the 2014 National Curriculum for England, the children will be introduced to properties and changes to materials. They will be given the opportunity to develop their observation skills, pose their own questions and carry out scientific enquiries to answer them. They will take on the role of the 'material mavericks' in their quest to find out more about materials. They will build fires and use storm kettles for cooking and heating materials. They will make their own filtration sieve and take part in a welly boot challenge in a quest to find out more about materials and their properties.

To support inclusive practice or to extend learning, the space, task, equipment and people (STEP) approach can be adopted throughout this unit. By changing the space, task, equipment or people, the activity can be made more challenging or easier to understand, enabling all pupils to take part in the activity, as explained in the assessment chapter in this book.

The children will be expected to work as a whole class directed by the teacher, together in small groups with support from adults, and independently.

The role of the adult is to lead the sessions safely and model the activities, allowing experimentation and independence whilst providing support and encouraging resilience.

You may wish to record the activities using a camera.

Natural connections

- Enhanced awareness of the local natural environment
- Understanding of natural materials and their properties.

Health and wellbeing

- Physical activity
- Being focused and attentive
- Teambuilding
- Emotional resilience
- Independent learning.
- Risk management.

Word bank

Materials

- absorbency
- strength
- durability
- insulator
- conductor
- thermal
- filtration
- irreversible
- change
- soluble
- insoluble
- transparency
- magnets
- solids
- liquids
- gases
- dissolving
- sieving
- evaporating

Scientific

- controlling variables
- measurement
- accuracy
- precision
- recording data
- diagrams
- classification
- bar and line graphs
- predictions
- comparative and fair tests
- conclusions
- scientific evidence
- explanations of results

Summary overview

Progression	Curriculum content	Learning experiences/activities
Lesson 1	Compare and group together everyday materials on the basis of their properties, including their hardness, solubility, transparency and conductivity (electrical and thermal).	Children will explore thermal insulators and thermal conductors in this session by carrying out investigations. They will investigate which materials are effective in insulating ice cubes so they do not melt. They will also find out which cups are the most effective at retaining heat to keep hot chocolate warm. Children will use a storm kettle and make observations in comparative tests to find answers to their questions.
Lesson 2	Give reasons, based on evidence from comparative tests, for the particular uses of everyday materials, including metals, wood and plastics.	Children will continue with their investigations to find out which everyday materials are thermal insulators and which materials are thermal conductors. They will make popcorn using a variety of saucepans and they will give reasons why some materials are better than others for transporting the popcorn they have made.
Lesson 3	Give reasons, based on evidence from comparative tests, for the particular uses of everyday materials, including metals, wood and plastics.	Children will investigate which materials are most absorbent. They will look at evidence from comparative tests and take part in a welly boot challenge to support their enquiry into everyday materials.
Lesson 4	Compare and group together everyday materials on the basis of their properties, including their solubility. Plan different types of scientific enquiry to answer questions and recognise and control variables.	Children will revisit solids, liquids and gases and determine which materials are soluble. They will be required to plan their own investigation and decide which variables to test, how they can ensure that it is a fair test and how to record their results.
Lesson 5	Use knowledge of solids, liquids and gases to decide how mixtures might be separated, including through filtering, sieving and evaporating.	Children will make their own sieve in this session using a variety of tools and knots. They will use the sieve they have made to carry out an investigation into the separation of materials, using a variety of methods including the use of sieving, evaporation, magnets and filtering.
Lesson 6	Explain that some changes result in the formation of new materials, and this kind of change is not usually reversible, including changes associated with burning.	Children will have the opportunity to investigate changes that occur when materials are heated, mixed or burned. They will consider what new materials are formed as they carry out their own enquiries as 'material mavericks'.

PREPARATION

Ensure that there is a selection of different materials available in the outdoor learning area.

Make question cards and 'key words' cards relating to materials.

Resources

- 'Key words' question cards
- Range of materials and tarpaulins
- Range of cups: plastic, paper, glass, tin
- Thermometers, pens and paper
- Storm kettles, hot chocolate powder, cups, measuring jugs and ice cubes
- Fire-making kit and water to extinguish fire

Previous learning

Ask children what they remember about materials and their properties before they go outside.

CONSIDER

Health & Safety

Assess and evaluate hazards and risks in your setting. See the health and safety chapter.

LESSON OBJECTIVES

We are learning to compare and group everyday materials based on their properties.

National Curriculum Content

- Compare and group together everyday materials on the basis of their properties, including their hardness, solubility, transparency and conductivity (electrical and thermal).

ADULT ROLES

- Support the children in carrying out their scientific enquiries.
- Encourage them to pose their own questions and find answers through their investigations.
- Support the children in making a hot drink using a storm kettle.

WARM UP IDEAS

Icebergs

Children are encouraged to take part in a problem-solving activity. Groups of four to six are each given a small piece of tarpaulin. They need to work out how they can all stand on the 'iceberg' without going onto the ground. Each group should discuss the challenge and plan what they are going to do.

Carry out the activity and then review it.

- What worked?
- What do they need to change?

Introductory activity

Continuing to work in small groups, children are challenged to sort a selection of materials. As the children sort the materials, they answer questions using the question cards provided.

Questions could include:

- What are the properties of the materials?
- Which materials are insulators?
- What does an insulator do?

Children could also sort the materials using the 'key words' cards, e.g. deciding which materials are soluble, thermal or magnetic.

This activity will identify what the children know about materials, what their understanding of key words is and in which areas they need further support. It will also identify areas in which they want to find out more and enable them to pose their own questions.

MAIN ACTIVITIES

Material mavericks – comparing and grouping

Challenge 1 (whole class and groups of four)
Cool investigation

Talk to the children about what they understand about thermal insulators and thermal conductors. Set up an investigation to see whether they can keep some ice cubes cool. Will the children need material that is a thermal insulator or a thermal conductor, i.e. do we need a material that enables heat to pass through? (Answer: No, we need to insulate the ice cubes so that they stay cool.)

Working in groups of four, using cups of the same size, set up an experiment to see how well insulated plastic cups, mugs, glasses, etc. are. Once the children have chosen some different cups, they will need to place the same amount of ice cubes into each cup to ensure that it is a fair test. Encourage the children to think about what they could measure during the experiment. Could they take the temperature of the ice cubes at regular intervals? Once the children have set up the investigation, they need to place the cups in a cool place. They should be encouraged to monitor and record their results at regular intervals.

Challenge 2 (whole class and groups of four)
Keeping warm

Talk to the children about the use of a storm kettle. Is a storm kettle a thermal conductor or a thermal insulator? Which part of the kettle acts as a thermal insulator? Which part is a thermal conductor? (The wooden handle is a thermal insulator, but the main body of the kettle is a thermal conductor.)

Working in groups of four, the children investigate heating water with hot chocolate powder in a storm kettle. They should use the step-by-step principles for using a storm kettle as shown in the health and safety chapter. This should be adult-led or modelled, depending on the experience of the children in using storm kettles. The children will need a range of different cups for keeping the hot chocolate warm. They will need to place the same amount of liquid into each cup using a measuring jug. They may require help in removing the liquid from the storm kettle.

Which cup is the best thermal insulator for keeping the hot chocolate warm? Encourage the children to record the temperature of the hot chocolate at regular intervals.

PLENARY

Talk to the children about what they have found out in both investigations.

- Which cup is the best thermal insulator for keeping ice cubes cool?

- Is this the same cup that also keeps the hot chocolate hottest for the longest time?

- What material are the cups made from?

- How long did the ice cubes remain in the cup? Which material was the best insulator for keeping things cool?

- How long did the hot chocolate stay warm in the cup? Which was the best insulator for this purpose?

- What other questions do they have about insulation and conduction?

- What other investigations would they like to do?

Back in the classroom

Build a class collection of materials, with 'big questions' that the children will answer through these progressions. Can they produce bar charts and graphs to present the findings of their investigations? Encourage the children to take the role of 'material mavericks'. Can they come up with a design for a cup that can store hot drinks and cold drinks based on their investigation findings?

EVALUATION/FOLLOW ON

- What went well today?

- Which children understood the concepts?

- Which children needed more help?

- Are there other resources you can use?

PREPARATION

Make 'question' cards for the introductory activity.

Resources

- A range of saucepans. Ideally these should all be similarly sized, but made from different materials. Ideally the saucepans should have transparent lids (to monitor popcorn as it cooks)
- 'Key words' and 'question' cards
- Fire-making kit and water to extinguish fire
- Material words, stop watches, whiteboard and pens
- Popcorn and oil
- Paper or cardboard

Previous learning

Talk to the children about what they know about materials. What do they understand about thermal insulators and thermal conductors?

CONSIDER

Health & Safety

Assess and evaluate hazards and risks in your setting. See the health and safety chapter.

LESSON OBJECTIVES

We are learning to carry out tests to determine which materials are more effective for different purposes.

National Curriculum Content

- Give reasons, based on evidence from comparative tests, for the particular uses of everyday materials, including metals, wood and plastics.

ADULT ROLES

- Support the children in carrying out their scientific enquiries.
- Encourage them to pose their own questions and find answers through their investigations.

WARM UP IDEAS

Line up

Encourage the whole class to stand on a line in the playground or use some tape or rope to mark out a line in the outdoor area.

- Give each child a word relating to materials that was used in the last progression, e.g. hardness, solubility, transparency and conductivity.
- Ask the children to order the words they have been given alphabetically on the line. They need to work cooperatively as a team and try not to step off the line as they change places.
- Once they are in alphabetical order, ask the children to discuss their word with the children either side of them.
- Then ask each child to say their word and explain to the whole class what that word means. If they do not know the meaning, they can step back and someone else in the line can help to explain the meaning of the word.

Introductory activity

Using the 'key words' cards, can they find their pair, e.g. solubility could pair with salt.

Can the children find the answer to a question card, e.g. What material could be used as a thermal insulator? There may be more than one answer to each question.

MAIN ACTIVITIES

Material mavericks – testing materials

Challenge 1 (whole class and groups of four)
Saucepan sorcery

Show the children a range of saucepans. Ask the children to explain what they know about the purpose of a saucepan. Is the saucepan a thermal conductor or a thermal insulator? Could there be parts of the saucepan that are thermal insulators?

Groups build a fire using the key safety principles from the health and safety chapter. Give each group a different saucepan. Ideally, the saucepans should all be of a similar size and they should only vary in one respect: for example, they could each be made out of a different material. Give each group the same amount of popcorn and the same amount of oil. Talk to the children about the importance of a fair test.

Encourage the children to cook the popcorn, measuring the length of time it takes for the popcorn to be cooked using a stopwatch. Ask the children to make observations of the changes that take place during the cooking of the popcorn and note these on a whiteboard or paper.

Once the popcorn is cooked, ask the children to consider the following:

- Which saucepan cooked the popcorn the quickest? How long did it take?
- Is the quality of the popcorn good, e.g. not burned or stuck to the pan?
- Which saucepan cooked the popcorn the slowest?
- What changes did they observe?
- What have they found out about the materials used in the investigation?
- What questions did they have prior to the investigation? Have they been answered?

Challenge 2 (whole class and groups of four)
Popcorn containers

Now the children have cooked the popcorn, they need to find the best way to transport the popcorn.

- What everyday material could they use to transport the popcorn?
- Could they make a container from paper or cardboard?
- Could the material they use be recycled?
- What shape does the container need to be?
- Look at some example containers.
- What tests can they carry out to see which container is the most effective at transporting the popcorn?

Allow time for the children to construct and test containers for the popcorn.

PLENARY

Discuss both investigations that have taken place.

- Which saucepan was most effective at heating the popcorn?
- What have the children found out about the saucepans they have used?
- Which container was the best for transporting popcorn?
- What tests did they carry out? Were they fair tests?
- What would they do differently? Could they improve their design?

Back in the classroom

Continue to build a class collection of materials, with 'big questions' that the children will answer through these progressions. Can they produce their results in an interesting way? Encourage the children to take the role of 'material mavericks'. Can they come up with a design for a popcorn container that can be used to transport popcorn?

EVALUATION/FOLLOW ON

- What went well today?
- Which children understood the concepts?
- Which children needed more help?
- Are there other resources you can use?

PREPARATION

Resources

- Two ropes
- Range of materials and cloths to test the absorbency of
- Water
- Tape
- Sand (or another similar material with which to fill a welly boot)
- Large plastic sheet, rubber gloves and measuring jugs
- Wellington boots and a range of different materials to make a wellington boot shape: cloth, newspaper, etc.

Previous learning

Talk to the children about what they have learned to date about materials. What do they understand about a fair test and a comparative test?

CONSIDER

Health & Safety

Assess and evaluate hazards and risks in your setting. See the health and safety chapter.

LESSON OBJECTIVES

We are learning to carry out comparative tests and explain why some materials are more absorbent than others.

National Curriculum Content

- Give reasons, based on evidence from comparative tests, for the particular uses of everyday materials, including metals, wood and plastics.

ADULT ROLES

- Support the children in carrying out their scientific enquiries.
- Encourage them to pose their own questions and find answers through their investigations.

WARM UP IDEAS

Through the wire

Place two ropes between two posts or trees. One of the ropes needs to be higher than the other to create a gap that the children could pass safely through. Working in teams of four to six, the children must get their whole team through the wire (rope) without touching either of the ropes. The children should be encouraged to plan what they are going to do, carry out their plan and then review it.

- Which team managed to get everyone through the wire first?
- Which plan worked most effectively?
- What would they do differently next time?
- Could they complete the challenge in a quicker time?

Introductory activity

Explain that the children are going to investigate the absorbency of different materials. Ask the children what they know about the meaning of the word 'absorbency'. Are there any everyday objects that they know that are absorbent?

Ask each child to select three different materials from a container and place them in absorbency order, with the one they think would be the most absorbent first to the least absorbent last. Discuss their predictions in pairs and give the children the opportunity to reorder the materials after discussion if they need to.

Now pour the same amount of liquid onto the same surface and ask the children to test out the material that they predicted to be the most absorbent. How long does it take to soak up the liquid? Is the material reusable? Can it be recycled?

Material mavericks – how absorbent?

Explain that children will now have a further opportunity to test materials for their absorbency properties and how effective they are in cleaning up a welly boot mess.

Challenge 1 (whole class and groups of four)

The welly boot mess clean

Encourage the children to look at the materials they used in the absorbency tests. Which materials were most effective at absorbing water? Allow the whole class to create a mess on a large plastic sheet with their muddy wellington boots. They then need to consider the following and pose their own questions to carry out their own investigations.

- Which material will be most effective at cleaning?
- Which material has durability? Which material will be absorbent?
- Which material will be able to cope with cleaning such a large mess, i.e. the volume of the clean-up?
- What other materials may be needed?

Groups carry out tests on a range of materials for all the factors listed above. They should ensure that all tests are comparative and fair. Model how to carry out a test, e.g. select four different types of cloth and cut them to the same size. Using rubber gloves, measure a selected area of the plastic sheet and try to clean it up using the cloth. Set a time limit. Make observations during the cleaning and again at the end of the process. What condition is the cloth? Could you measure the amount of water that has been collected?

Challenge 2 (whole class and groups of four)

Making wellies

Talk to the children about the results of Challenge 1. Did they need to use a range of materials to clear the mess? Which materials were the most effective? Why were these the most effective?

Could these materials be used to make a welly boot? Should welly boots be made of a different material? Working in groups, the children make welly boots out of different materials. The children could use their own welly boots as a mould, i.e. they could make a cloth welly boot by wrapping cloth around the boot and then using tape to secure it once the shape has been made. Then slip the shape off from the welly boot. Children will need to improvise by filling the welly boot with sand or another material to ensure that it has weight instead of a human foot.

This challenge could involve devising and marking out a course that the welly boots need to go on to test them: through mud, through bushes, through water, etc. Which material stands up best to the challenge? Would this material last over time?

PLENARY

Talk to the children about the results of the investigations they have carried out.

- What have they found out about materials?
- Are the materials that are the most absorbent also the most durable?
- Which material is best for cleaning?
- Which material is the best boot? Why?
- Can they sort the materials into categories of properties?

EVALUATION/FOLLOW ON

- What went well today?
- Which children understood the concepts?
- Which children needed more help?
- Are there other resources you can use?

Back in the classroom

Can they produce bar charts and graphs to present the findings of their investigations? Encourage the children to take the role of 'material mavericks'. Can they come up with a design for a wellington boot that is a 'super welly' and is waterproof, warm and resistant?

PREPARATION

Review ideas in: www.bbc.com/bitesize/articles/zpd6hyc.

Resources

- Three cones
- A range of materials that are soluble and insoluble, e.g. salt, soil, sugar, cornflour, sand, grit, gravel, etc.
- Measuring jugs, spoons, water and empty containers

Previous learning

Talk to the children about previous sessions they have completed on solids, liquids and gases. What do they understand about the differences between these three materials?

CONSIDER

Health & Safety

Assess and evaluate hazards and risks in your setting. See the health and safety chapter.

LESSON OBJECTIVES

We are learning to compare and group everyday materials on the basis of their properties, including their solubility.

National Curriculum Content

- Compare and group together everyday materials on the basis of their properties, including their solubility.
- Plan different types of scientific enquiry to answer questions and recognise and control variables.

ADULT ROLES

- Support the children in carrying out their scientific enquiries.
- Encourage them to pose their own questions and find answers through their investigations.
- Support the children in planning and delivering their investigations.

WARM UP IDEAS

Recap the children's understanding of liquids, solids and gases. Have three cones spaced apart, labelled solid, liquid and gas. Call out the name of an object, then children run to the correct cone and behave like the atoms in that matter (e.g. closely packed and still for solid and racing about and far apart for gas). Include an ice cube, water and steam in the objects.

Introductory activity

Talk to the children about 'pair and share'. This is where the children work in pairs and think about the question asked, then share their ideas. Ask the pairs: What material can sometimes be a solid, a liquid and a gas? (Hint: All three objects were used in the cones activity, detailed above).

Explain that all things are made up from atoms and whether the matter is a solid, liquid or gas will depend on how the atoms behave. In a solid, the atoms are tightly packed and can hardly move, e.g. in a stick. In a liquid, they are not so tightly packed and can move around more, e.g. water in a container will slop around. A gas not only doesn't hold its shape at room temperature but it does not even stay put, unless in a sealed container. It moves around all the time. The atoms in a gas move around very freely. Think of a balloon – air is blown into the balloon and, when sealed, it stays in there, but it is still moving around inside.

MAIN ACTIVITIES

Material mavericks – soluble problems

Discuss the scientific enquiries children have completed in this unit. In this session they will be given the opportunity to decide their own enquiry questions and variables. They will need to decide what to measure, what equipment they will need, and finally how to record their results so that they can put these into graphs and results tables.

Challenge 1 (whole class and groups of four)
Solutions to soluble problems

The first investigation they will carry out is about soluble materials. What do they know about soluble materials? What do they want to find out? Looking at the range of materials available, can they devise their own enquiry about these materials?

Model an example using a measure of water and a measure of sugar. Ask the children to first predict what they think will happen. Is sugar soluble? Using a spoon, place the sugar into the water and stir it. What has happened? Is the sugar still in the water? How would we test this?

Ensure that the children understand key safety principles. There will be some food items that they can test using taste, but it would not be safe to test soil by tasting the water, for example.

Talk to the children about the variables in this enquiry (the materials), what they are going to measure (the solubility), and the length of time it takes to dissolve something.

- What are they going to keep the same? (The amount of water and amount of material.)

- Will this ensure that it is a fair test?

- By making observations and collecting this data, will they be able to use the results to develop a bar chart/line graph?

- Is there another variable they could measure?

Working in groups, ask the children to devise and carry out an enquiry about soluble materials.

Talk to the children about their findings. Explain that some substances dissolve when you mix them with water. When a substance dissolves, it may look like it has disappeared, but it has mixed with the water to make a transparent, see-through liquid. Substances that dissolve in water are called soluble substances.

Challenge 2 (groups of four)
Presenting results

Encourage the children to discuss the results of their investigations, including any problems they had and whether it was a fair test. Ask them to prepare a five-minute presentation, in which they can present to the rest of the class the results of their investigations. They should make sure that everyone has a role in the preparation and presentation.

PLENARY

Discuss with the class the results of all their findings and how the groups presented these findings.

- What have they learned about soluble materials?

- What do they still want to find out?

- How could their reporting of results be improved?

- What else do they need to think about to be scientific in their investigations?

Back in the classroom

Encourage the children to take the role of 'material mavericks'. Can they come up with an idea for a soluble substance that turns drinks a different colour? Or think of their own question that they would like to answer through design?

EVALUATION/FOLLOW ON

- What went well today?
- Which children understood the concepts?
- Which children needed more help?
- Are there other resources you can use?

PREPARATION

Resources

- A range of materials to separate, including coffee, salt in water, pasta, paperclips, sand, gravel, soil, rice, nails, etc.

- Hazel wood, loppers, folding saws, string and secateurs

- A range of materials for making a sieve, e.g. tights, net, cloth, etc.

- Sieves and magnets

- Optional: fire-making kit and water to extinguish fire

Previous learning

Discuss with the children what they have learned to date about materials. What do they know about material properties? Have they answered some of the questions they had about materials? What do they still want to find out?

CONSIDER

Health & Safety

Assess and evaluate hazards and risks in your setting. See the health and safety chapter.

LESSON OBJECTIVES

We are learning to use sieving, evaporation and filtration as ways of separating materials.

National Curriculum Content

- Use knowledge of solids, liquids and gases to decide how mixtures might be separated, including through filtering, sieving and evaporating.

ADULT ROLES

- Support the children in carrying out their scientific enquiries.

- Encourage them to pose their own questions and find answers through their investigations.

- Support the children in making a sieve using tools and knots.

WARM UP IDEAS

(Groups of four)

Working in groups, encourage the children to build their own stick tower. Once they have built a stick tower, they should swap with another group. In the group, they then each take it in turns to remove one stick at a time until the tower falls. The groups could be timed as to which tower is standing for the longest. Which structure was most effective in this game? Ask the children what properties the longest-standing stick tower has.

Introductory activity

(Groups of four)

Using their knowledge of materials, children will now have the opportunity to separate a range of materials such as pasta, salt in water, paper clips, sand, gravel, soil, flour, rice, coffee, etc. Give each group a selection of materials that have been placed all together in a tub. Include some water that contains salt in a plastic container. Give the children a range of equipment, including sieves and magnets. Can the children come up with ways to separate the materials? Talk to the children about their understanding of sieving, filtering and evaporation.

MAIN ACTIVITIES

Material mavericks – separation of materials

Explain that in this session children are going to make their own frame as part of making a sieve, which they will use to separate some materials.

Challenge 1 (individual and groups of four)

Making sieves

Ask the children to collect four sticks that are similar in length. Children may need to use tools to cut the sticks into equal lengths. When using tools, ensure that they are using the appropriate tools for the task and follow the guidance for safe use of tools in the health and safety chapter. Once the children have four sticks of equal length, remind them of how to do a clove hitch knot. Further information about tying knots can be found at www.bloomsbury.com/NC-Outdoors.

Once they have connected two sticks using the clove hitch knot, they will then need to square-lash the knot to secure the two sticks together. Again, further information can be found at www.bloomsbury.com/NC-Outdoors.

They need to repeat this for each of the four corners of the square to make a frame.

In groups, the children should then select a different material that they are going to place over the frame and secure for a sieve. This could include cloth, tights, netting, filter paper, etc. They should discuss between them which would be most suitable material and why. They then need to secure their selected material over the frame to complete their sieve.

Challenge 2 (groups of four)

Sieve separations

The children in their groups select items that they predict could be separated using the sieves they have made. They may select just one substance, e.g. salt in water, and test it using a variety of different sieves. They may choose a range of materials and try to separate them using one of the sieves. They could place some of the materials in water and try to separate them using the sieve, e.g. sand, soil or gravel. Encourage the children to pose their own questions, set up their own investigations and record their results.

Talk to the children about what they have found out.

- Do the sieves work in separating materials?
- Has the salt separated from the water?
- What other materials have they managed to separate using the sieves?

Challenge 3 (groups of four)

Possible extension – evaporation solutions

Children may have predicted in the introductory activity that the only way to separate some materials is through the process of heating and evaporation. In this extension activity, the groups build a fire, using the safety principles in the health and safety chapter, and boil the water to separate the salt from it, using a pan. Can they predict what might happen? Does heating the water separate the salt? Why does heating the water work?

PLENARY

Discuss with the children what they have learned about separating materials.

- Which materials separate easily, using physical barriers like sieves, and which materials require other processes to separate them?
- What do the materials that are more difficult or easy to separate have in common?

Back in the classroom

Continue to build a class collection of materials, with 'big questions' that the children will answer through these progressions. Can they produce bar charts and graphs to present the findings of their investigations? Encourage the children to take the role of 'material mavericks'. Can they come up with a design for a large sieve machine that can sort materials on a large scale?

EVALUATION/FOLLOW ON

- What went well today?
- Which children understood the concepts?
- Which children needed more help?
- Are there other resources you can use?

PREPARATION

Gather a selection of recipes and ingredients, some of which when heated will result in reversible change, e.g. chocolate and jelly. Some ingredients will have irreversible change once heated, e.g. eggs.

Review the ideas in https://sciencebob.com/blow-up-a-balloon-with-yeast and www.hamilton-trust.org.uk/science/year-5-science/changes-materials-changing-materials-education-pack.

Resources

- A selection of recipes and ingredients
- Hoops, ropes, tarpaulins, sticks and cones
- Bread, toast, eggs, oil, frying pan and cooking utensils
- Test tubes or other transparent containers, balloons and warm water
- Baking powder, yeast, sugar and vinegar
- Fire-making kit and water to extinguish fire

Previous learning

Talk to the children about their investigations to date. What have they discovered as 'material mavericks'? What questions have they answered that they posed at the beginning of this unit? Are there still some things that they want to find out?

CONSIDER

Health & Safety

Assess and evaluate hazards and risks in your setting. See the health and safety chapter.

LESSON OBJECTIVES

We are learning to carry out investigations to find out which materials when mixed, heated or burned create changes that are not reversible and result in the creation of new materials.

National Curriculum Content

- Explain that some changes result in the formation of new materials, and this kind of change is not usually reversible, including changes associated with burning.

ADULT ROLES

- Support the children in carrying out their scientific enquiries.
- Encourage them to pose their own questions and find answers through their investigations.
- Support the children in cooking a variety of items to investigate reversible and irreversible change.

WARM UP IDEAS

Ask the children to recap the warm up games they have played in previous sessions.

- Which activities have they enjoyed?
- Can they lead an activity from a previous session?
- Who will lead the activity?
- Can they change the challenge to make it more difficult?

Introductory activity

Look at the range of recipes and ingredients and decide whether, once cooked, an irreversible change has taken place or a reversible change. This could include pictures and samples of various foods, e.g. chocolate and jelly (reversible change), or recipes and ingredients for a cake (once cooked, irreversible change).

Ask the children to consider the following:

- What do they understand about reversible change?
- What do they understand about irreversible change?

MAIN ACTIVITIES

Materials mavericks – irreversible changes

Discuss what children know about irreversible changes. Explain that some changes can happen when substances are mixed, and some changes occur when substances are heated or burned. Children will plan their own investigations, working in small groups. They will investigate heating, mixing and burning.

Challenge 1 (groups of four)
Changes from heating materials

Encourage the children to look at the range of ingredients available. They need to decide what they are going to heat, e.g. by selecting bread and eggs, they could make eggs on toast. They will need to decide on a scientific question they want to answer about the heating of these materials and predict what might happen. They will then need to make a fire, following the safety steps in the health and safety chapter. Once the fire is made and it is safe to cook, they heat their chosen ingredients, making observations of the process.

Discuss the results with the children.

- What happened to the ingredients?
- Is this an irreversible change?
- Were any substances produced as a result of heating, e.g. carbon produced from burnt toast?
- Use your review of the websites referenced in the preparation section to explain this process further to the children.

Note: The children should not eat burnt toast, due to the chemical changes that have taken place.

Challenge 2 (groups of four)
Changes from mixing materials

In the same groups, children investigate the mixing of substances. They could select yeast and sugar or baking powder and vinegar. Encourage the children to think about when these substances are used in cooking and what changes take place. They will need to use test tubes or other transparent containers. They will need to think about how to set up the investigation, e.g. three test tubes: one with sugar, yeast and warm water, one with just sugar, and one with just yeast. What will they use as a control? What if they used cold water? What do they predict will happen in each case? Why do they need a balloon for this investigation? How will they record their results?

Discuss the results with the children.

- What changes have happened?
- Are these irreversible changes?
- What has been produced as a result of mixing the substances?
- What have the children found out about changes from mixing materials?

Challenge 3 (whole class)
Extension activity – burning materials

What has happened to the wood in the fire? Look at the charcoal. What change has taken place? What has been burned? What has been produced? What could this now be used for? Consider what this means in relation to the burnt toast. Remind them about the fire triangle of fuel, oxygen and heat.

PLENARY

Discuss with the children the results of all their investigations carried out to date.

- What have they learned about materials and their properties?
- What big questions have they answered?
- What do the children still want to know?

Back in the classroom

Finalise the class display with answers to the questions they had. They could include pictorial examples of irreversible and reversible changes in their heating and mixing experiments, and their ideas for an irreversible change as a result of heating, mixing or burning.

EVALUATION/FOLLOW ON

- What went well today?
- Which children understood the concepts?
- Which children needed more help?
- Are there other resources you can use?

Geography

Based on the Key Stage 2 geography objectives identified in the 2014 National Curriculum for England, in this unit children develop their geographical and world knowledge through the use of orienteering and fieldwork. Previous map-reading skills are reinforced and extended as they read, follow and create maps and trails to collect and process information about the wider world, working together to complete challenges along the way.

The unit models the use of orienteering to collect geographical information, which is then transformed or interpreted in some way; however, the methodology can be applied to any curriculum area. British Orienteering, the national governing body for the sport of orienteering in the UK, provides support for the unit in the form of the free resource 'Tri-O: Orienteering made easy (a complete introductory orienteering activity package for schools)', available to download from www.britishorienteering.org.uk.

To support inclusive practice or to extend learning, the space, task, equipment and people (STEP) approach can be adopted throughout this unit. By changing the space, task, equipment or people, the activity can be made more challenging or easier to understand, enabling all pupils to take part in the activity, as explained in the assessment chapter in this book.

The children will be expected to work as a whole class directed by the teacher or in small groups or pairs, with support from adults or independently. The role of the adult is to lead the sessions safely, and model the activities, encouraging independence by giving the children time to come up with their own ideas, whilst providing positive support where appropriate.

The activities in this unit involve marking letters on a playground using chalk, like this. For further information, see www.bloomsbury.com/NC-Outdoors.

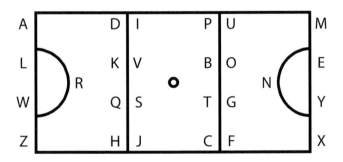

Natural connections

- Awareness of human and physical geographical features in the local environment
- Awareness of the properties and uniqueness of the world
- Connection through the recognition of natural features
- Tree identification.

Health and wellbeing

- Increased confidence through acquiring and developing skills
- Physical activity
- Selecting and applying skills and tactics
- Working together to solve problems
- Developing a responsible attitude to safety
- Being trusted to be 'away from sight' within the setting
- Appreciating their own and others' performance.

Word bank

- physical and human geographical features
- symbols
- key
- controls
- control point
- control point markers
- northern hemisphere
- southern hemisphere
- equator
- names of countries
- eight-point compass

Summary overview

Progression	Curriculum content	Learning experiences/activities
Lesson 1	Use maps, atlases, globes and digital/computer mapping to locate countries. Identify the position and significance of latitude, longitude, equator, northern hemisphere and southern hemisphere. Use fieldwork to observe human features in the local area.	Using lines on the playground, children warm up by making 'human alphabet' shapes. They learn to orientate a map, before following arrows trails to collect letters forming the names of northern hemisphere countries. They may also create their own arrows trail map.
Lesson 2	Use maps, atlases, globes and digital/computer mapping to locate countries. Identify the position and significance of latitude, longitude, equator, northern hemisphere and southern hemisphere. Use fieldwork to observe human features in the local area.	Using lines on the playground, the children take part in a 'Line up' challenge. They learn to orientate a map and use control points marked by circles to collect letters forming the names of southern hemisphere countries, recording these on a control card. They may also create their own map.
Lesson 3	Use maps, atlases, globes and digital/computer mapping to locate countries. Use fieldwork to observe human features in the local area.	Using lines on the playground, the children take part in a 'Jump the line' challenge. They work in teams to collect letters forming the names of countries on a control card, and find their locations using an atlas. They may also create their own map.
Lesson 4	Use maps, atlases, globes and digital/computer mapping to locate countries. Use fieldwork to observe human features in the local area.	Children take part in a team map-symbol running game, matching words to symbols using a key. They use a map of the outdoor area to find ten control points with country names as control marks. They collect these on a control card, then use atlases to locate the countries, classifying them by which hemisphere they are in.
Lesson 5	Use the eight points of a compass. Use fieldwork to observe human and physical features in the local area.	Children practise tactics in a 'Countdown' activity. They practise using eight compass points. On a marked grid, they work out a 'safe route' across a swamp.
Lesson 6	Use the eight points of a compass, symbols and keys. Use fieldwork to observe, measure, record and present the human and physical features in the local area, using a range of methods, including sketch maps.	Children reinforce their recognition of map symbols using a matching pairs team relay. The children match the symbols to physical features in the setting. They use basic maps of the setting to make their own trails and routes, using arrows and eight compass points to describe direction of travel. They give their map to others to try out. They evaluate the unit and their own learning.

PREPARATION

On playground markings, e.g. a netball court, mark the letters of the alphabet in chalk, placing a cone at one corner to represent the start.

Mark the position of the letters on a master map and keep this as your record. The letters should only be marked on the master map (not the maps for the children to use).

Draw arrows on a playground markings map to identify the route that needs to be taken to collect all the letters in the name of a country in the northern hemisphere – one map for each country used (different-coloured paper for each map can make them easier to identify when handing out).

Mark the start position (Δ) on the map.

Label each map 1, 2, 3, 4, 5, etc., making a note of the name of the country corresponding to each map on an answer sheet.

Resources

- Playground labelled with letters of the alphabet, with a cone placed at one corner to represent the start
- Five large copies of map number 1
- Copies of each 'northern hemisphere country' arrows trail map
- Basic copies of the playground markings map (with lines and letters but no route marked)
- Copies of the master map and answers
- Clipboards, paper and pencils and playground chalks
- Atlases (and globes)

Previous learning

Use questioning to evaluate previous learning.

LESSON OBJECTIVES

We are learning to identify points on a map to collect letters making the names of countries in the northern hemisphere.

National Curriculum Content

- Use maps, atlases, globes and digital/computer mapping to locate countries.
- Identify the position and significance of latitude, longitude, equator, northern hemisphere and southern hemisphere.
- Use fieldwork to observe human features in the local area.

ADULT ROLES

- Model the activity.
- Support with orientating the maps.
- Verify the answers.

CONSIDER

Health & Safety

Assess and evaluate hazards and risks in your setting. See the health and safety chapter.

WARM UP IDEAS

Explain that for the next six weeks, the children will be using orienteering to find clues to help them develop their geographical knowledge. Clarify the term 'orienteering'.

Using 'follow the leader', walk the class along the marked lines on the playground to explore the chalk-marked letters. What are they? Where are they placed? Point out that some letters are on one side of a line and others are on the other side of a line. What do they think they will be used for?

Introductory activity

Human alphabet

For a more physical warm up, use the lines as markers on which to make a shape.

1. The children jog around the playground in different directions.
2. When the teacher calls out a letter in the alphabet, they stop, run to the nearest line and make the shape of that letter with their bodies, using a partner to help balance or form the letter.

MAIN ACTIVITIES

Northern hemisphere country hunt

Observe how to orientate a map of the playground

Using the enlarged copies of map number 1, point out the map number, the start position (marked on the map by the triangle and on the ground by the cone) and how the map matches the netball court markings on the ground. Point out that arrows are drawn on the paper maps and that the arrows point to a letter (control point) on the ground.

Model how to set the map (using the start position as a guide) and move around the playground, keeping the map in line with the markings on the ground (orientating it).

Give each group a copy of the enlarged map. Can they 'set their map' to match the lines on the ground?

1. Children move to a different position, e.g. to the other side of the court. Can they set their maps?
2. They move to a third position, e.g. to the end of the court. Can they set their maps?
3. Explain that this is called 'map orientation', where the map is orientated to features on the ground.
4. Point out the start cone (marked with a triangle on the map) and ask a volunteer pair to stand at that point.
5. Point out the arrows on the map, explaining that the arrows mark a route to be followed.
6. Ask the volunteer pair to move to the place indicated by the first arrow. What letter do they find there? Repeat with the rest of the route.

You could give children further support by placing physical arrows on the ground (e.g. PE rubber markings or large printed arrows) to help reinforce the direction of travel when modeling this activity.

Challenge 1 (in pairs or groups of four)

Follow an arrows trail to collect letters to spell out countries' names

The children's task will be to follow the arrows to each control point to collect letters.

The letters make up the letters in the name of a northern hemisphere country. Can they explain this terminology from prior maths learning? A hemisphere is a three-dimensional shape that is half of a sphere. Use a globe to reinforce how the northern and southern halves of the world are described as the northern hemisphere and southern hemisphere, pointing out the equator as the divisor.

Pairs or groups have to:

1. Find each control point on the map, 'recording' the control points letter by letter and writing down the letters to spell the name of a country.

2. They then need to use an atlas or a globe to find the location of the country.
3. When they have the country name, they will need to take the number of their map and their answer to an adult, who will tell them whether it is correct or not (the spelling must be correct).
4. If it is correct, they can choose another map to find another country.
5. If it is not correct, then they must repeat that trail again to check their route.

Extension

Some children may be able to draw their own arrows trail map identifying a different country, to give to another group to complete.

PLENARY

Encourage the children to explain what they have been doing in the session and state what they have found out about following arrows on a map and any new countries in the northern hemisphere that they have found.

Leave the chalk marks on the ground for the children to practise with or use during playtimes.

EVALUATION/FOLLOW ON

- What went well and why?
- What didn't go as well as expected?
- What could be changed?
- Who stood out and why?

PREPARATION

On playground markings, e.g. a netball court, mark the letters of the alphabet in chalk, placing a cone at one corner to represent the start.

Mark the position of the letters on a master map to keep for reference.

Circle letters on the playground map to identify the positions of letters in the names of countries in the southern hemisphere – one map for each country used.

Make control cards (see the example on page 63).

Ensure that the start position is marked Δ.

Label each map 1, 2, 3, 4, 5, etc., making a note of the name of the country corresponding to each map on an answer sheet.

Resources

- Netball court chalked with letters of the alphabet, with a cone placed at one corner to represent the start
- Five large copies of map number 1
- Copies of each 'southern hemisphere country' map
- Control cards (one per pair or group)
- Un-circled copies of the playground map
- Copies of the master map and answers
- Whiteboards, whiteboard pens, pencils and rubbers
- Playground chalks
- Atlases or globes

Previous learning

This extends previous learning children may have done using orienteering activities.

LESSON OBJECTIVES

We are learning to identify control points on a map to collect letters making the names of countries in the southern hemisphere.

National Curriculum Content

- Use maps, atlases, globes and digital/computer mapping to locate countries.
- Identify the position and significance of latitude, longitude, equator, northern hemisphere and southern hemisphere.
- Use fieldwork to observe human features in the local area.

ADULT ROLES

- Model the activity.
- Support with orientating the maps.
- Verify the answers.

CONSIDER

Health & Safety

Assess and evaluate hazards and risks in your setting. See the health and safety chapter.

WARM UP IDEAS

Explain that children will be using the playground markings to find letters of countries in the southern hemisphere. Choosing a leader, the group moves along the playground markings in different ways, such as hopping or jumping along the lines, while revising the chalk-marked letters.

Introductory activity (class divided into four)

Line up

For a more physical warm up, use the lines for a group problem-solving activity: 'Line up'.

1. Groups stand on a line, all facing the same way.
2. Without stepping off the line, they need to change places to create an order of some kind. If anyone steps off the line, then that group must start again.
3. Give an example by asking the groups to line up in height order.
4. Other examples might include: line up in alphabetical order by their first name, age, number of siblings, who has the oldest living relative, etc. Can other groups guess the order they have used?
5. How did they come up with a plan of action? Did they all know what to do? Were they effective?

Southern hemisphere country hunt

Observe how to orientate a map of the playground

Show the enlarged copy of map number 1. What do the children notice? The positions (control points) are represented by circles on the map rather than as an arrows route.

What difference will this make to collecting the letters, i.e. that they can be visited in any order?

Revise how to set the map and move around the playground, keeping it orientated to the markings (indicated by the start position) and addressing any difficulties experienced in Progression 1.

Challenge 1 (in pairs)

Collect letters to spell out countries' names

Explain that the letters the children collect will make up the letters in the name of a country in the southern hemisphere but, because the letters can be collected in any order, the name may be scrambled.

1. Show how the control card has a row for each map number, columns to collect the letters and a space for the answer at the end of the row.

2. In pairs, children find each control point on the map and collect the control point letters, writing them on a control card.

3. They must work out which country it is by unscrambling the letters to spell the name of a country. They can use their whiteboards to descramble the letters and atlases to help them spell and locate the country.

4. When they have the country name and have found its location on a map, they take the control card to an adult, who tells them whether it is correct or not (the spelling must be correct).

5. If it is correct, they can choose another map to find another country.

6. If it is not correct, then they must repeat that map to check where they went wrong.

7. Adults can support those finding it difficult by providing the first letter.

Extension

Some children may be able to draw their own circles map identifying a different country, to give to another group to complete.

Control card example

Map no.	Letter	Letter	Letter	Letter	Letter	Letter	Letter	Letter	Letter	Answer
1										
2										
3										
4	T	R	A	U	A	S	A	I	L	AUSTRALIA
5										
6										
X										

PREPARATION

On playground markings, mark the letters of the alphabet in chalk, as in the previous progressions.

Circle letters on playground markings maps to identify the positions of letters in the names of countries in either hemisphere – one map for each country (using different colours for each map makes them easier to identify when handing them out). Ensure that the start position is indicated, as this helps to orientate the map.

Label each map 1, 2, 3, 4, 5, 6, etc. making a note of the name of the county corresponding to each map on an answer sheet.

Make the control cards as in Progression 2.

Resources

- Playground labelled with letters of the alphabet
- Five large copies of map number 1
- Copies of each country map, with the position of each letter in the name marked with a circle
- Copies of the playground markings map
- Copies of the master map and answers
- Control cards, pencils and playground chalks
- Maps and atlases

Previous learning

Has anyone used the playground markings during playtime to make their own map?

LESSON OBJECTIVES

We are learning to follow a map to collect the names of (and locate) countries from anywhere in the world.

National Curriculum Content

- Use maps, atlases, globes and digital/computer mapping to locate countries.
- Use fieldwork to observe human features in the local area.

ADULT ROLES

- Model the activity and verify the answers.
- Support with orientating the maps.

CONSIDER

Health & Safety

Assess and evaluate hazards and risks in your setting. See the health and safety chapter.

WARM UP IDEAS

Explain that today's session will again be taking place in the playground.

Choosing a leader, the class 'follows the leader' along the playground markings to revise the chalk-marked letters.

Introductory activity (class divided into four)

Jump over the line

For a more physical warm up, use the lines as markers to jump over, but with a challenge to all land at the same time.

1. Groups line up with their toes touching a line on the playground (e.g. a netball court line). Explain that the aim of the group is to jump over the line and land at exactly the same time.
2. Try it once or twice. What happens?
3. This time work out a plan, e.g. what number will they jump on ('1, 2, 3, jump' or 'jump on 3')?
4. How many goes does it take to all land at the same time? Did they have a leader?

Worldwide country hunt

Relay team orienteering

Explain that this week, the letters that children collect will form the name of a country anywhere in the world, i.e. in either hemisphere. The task this week is a relay team challenge, with the team having a 'base' at one side of the court, and with one team member at time collecting one control mark (letter) each. Give each team of four a control card, pencil and atlas.

Challenge 1 (groups of four)

Use relay teamwork to collect letters to spell the names of countries

Model the activity with a demonstration group to ensure that all the children understand the task.

1. Each team stands at a start position at one side of the court and studies their map, taking note of the number. This is important, as they need to check that they are going to be placing the control marks in the correct row on the control card.

2. They decide on the order of runners and which control point (marked using a circle on the map) each team member will go to, e.g. the fittest or fastest runner going the furthest.

3. On a signal from the teacher, the first team member runs with the control card and pencil to collect one control mark (letter) at a control point marked on their map, writing it in the correct row of the control card and running back to base (taking care to avoid bumping into other people).

4. The returning runner gives the pencil and control card to the next team member, who then runs to their control point to record the control mark on the control card and returns to base. They take it in turns for each team member to run until all the letters have been collected.

5. Together, they then work out which county it is by unscrambling the letters to spell the name, using maps and atlases to help them locate the country, and identifying whether it is in the northern or southern hemisphere.

6. When they have the country name and location, they take their control card to an adult, who verifies whether it is correct or not (the spelling and location must be correct).

7. If it is correct, they get given another map to find another country.

8. If it is not correct, then they must repeat the relay and unscrambling.

Adults can support those finding it difficult by providing the first letter.

Which team is the quickest?

Extension

Some children may be able to draw their own circles map to give to another group to complete.

Encourage the children to explain what they have been doing in the session and state what they have found out about effective team planning. Was it more challenging doing this as a group? In what way and how were these challenges overcome? How could they improve next time? Who can share something they know about the countries they found?

- What went well and why?
- What didn't go as well as expected?
- What could be changed?
- Who stood out and why?

PREPARATION

Prepare the map symbols cards and draw a map of the area with key features marked with symbols.

Mark control points on the map to identify the position of each control point on the ground, using a circle with a number in it, e.g. ①②③.

Write the names of ten countries onto card and suspend these from trees and fences, together with the corresponding control point markers.

Prepare the control cards (see the example on page 67).

Resources

- Map symbols cards and one key card per group (see pages 20–28 of the British Orienteering Tri-O resource, available to download from www.britishorienteering.org. uk)
- Container for the symbol name cards
- Map of the learning area (marked with geographical feature symbols and numbered circles marking the position of control points)
- Ten cards of country names, with string attached
- Red and white control point markers (Tri-O, pages 33–37)
- Control cards
- Maps and atlases

Previous learning

Ask the children if they have ever been cross-country orienteering or geocaching. Discuss.

LESSON OBJECTIVES

We are learning to follow a 'cross-country' trail marked on a map to collect information.

National Curriculum Content

- Use maps, atlases, globes and digital/computer mapping to locate countries.
- Use fieldwork to observe human and physical features in the local area.

ADULT ROLES

- Model the activity.
- Reinforce and clarify the use of keys and symbols.

CONSIDER

Health & Safety

Assess and evaluate hazards and risks in your setting. See the health and safety chapter.

WARM UP IDEAS

Explain that today the children will be finding control points marked on a map of the area.

What is a geographical feature? What examples can they point out in the outdoor learning area?

Hand out the 'keys' to the map symbols to each group, identifying the symbols and their meanings and matching them with examples in the setting.

Introductory activity

Map symbols running relay

1. Groups line up behind a line on the playground.
2. Lay the map symbols cards face up in a grid pattern on the other side of the playground, in line with each group.
3. Place the corresponding symbol names in a container in front of each group.
4. On the start signal, the first person picks up a name card, reads it and runs to the symbol cards, returning with the correct matching card.
5. The group checks that it is correct, using the map symbols key.
6. If they match, e.g. the symbol for 'pond' and the word 'pond', then those two cards are kept by the group. If they don't match, they are replaced where they came from.
7. The rest of the team take it in turns to pick up a name card and run to the symbol cards, returning with the correct matching card, until all the cards have been matched.

Cross-country trail

Match map symbols to real examples in the setting

Explore the outdoor learning area, identifying key features and discussing how these would be marked on a map in the form of a symbol. Include buildings, walls, fences, open land, trees, play apparatus, footpaths, ponds, forests, steps, slopes, etc. Can children classify them as human or physical geographical features?

Challenge 1 (whole class)

Model collecting countries' names to identify their hemisphere

1. Hand out the maps of the learning area, pointing out the control points marked on the map in circled numbers, e.g. ①②③, and identifying the symbols indicating human and physical geographical features.

2. Explain that children will use the map to find ten controls (ten cards with the names of countries written on them).

3. Show an example of the controls (cards suspended from trees or fences) and control point markers (red and white numbered markers) so that they know what to look for.

4. Explain that they must leave the controls in place but write the name of the country on their control cards in the correct place, i.e. to match the number of the control point (see the example below).

5. Show the control cards to the groups.

6. Explain that when they have all ten names, they should return to 'base' to find the countries in atlases, identifying whether they are in the southern or northern hemisphere, and then take their control cards to an adult to check their answers.

Challenge 2 (groups of four)

Find the locations of control points, collecting names

Start groups at different points on the route to identify the position of the control points and complete the task as described above.

Encourage the children to explain what they have been doing in the lesson and state what they have found out about following map trails, map symbols and countries. How did they overcome any problems? Explain where and when they can take part in orienteering out of school (e.g. a local club).

- What went well and why?
- What didn't go as well as expected?
- What could be changed?
- Who stood out and why?

Control card example

TEAM NAME					
Control point	Country	Hemisphere	Control point	Country	Hemisphere
1			6		
2	New Zealand	Southern	7		
3			8		
4			9		
5			10		

PREPARATION

Mark out four or five grids (six squares by six squares on the ground) or use a paved area, marking the perimeter and labelling them with N, S, E and W. This could be linked to a maths activity, where the children measure and mark out the grid.

Resources

- Tubular webbing or rope
- Playground chalk
- Grids, such as a paved area (one for each group)
- Corresponding squared paper (e.g. six by six squares)

Previous learning

This progression reinforces and applies maths learning.

CONSIDER

Health & Safety

Assess and evaluate hazards and risks in your setting. See the health and safety chapter.

LESSON OBJECTIVES

We are working as a team to find a safe path to cross a swamp using compass points.

National Curriculum Content

- Use the eight points of a compass.
- Use fieldwork to observe human and physical features in the local area.

ADULT ROLES

- Model the activity.
- Clarify the positions of the hazards in the swamp.
- Take part in the 'Countdown' activity but let the children make the tactical choices in order to complete the task.

WARM UP IDEAS

Explain that today the children will be using compass points to cross a dangerous swamp, but before they do that, they will need to practise team communication and awareness of others.

Introductory activity

Countdown (whole class)

Ask the children to make a circle using tubular webbing or rope and stand around the perimeter.

Explain that the aim of this activity is to count down from the number of children in the class (e.g. 30) to zero in consecutive descending numbers, i.e. 30, 29, 28, 27, etc.

1. One person jumps in and out of the circle, calling out 30.
2. Another person jumps in and out of the circle, calling out 29.
3. One at a time the children step (or jump) into and then out of the circle, calling out the next descending consecutive number.
4. Any child can step or jump into the circle, but they can only do so once.
5. If two or more children enter the circle at the same time, then the countdown restarts.
6. They will need to watch one another, pick up on the body language of a person preparing to enter the circle, make eye contact, etc., to avoid having to start again.
7. Discuss: Did the class decide on a plan? Did it work? How would they rate their success?

Compass swamp-crossing

Revise the eight points of a compass and follow turn directions

Using the circle from the warm up, mark north at the top of the circle.

Ask for volunteers to write and place south, west and east. What other points of a compass do they know? Ask for volunteers to write south west (SW), north west (NW), south east (SE) and north east (NE) in the appropriate positions.

All of the children stand in the centre of the circle facing the same way, e.g. north.

Asking the children to predict the outcomes before moving, give instructions, such as 'Make a half turn clockwise. What direction will you be facing?'. For example, 'Facing north west, make a quarter turn anticlockwise. Where will you face?'

Challenge 1 (groups of six)

Use teamwork and tactics to cross the dangerous swamp with compass directions

Each team stands at the edge of the grid on the south bank.

Explain that this is the 'swamp' and each square is a clump of harder ground, which may or may not support their weight. A 'swamp guardian' for each team stands on the north bank.

1. The guardian has a clipboard and copy of the grid on paper, on which they mark a 'safe route' across the swamp. See the example below. This is not shared with the team.

2. Taking it in turns (one person at a time), each team member attempts to find the safe path through the swamp by moving from square to square.

3. They can move in any direction, including south and diagonally, but can only move one square at a time.

4. If they deviate from the safe path, then the swamp guardian calls out 'You're sinking!' and the team member must return to the south bank.

5. The team needs to remember which squares are safe and avoid the 'dangerous' ones when it is their turn, or risk having to return to the south bank.

6. Encourage the team to communicate, giving instructions such as 'north east square, west square, west square', etc., to support the team member attempting to cross the swamp to find the safe squares.

7. Once the safe path is found, the whole group need to follow it to get to the north bank.

Swamp guardian safe route example

North bank

	✓				
	✓				
		✓	✓	✓	
	✓			✓	
✓		✓	✓	✓	
	✓				

South bank

Encourage the children to explain what they have been doing in the session and state what they have found out about communication and teamwork. Did they use 'trial and error' or 'analysis, planning, then action'? Which tactics worked well? How much did the compass directions help? In what way?

- What went well and why?
- What didn't go as well as expected?
- What could be changed?
- Who stood out and why?

PREPARATION

Ensure that the outdoor learning area is clear of hazards.

Use the symbol cards from Progression 4.

Prepare basic maps of the setting area (without symbols).

Resources

• Sets of map symbols cards where each 'symbol' card has a matching card that gives its meaning (one set per group), available from pages 20–28 of the British Orienteering Tri-O resource, available to download from www.britishorienteering.org.uk)

• Basic maps of the learning area without symbols

• Clipboards, paper and pencils

Previous learning

This progression reinforces and extends previous learning children may have done using orienteering activities.

CONSIDER

Health & Safety

Assess and evaluate hazards and risks in your setting. See the health and safety chapter.

LESSON OBJECTIVES

We are learning to make our own map of an area using compass directions and symbols.

National Curriculum Content

• Use the eight points of a compass, symbols and keys.

• Use fieldwork to observe, measure, record and present the human and physical features in the local area, using a range of methods, including sketch maps.

ADULT ROLES

• Model the activity.

• Support with the positioning of features.

• Clarify the use of keys and symbols.

WARM UP IDEAS

Explain that today the children will be making their own arrows trail on a map of the area, using what they know about the eight points of the compass to provide directions. To make their map really clear, they will have to use symbols to represent key features.

Introductory activity (groups of four)

Reinforce map symbol recognition by playing a pair-matching relay game

This is a variation of the map symbols relay from Progression 4.

1. Lay the pairs of map symbols cards face down in a grid pattern – one grid per group.
2. Each group lines up behind a line facing their grid pattern.
3. On the signal to start, the first person runs to the grid and turns over two cards.
4. If they match, e.g. the symbol for 'tree' and the word 'tree', then those two cards can be kept by the group; if not, they are replaced face down (use a map key to help).
5. The next person runs to the grid and turns over two cards.
6. The team must pay careful attention to the position of the cards so that they gradually learn the position of possible matching cards.
7. The rest of the team take it in turns to pick up and turn two cards over until all the cards have been matched.
8. The aim is to be the first team to pick up all their cards.

Mapping our outdoor learning area

Revise and match the map symbols to real examples in the setting

Explore the outdoor learning area, identifying key features, and classifying them as human or physical geographical features. Revise how these can be marked on a map.

Show how to mark these features on a basic map of the area, so that outlines of the key features, such as buildings and paths, are shown, but no smaller features are yet marked with symbols.

Challenge 1 (pairs)

Mark arrows on a map using an eight-point compass to describe their direction

1. Using copies of the basic map of the area, pairs draw their own arrows trail for another pair to follow.

2. They decide what controls need to be collected (e.g. chalk-marked letters or shapes) and place them in position, marking them with circled numbers, and deciding whether the control marks can be collected on the map or on paper.

3. They write the direction of travel next to each arrow. Note: Using north as the top of the page and south as the bottom of the page might be more accessible for some, or find out the direction of north and mark this on the map for reference.

4. Once complete, they walk their trail, checking that it is accurate and adding more detail such as key features using symbols. Additional detail, such as the species of tree, could also be marked with a symbol in the form of an appropriately shaped leaf.

5. Pairs swap maps and try out a different map.

6. They assess for accuracy, considering whether it is easy to follow. Why? Why not? The pair that made the map makes improvements or adjustments in the light of the feedback.

Some children may need a peer leader or adult to support with the positioning of features on the map or the use of the eight-point compass.

Some children might be able to use more precise compass terms, such as SSW or WNW, etc.

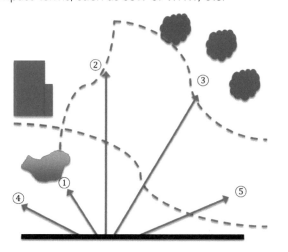

Encourage the children to explain what they have been doing and state what they have found out about making and following maps. Review the unit, considering what they now know and how they have developed as learners. What were the best things they learned from completing the unit and why? Encourage well-considered answers and explanations.

- What went well and why?
- What didn't go as well as expected?
- What could be changed?
- Who stood out and why?

History

Based on the Year 5 statutory attainment targets, matters, skills and processes for history identified in the 2014 National Curriculum for England, children use a religious building and its grounds as a primary source to explore local history in this unit. They raise questions and use these as a focus to gather information and evidence, considering similarities, differences and possible causes, undertaking investigations and collecting data to be analysed back in the classroom. There are links to Year 5 mathematics (number, fractions and statistics). They use the available evidence to reflect on the lives of past members of the community, working forensically to gather clues from headstones and other memorials to establish a chronologically secure local historical narrative. They discover that nature can also be used to measure the passing of time.

Although the progressions describe the use of a local religious building and its grounds, they could easily be adapted to a local study of key historical figures through the use of memorials, statues, commemorative plaques at the school or dedicated green spaces and parks in the immediate surroundings.

To support inclusive practice or to extend learning, the space, task, equipment and people (STEP) approach can be adopted throughout this unit. By changing the space, task, equipment or people, the activity can be made more challenging or easier to understand, enabling all pupils to take part in the activity, as explained in the assessment chapter in this book.

The children will be expected to work as a whole class directed by the teacher or in small groups or pairs, with support from adults or independently. The role of the adult is to lead the sessions safely, modelling the activities and providing positive support where appropriate.

You may wish to record the activities using a camera.

Natural connections

- Appreciation of wildlife and and interpretation of information from nature
- Use of the senses
- Investigation of nature as the inspiration for imagery
- Investigation of lichens and trees as a measure of time.

Health and wellbeing

- Reflective practice
- Development of observation skills
- Justifying viewpoints and opinions
- Considering and valuing the opinions of others
- Problem-solving
- Appreciation of safe practices.

Word bank

- chronological
- evidence
- forensic
- plaques
- memorial
- lichens
- lichenometry
- data

Summary overview

Progression	Curriculum content	Learning experiences/activities
Lesson 1	A study over time, tracing how several aspects of national history are reflected in the locality. A study of an aspect of history or a site dating from a period beyond 1066 that is significant in the locality. Understand how our knowledge of the past is constructed from a range of sources.	Children are introduced to a local historical building: a Christian church. They explore its features before investigating it as a source of local history, recording paintings, plaques, carvings and sculptures. They use their evidence to create a digital plan of the building, including information text boxes.
Lesson 2	A study of a site dating from a period beyond 1066 that is significant in the locality. Note connections, contrasts and trends over time.	Children explore the graveyard around the church. They study information from headstones, before gathering a range of historical evidence. They reflect on their information to find out more about what life was like in the past, observing similarities and differences.
Lesson 3	A study of a site dating from a period beyond 1066 that is significant in the locality. Note connections, contrasts and trends over time.	Children gather historical information to answer a question or to test a hypothesis. They use maps to organise information. They use the information collected to answer their own questions. They compose more questions, which can be applied to a particular person.
Lesson 4	A study of a site dating from a period beyond 1066 that is significant in the locality. Note connections, contrasts and trends over time.	Children share information about their findings. They investigate in detail the life of a particular person, recording their evidence in a range of ways. They use the information to create a 'snapshot' or narrative, with thoughtful selection and organisation of relevant historical data.
Lesson 5	A study of an aspect of history or a site dating from a period beyond 1066 that is significant in the locality. Understand how our knowledge of the past is constructed from a range of sources.	Children are shown how lichenometry can be used to measure the passing of time and to place an approximate age on stones and trees. They calculate the age of lichens on headstones in the graveyard.
Lesson 6	A study of a site dating from a period beyond 1066 that is significant in the locality. Note connections, contrasts and trends over time.	Children learn how to measure tree growth (and measure time) by counting tree rings. They measure tree growth using girth measurements as a source of historical data. They estimate the ages of trees in the graveyard and use the dates to find out more information about that time span.

PREPARATION

Before the visit, contact the church to arrange access, permission for the planned activities and perhaps a guided historical tour.

Prepare an outline map of the building if required.

Assess off-site risks in accordance with your school policies.

Be aware and sensitive to the facts that children in the class may feel unsure or uncomfortable about visiting a Christian church or they may have friends or relatives buried on the site.

Resources

- Clipboards, paper and pencils
- Wax crayons for rubbings
- Prepared outline map of the building (if the children are not doing this themselves)
- Cameras

Previous learning

Discuss what the children know about Christianity and churches already. Explain that in Britain, churches are useful historical resources as they are often very old and were at the centre of community life.

CONSIDER

Health & Safety

Assess and evaluate hazards and risks in your setting. See the health and safety chapter.

LESSON OBJECTIVES

We are exploring a historical building and its importance in the community over time.

National Curriculum Content

- A study over time, tracing how several aspects of national history are reflected in the locality.
- A study of an aspect of history or a site dating from a period beyond 1066 that is significant in the locality.
- Understand how our knowledge of the past is constructed from a range of sources.

ADULT ROLES

- Support with naming parts of the building, based on the clues provided.
- Support with the correct placement of architectural features and other elements on the map.

WARM UP IDEAS

Explain that for the next six lessons children will be using the grounds of a historical building for a local historical investigation. Ask them what they think they might be finding out.

Ask what evidence could be provided on the site and over what time period, concluding that a building holds an importance and significance in the community over time, which in some cases could be decades or even centuries, and is thus an important source of historical evidence.

Discuss its importance and relevance within the community and what children might need to consider when visiting, e.g. respectful behaviour, religious customs, safety, etc. Allow time to discuss, then share ideas.

Introductory activity

As children approach the area, what clues to the history of the setting can be found, e.g. the use of stone, established trees, gravestones and plaques? Look around the new area, observing features of the setting. Have they visited before? When and why was that?

How does it make them feel? Do they get a sense of the past? Encourage speculation about how far back it dates and what the people who lived near the church might have been like and why it was built. Why was this place chosen and what might have been here before?

MAIN ACTIVITIES

Features of a historical building

Exploring a historical building

Enter the building and sit. Take some time for reflection by using the senses of smell, hearing and touch, to explore how it makes the children feel. Why is this?

If possible, ask for a guided tour or, using prior research, walk the children around the building yourself, looking for evidence of the age of the building and its use.

Challenge 1 (in pairs)

Label a map of the church with its features

Ask the pairs to mark on a map of the church the significant architectural elements, using clues from the tour to help. For example:

- The main section of the church – the nave.

- Any other sections, such as seating areas, side aisles or side chapels .

- The altar – the holiest part of the church, often separated from the main body of the church by an 'altar rail', screen or railings.

Challenge 2 (in pairs)

Mark the position of historical evidence on the map

Pairs explore again but this time they note the positions of any of historically significant stained glass windows, paintings, monuments, plaques, carvings and symbols. How do they know if something is 'historically significant'? E.g. does it include names of people, places or dates?

This could provide an opportunity to make brass and stone rubbings (with permission from the setting).

Ask the children to take photographs, to add to a digital plan of the church back in the classroom.

When as much evidence as possible has been collected, the pairs should take time to place and record the evidence in chronological order to create a timeline.

Discuss how the features they have been investigating could be a primary source of historical information. What questions do they raise? Write some of these questions down.

Challenge 3 (individual)

Quiet reflection

Let the children sit quietly and take time for a moment of reflection about the historical features they have seen. They could reflect on how they would like to be remembered. Why is it important to be remembered?

PLENARY

Pairs join other pairs to share their findings about the church. What surprising things did they find? What is the most interesting thing they found?

Back in the classroom

Create a digital plan of the church, including information text boxes for plaques, carvings and symbols.

Groups investigate the history of one of the plaques, e.g. a notable local person or major historical figure. They find out more about the person. Are there any local stories or legends about them?

EVALUATION/FOLLOW ON

- What went well and why?

- What didn't go as well as expected?

- What could be changed?

- Who stood out and why?

PREPARATION

Check the graveyard for any hazards and make the children and other staff aware of them.

Draw and make copies of a map of the graveyard.

Resources

- Compass
- Clipboards, paper and pencils
- Wax crayons for rubbings
- Prepared outline map of the graveyard (if the children are not doing this themselves)
- Cameras

Previous learning

This extends previous learning children may have done using orienteering activities (see the geography progressions).

CONSIDER

Health & Safety

Assess and evaluate hazards and risks in your setting. See the health and safety chapter.

LESSON OBJECTIVES

We are exploring a graveyard as a primary source to gather local historical information.

National Curriculum Content

- A study over time, tracing how several aspects of national history are reflected in the locality.
- A study of a site dating from a period beyond 1066 that is significant in the locality.
- Note connections, addressing historically valid questions about similarity, difference and significance.

ADULT ROLES

- Ensure safe and respectful behaviour and practice.
- Support with the orientation of the map.
- Support with maths calculations, applying classroom methods and strategies and making links.

WARM UP IDEAS

Arriving back at the graveyard of the church or religious building, discuss the importance and relevance of this place within the community.

What might children need to consider when visiting a graveyard, e.g. respectful behaviour, religious customs, safety, etc.? Allow time to think and discuss, then share ideas.

Allow time to look around the new area, observing features of the setting. Have children visited before? When and why was that? Explore how it makes them feel, using an 'inner narrative' to express their feelings.

Introductory activity (Individual)

Use the senses to reflect on the setting

Clarify and define the meaning of what a 'sound' is by becoming 'graveyard listeners', guiding the children to tune in to the sounds around them by finding a quiet place to sit nearby with eyes closed.

1. Zoom in... What is the closest sound they can hear? Is it a natural or man-made sound?
2. Gradually zoom out. Can they identify sounds further away? What is the furthest-away sound they can hear? How many different sounds are there? Any similar sounds? Can they name any of them?
3. Zoom in again. Are there pleasing or displeasing sounds? How do the sounds make them feel or imagine?
4. From their listening spot, identify where in the landscape each sound is being created.
5. Quietly share the sounds with a partner. Did they hear the same sounds?
6. What do the noises tell us about the area, such as its wildlife or proximity to busy roads?

Graveyard evidence

Challenge 1 (whole class)

How to gather information through an overview of a graveyard

Look at headstones and other memorials. How could these provide a source of historical evidence or a glimpse of the past? Explain that in the past, only wealthy people had stone memorials, but nowadays the names and dates of 'everyday' people are remembered on headstones.

- What clues are in the wording on the headstones?

- What form of language is used? How does this give us information about the time and society?

- What differences can the children spot, e.g. why are some stones (ledgers) laid flat? How old are these ledgers compared to other headstones?

Using a compass, explore the orientation of the site, linking to geography.

- What do they notice about the orientation of the headstones, e.g. they often face east?

- What is the significance of this and how is this similar to other religious practices?

- Does the position of the headstone in the graveyard matter, e.g. do they think there might be 'poor' and 'rich' areas? Why? What evidence can they find for this hypothesis? What does this tell us about society in the past?

Challenge 2 (groups of four to six)

Gather historical evidence

- In forensic teams of four or five, children capture historical evidence from each area of the graveyard, i.e. north, south, east, west and the rough centre of the area.

- Groups draw an outline map of the graveyard and mark the areas they are investigating (or mark this on their copy of the prepared map).

- Evidence could include shapes of headstones or decorative motifs, which could be drawn from observation, drawing outline shapes or taking rubbings.

- Do they notice any lichens growing on the stones? How long do they think they've been there?

- Take close-up photographs for use with computing back in the classroom, linking to art.

- Gather a date of birth and death from a headstone in each area. Can children calculate the age at death? Are there any surprising results? Hypothesise why this might be the case.

- Gather inscriptions, epitaphs, poetry or prose.

- What is the oldest reference they can find in the graveyard?

Challenge 3 (individual)

Quiet reflection

Ask the children to imagine what one of the people whose graves they have investigated might have been like. What might they have worn? How might they have behaved? What might their job have been?

Ask them to write their ideas down on paper or leaves. This could be brought back to school to form a display.

Pairs share information that they have found that is particularly interesting, expressing personal opinions and giving well-structured descriptions and explanations.

Encourage the children to explain what they have found out about graveyards as possible primary sources of information. What were the challenges and how were these overcome?

Back in the classroom

Collate the evidence and contextualise it, e.g. by finding out what life was like at the birth or death date or describing historical events from that period.

Can the children extend their learning to find out differences and similarities between then and now?

Children compose questions and hypotheses that they will try to answer or check on their next visit. See the next progression for example questions.

- What went well and why?

- What didn't go as well as expected?

- What could be changed?

- Who stood out and why?

PREPARATION

Check the setting for any hazards and make the children and other staff aware of them.

Prepare an outline map of the graveyard if the children are not doing this themselves.

Resources

- Clipboards, paper and pencils
- Prepared outline map of the graveyard

Previous learning

Children will have devised questions in the previous progression, for use in this session.

CONSIDER

Health & Safety

Assess and evaluate hazards and risks in your setting. See the health and safety chapter.

LESSON OBJECTIVES

We are collecting historical information from a graveyard as a primary source to test a hypothesis.

National Curriculum Content

- A study over time, tracing how several aspects of national history are reflected in the locality.
- A study of a site dating from a period beyond 1066 that is significant in the locality.
- Note connections, addressing historically valid questions about similarity, difference and significance.

ADULT ROLES

- Ensure safe and respectful behaviour and practice.
- Support with maths calculations, applying classroom methods and strategies and making links.

WARM UP IDEAS

Arriving at the graveyard, revise respectful behaviour, religious customs and safety.

Look around the area, observing any new features or changes in the setting and discussing possible reasons for these.

Introductory activity (in pairs)

Spotters

1. Pairs walk around the area, looking for changes since their last visit.
2. They carefully explore until something catches their attention. This could be something big or small, a glint of wetness, a small detail or part of something bigger, the shape of lichen on a stone, maybe a new smell, the call of a crow, etc.
3. The spotter whispers 'I can see something!' and their partner whispers 'What can you see?'
4. Encourage the use of dramatic and powerful words as the spotter describes what they are looking at, e.g. 'I heard a deep throated croak. I see two eyes staring at me from that gnarled and twisted branch. I think it is watching us.'
5. The partner asks, 'How does it make you feel?'
6. The spotter tries to explain.
   - How did it make them feel when they spotted it?
   - What has caused their reaction to seeing it?
   - How it is making them feel now?
7. Pairs continue to explore the area, taking it in turns to spot things that catch their eye, describing it in detail and explaining how it makes them feel.

Checking a hypothesis

Challenge 1 (in pairs)

Gather historical evidence to answer a question or to test a hypothesis

Using the questions that they devised in the classroom as part of the previous progression, the children engage in focused and detailed data collection in the graveyard.

They decide how their findings will be recorded to answer specific questions, exploring similarities and differences between the past and now, such as:

- Did women live longer than men?
- Is there a particular century or decade in which many people died, and what could the reason be for this, e.g. epidemics, wartime?
- Have Christian names changed over time?
- Which names are common to the locality?
- Is there evidence to support an enquiry into changing occupations over time?
- Is there evidence to find out whether people died at an earlier age long ago by calculating their life spans?

Pairs discuss their findings, e.g. things that have changed and things that might have stayed the same.

They mark their investigation area on their maps.

This will be used for discussion and drawing conclusions back in the classroom and in the next progression.

What conclusions can the children make about the data they have collected?

Encourage the children to explain what they have found out about similarities and differences over time. Is there a particular gravestone that they are fascinated by? Why is this?

Could they find out more information about a specific person, and what questions would they need to find the answers to in order to do this?

Back in the classroom

Children process the data to answer questions such as what the average life span within a given time period is, linking to maths to calculate mean, mode, median, etc.

Children write more questions that they would like to find the answers to and which could be applied to a specific person.

- What went well and why?
- What didn't go as well as expected?
- What could be changed?
- Who stood out and why?

PREPARATION

Check the setting for any hazards and make the children and other staff aware of them.

Resources

- Clipboards, paper and pencils
- Wax crayons for rubbings
- Maps of the graveyard
- Cameras

Previous learning

Children will have devised questions in the previous progression, for use in this session.

CONSIDER

Health & Safety

Assess and evaluate hazards and risks in your setting. See the health and safety chapter.

LESSON OBJECTIVES

We are collecting historical information from a graveyard as a primary source to conduct a focused study about one person.

National Curriculum Content

- A study over time, tracing how several aspects of national history are reflected in the locality.
- A study of a site dating from a period beyond 1066 that is significant in the locality.
- Note connections, addressing historically valid questions about similarity, difference and significance.

ADULT ROLES

- Ensure safe and respectful behaviour and practice.
- Support with applying classroom methods and strategies and making links.

WARM UP IDEAS

Arriving back at the graveyard, revise respectful behaviour, religious customs and safety.

Explain that today children will become forensic historians to collect all possible data about one particular person.

Look around the area, observing any new features or changes in the setting and discussing possible reasons for these.

Introductory activity

Share the data

Ask each pair to share their research and findings from Progression 3 with the class in the context of the areas where they gathered their data (using their maps to identify the explored locations).

- What information was found in each area of the graveyard? How was it used? What conclusions did they come to?
- Which areas were a rich source of data and historical information? Give reasons for this.
- Ask for possible reasons for the similarities and differences that were found, encouraging the children to give well-structured descriptions and explanations, speculating, hypothesising and exploring ideas in line with National Curriculum spoken-language guidance.

A particular life

Challenge 1 (in pairs or individual)

Conduct research into the life of one person

Using the questions prepared for their investigation, children focus on one person and forensically record any evidence they can find in the graveyard about that person.

This could include:

- Name
- Date of birth
- Date of death
- Mention of other relatives, such as parents, brothers, sisters or children, which could be used to create a family tree.
- Are these relatives buried nearby or in the same graveyard, or still alive?

- Dates of birth and death of parents, brothers, sisters or children, which could be used to create a timeline
- An inscribed dedicated prayer
- An inscribed message or epitaph
- A carving or artwork
- An image of the person
- A symbol
- The quality of the gravestone or size of the plot (to reflect their wealth).

This data can be recorded by making careful observational drawings, taking rubbings or taking photographs to be used back in the classroom.

PLENARY

Encourage the children to explain what they have found out about their chosen person. Are there any surprises or information they are excited about? Share this.

What were the challenges and how were these overcome?

EVALUATION/FOLLOW ON

- What went well and why?
- What didn't go as well as expected?
- What could be changed?
- Who stood out and why?

Back in the classroom

Children find out more about their chosen person, the people that lived in the locality and their context in time, asking questions such as:

- If there was evidence found of employment, what jobs did people do during that date span? What was a typical day at work like, how far did they travel to work and how did they get there?
- What might their home have been like and what objects might they have had in their home?

Children use the information to create a chronologically secure 'snapshot' or narrative of their focus person, using informed and thoughtful selection and organisation of the relevant historical information they have gathered.

Children can link to English by writing a diary entry or newspaper article for the person and/or use the language of the epitaphs to create their own poetry.

PREPARATION

Check the off-site area for any hazards and make the children and other staff aware of them.

Prepare an outline map of the graveyard if the children are not doing this themselves.

Resources

- Clipboards, paper, pencils and rulers with measurements in millimeters
- Prepared outline maps of the graveyard
- Cameras
- Churchyard lichen identification sheet e.g. https://www. opalexplorenature.org/ lichen-identification-guide or https://www.field-studies-council.org/shop/ publications/churchyard-lichens-identification-chart/

Previous learning

This session builds on the previous progressions in this unit.

CONSIDER

Health & Safety

Assess and evaluate hazards and risks in your setting. See the health and safety chapter.

LESSON OBJECTIVES

We are using lichen as a primary source of time measurement.

National Curriculum Content

- A study over time, tracing how several aspects of national history are reflected in the locality.
- A study of a site dating from a period beyond 1066 that is significant in the locality.
- Understand how our knowledge of the past is constructed from a range of sources.

ADULT ROLES

- Ensure safe and respectful behaviour and practice.
- Model the activities, acknowledging the difficulties and exploring ways to overcome them.

WARM UP IDEAS

Arriving back at the graveyard, revise respectful behaviour, religious customs and safety.

Look around, observing any new features or changes in the setting and discussing possible reasons for these.

Introductory activity

Using the senses to reflect on the setting

Repeat the warm up activity from Progression 2, 'graveyard listeners'. Individuals tune in to the sounds around them by finding a quiet place to sit nearby with their eyes closed.

1. Zoom in... What is the closest sound they can hear? Is it a natural or man-made sound? How might the sounds have differed in the past?
2. Gradually zoom out. Can they identify sounds further away? What is the furthest-away sound they can hear? How might the sounds have differed in the past?
3. From the listening spot, identify where in the landscape each sound is being created. Does the fact that the area is now familiar to them make a difference to what they can hear and how easily they can locate sounds?
4. Record these sounds in some way, e.g. dashes and lines on paper.
5. Quietly share the sounds with a partner. Did they hear the same sounds? What questions arise from the noises?

MAIN ACTIVITIES

Approximating time measurement from nature

Challenge 1 (whole class)

How nature can give us clues to time

Did the children know that nature can provide clues about the passing of time? Can they think of examples of this?

Ask whether the children have noticed lichen growing on the headstones. How old do they think it is and why?

It has probably only been growing there since the stone was put in place and, since lichens tend to have a slow and steady growth of approximately 1 mm a year, they can be used to estimate the passing of time. This has a name: 'lichenometry'.

Show how to conduct a historical investigation using lichens, comparing the dates on the gravestone to corroborate the results or disprove their findings.

1. Use the identification guide to spot differences in the lichens.
2. In particular, look for the pale green-yellow-black 'encrusted' 'map lichen' species, which grows approximately 1 mm a year.

3. Show how to take the maximum diameter measurement in millimetres from edge to edge to calculate the age. Taking multiple measurements from a known time period, i.e. the same date of death on different headstones, will provide comparable and corroborative data. This can be entered on a table.
4. Does the age of the lichen fit with the history or date on the gravestone?

Challenge 2 (pairs and small groups)

Conduct a historical investigation using nature

The children conduct a historical investigation using lichens as modelled above, recording their measurements, calculations and results, and taking close-up photographs, which can be used back in the classroom to supplement the data.

PLENARY

Encourage the children to explain what they have found out. What were the challenges to carrying out this investigation and how were these overcome? Discuss what the problems could be of using lichenometry to age stones, e.g. that the lichens might not grow as soon as a headstone is put into place, or that lichens are very sensitive to air pollution, which stunts their growth, so this might affect the accuracy of any measurement.

Back in the classroom

Find out more about lichens and lichenometry. Does nature provide any other clues to history?

EVALUATION/FOLLOW ON

- What went well and why?
- What didn't go as well as expected?
- What could be changed?
- Who stood out and why?

PREPARATION

Check the graveyard for any hazards and make the children and other staff aware of them.

Resources

- Clipboards, paper, pencils and rulers with measurements in millimeters
- Two or three log stumps
- Prepared outline map of the graveyard
- Tape measures
- Cameras
- Tree identification chart or sheet

Previous learning

Have the children used lichenometry or other nature-based time indicators since the last session?

CONSIDER

Health & Safety

Assess and evaluate hazards and risks in your setting. See the health and safety chapter.

LESSON OBJECTIVES

We are collecting historical information from a tree as a primary source.

National Curriculum Content

- A study over time, tracing how several aspects of national history are reflected in the locality.
- A study of a site dating from a period beyond 1066 that is significant in the locality.
- Note connections, addressing historically valid questions about similarity, difference and significance.

ADULT ROLES

- Ensure safe and respectful behaviour and practice.
- Model the activities, acknowledging the difficulties and exploring ways to overcome them.

WARM UP IDEAS

Arriving at the graveyard, revise respectful behaviour, religious customs and safety.

Look around, observing any new features or changes in the setting and discussing possible reasons for these.

Introductory activity (whole class and groups of four to six)

Count tree rings

In the last lesson, children used nature to measure the passing of time. Did anyone find out about other nature-based methods of estimating time? Share these.

Show the children the log stumps and how the concentric rings show the growth of the tree.

Point out the darker and lighter bands, which together represent one year of growth.

The rings can also provide historical evidence of environmental information. Narrow bands represent slow growth, which could indicate cold or dry conditions, and thicker bands represent good growing conditions.

Groups count the dark rings to estimate the age of the tree, counting from the centre to the outer edge up to the bark. They study the stumps to see what historical information they can gather.

Groups share their findings with the rest of the class.

Tree time

Explain that trees can also be used in other ways to provide historical evidence. What examples can the children give?

Challenge 1 (groups of four)

What can trees tell us about the history of the area?

Can children test out a hypothesis to answer a question, such as 'Are all trees of the same species in the graveyard the same age, and what can this tell us about the history of the area?'

As an approximation, trees grow 2.5 cm a year, so to calculate the rough age of a tree, divide the girth by 2.5, e.g. a tree with a girth of 30 cm will be 12 years old.

Groups identify trees using a tree guide (or link to science by using a dichotomous classification key), and collect data by measuring the girth of each tree at 1 m from the ground, measuring to the nearest centimetre and recording the results.

Use the information to order the trees of each species in the area, from oldest to youngest.

What other questions could be posed relating to the trees?

PLENARY

Encourage the children to explain what they have found out about using nature as a measure of time. What were the challenges and how were these overcome?

Back in the classroom

Children draw a timeline or chart to present the information they collected in their group, using computing. Which is the most common tree species in the learning area and were these trees all planted at the same time?

Gather information about what was happening when the trees were planted. What major events have occurred over the time of their growth?

Which tree is the oldest? Might it be a yew tree? Investigate the significance of tree species in and around graveyards.

Link to creative writing by telling historical tales from the tree's viewpoint. For example, what dramatic events and changes over time has the yew tree seen in its long life? Make a class book of these tales from different trees' perspectives.

EVALUATION/FOLLOW ON

- What went well and why?
- What didn't go as well as expected?
- What could be changed?
- Who stood out and why?

Art and Design

In this unit, based on the Key Stage 2 art and design objectives identified in the 2014 National Curriculum for England, children reflect on the work of great artists and designers. They apply their findings to their own artwork, aiming to capture an 'essence of place' through the expression of meaning in the context of the natural environment. They develop their understanding of line, colour and pattern, experiment with a limited palette, tone and intensity and observe negative shapes. Using nature as a starting point for design, the children learn to convey meaning through their images, experimenting with new art techniques and materials, such as the wet-on-wet technique and natural printing into clay. There are also links to the National Curriculum Year 5 science content (living things and their habitats).

To support inclusive practice or to extend learning, the space, task, equipment and people (STEP) approach can be adopted throughout this unit. By changing the space, task, equipment or people, the activity can be made more challenging or easier to understand, enabling all pupils to take part in the activity, as explained in the assessment chapter in this book.

The children will work as a whole class directed by the teacher or together in small groups, either with support from adults or independently. Art education should be organic and worked through by doing it, so the role of the adult is to lead the sessions safely and to model the activities using appropriate art vocabulary. Throughout the unit, children should be encouraged to own the whole process, and therefore it is strongly recommended that the adult does not draw on the children's work, instead modelling examples in their own sketchbook.

You may wish to record the activities using a camera.

Natural connections

- Studying colours, lines, patterns and shapes in nature
- Reflecting on reasons and purposes
- Observing plant reproduction and life cycle changes
- Describing seasonal changes and the resulting impact on nature
- Developing awareness of human impact on environments.

Health and wellbeing

- Physical activity
- Development of observational and fine motor skills

- Appreciation of beauty and increased aesthetic awareness
- Offering and justifying viewpoints and opinions and considering others' opinions
- Expression of emotions and feelings
- Problem-solving
- Learning and applying new skills
- Reflecting on their own and others' achievements.

Word bank

Colour

- primary and secondary colours
- limited palette
- tone
- shade
- blending
- monochrome
- shading
- neutral
- intensity
- wet-on-wet

Texture, pattern

- repeating
- symmetry
- orientation

Line, shape, form

- sketch
- contour (outline)
- hatching
- cross-hatching
- blind contour drawing
- hand–eye coordination
- overlapping

Composition

- composition
- placement
- spatial organisation
- adjacent

Summary overview

Progression	Curriculum content	Learning experiences/activities
Lesson 1	Create sketch books to record their observations and use them to review and revisit ideas. Improve their mastery of art and design techniques, including drawing with a range of materials. Learn about great artists in history.	Children explore line using tubular webbing to make outline shapes of known leaves. They observe the use of line by Da Vinci and Kelly, and experiment with blind contour drawing. They try mark-making using pressure, dots and dashes.
Lesson 2	Create sketch books to record their observations and use them to review and revisit ideas. Improve their mastery of art and design techniques, including drawing and painting with a range of materials.	Children explore the use of line to communicate meaning, using drawing tools and mark-making to record the journey or route taken by wildlife in the area. They overlap and draw around leaves in their sketchbooks and colour them in using crayons or watercolours, ensuring that no two adjacent colours are the same.
Lesson 3	Create sketch books to record observations and use them to review and revisit ideas. Improve mastery of art and design techniques, including drawing and painting with a range of materials. Learn about great artists in history and understand the historical and cultural development of their art forms.	Children explore using a limited palette, sorting grasses and green leaves by lightness and darkness, colour tone and intensity. They study works by Claude Monet and his use of a limited palette. They explore the effect of dark and shadow and draw enlarged grasses or leaves, painting them in different shades of green, studying the outlines, shapes and spaces between them.
Lesson 4	Create sketch books to record their observations and use them to review and revisit ideas. Improve their mastery of art and design techniques, including drawing and painting with a range of materials. Learn about great artists in history.	The children are introduced to the wet-on-wet watercolour technique. They study work by Paul Cézanne, observing the use of soft edges and the blending of colour produced by the technique. They experiment with the technique, painting a leaf outline with clean water and then touching it with colour, making choices to mix colours to match the original leaf.
Lesson 5	Create sketch books to record their observations and use them to review and revisit ideas. Improve their mastery of art and design techniques, including drawing and painting with a range of materials. Learn about great artists in history.	The children explore pattern, using a leaf to create a repeating regular pattern, based on William Morris designs. They decide how to create their own repeating patterns based on nature.
Lesson 6	Improve their mastery of art and design techniques, including sculpture with a range of materials. Learn about great artists in history and understand the historical and cultural development of their art forms.	Children go on a hunt to find leaves with prominent veins, discussing their shape, pattern and lines. They classify the leaves, linking to science. They make clay leaf print tiles in the style of William Morris, with the option to create shallow dishes. They review the unit, assessing how they have developed as artists and how they have expressed the essence of place in their artwork.

PREPARATION

At the start of the session, make the children aware of poisonous or hazardous plants and berries in the outdoor area.

For information, Leonardo Da Vinci (1452–1519) was an Italian Renaissance artist. Ellsworth Kelly (1923–2015) was an American minimalist artist inspired by the natural world (see www.bonhams.com/auctions/14799/lot/324).

Resources

- Lengths of tubular webbing (or soft cord)
- Images of Leonardo da Vinci's *Sprigs of oak and Dyer's Green Weed* (c.1506–12)
- An example of Ellsworth Kelly's contour leaf studies, such as *Oak VI* (1992)
- Selection of leaves to draw around
- Clipboards, sketchbooks or paper
- Pencils and pencil sharpeners
- Plant / leaf identification guides

CONSIDER

Health & Safety

Assess and evaluate hazards and risks in your setting. See the health and safety chapter.

LESSON OBJECTIVES

We are exploring how line can be used to capture the 'essence' of nature.

National Curriculum Content

- Create sketch books to record their observations and use them to review and revisit ideas.
- Improve their mastery of art and design techniques, including drawing with a range of materials.
- Learn about great artists in history.

ADULT ROLES

- Have a go at the blind contour drawing activity.
- Ask questions such as 'Can you see how… ?'
- Encourage well-structured descriptions.
- Ensure that the plants being collected or observed are not hazardous.

WARM UP IDEAS

Explain that for the next six lessons, the children will be using the outdoor learning area for their art, aiming to capture the 'essence of place'. What could this mean? What are 'place' and 'essence'?

Ask the children what they know about the area, its timeline and why it looks the way it does. Ask them to identify features of the natural and built environment, and to say how they think the environment has been changed and shaped for different purposes.

What will it be like to do art lessons outdoors? What experience do they have of drawing and painting in the outdoors?

Explain that today is about exploring lines in nature. What is their understanding of 'line'?

Introductory activity (groups of five to six)

Using lengths of tubular webbing with the ends joined with a water knot (see www.bloomsbury.com/NC-Outdoors), groups should:

1. Hold the webbing at waist height and make a perfect circle.
2. Carefully work together to place it on the ground.
3. Walk around the outside of the circle, checking to see whether it matches the properties of a circle.
4. Repeat but this time make a specific leaf shape, e.g. oak, beech, etc. How do they know whether it's right?
5. Check it against a leaf identification guide.

Lines in nature

Share images of leaf studies by Leonardo da Vinci and Ellsworth Kelly (whole class and in pairs)

Share the images, generating discussion about Da Vinci's botanical studies, created as preparation for his paintings. Explore the fine detail. How is it created? Point out the use of tones (using chalks) and use of hatched lines (parallel lines on an angle) and cross-hatching (parallel lines crossing at an angle) in the background. Can the children see how the lines create 'movement' around the plants and inside the sprig of oak?

By contrast, Kelly uses a technique called 'contour line drawing', with only leaf outlines being drawn. Kelly often used to draw without looking at his drawing hand – a technique called 'blind contour drawing'. He would fix his eyes on his subject and, using hand–eye coordination, his hand would record the shape in a continuous line, not removing his pencil from the paper. It is a technique to train the eye to draw what it sees. What benefits might there be in doing this? Is it easy to lose your place? What could go wrong?

Allow time for pairs to study and talk about both drawings. What can they see in the pictures? How have the artists used lines and layout (composition and placement) and what effect does this have? Is it effective and why? Encourage well-structured answers and descriptions from careful observation to share with the class.

Challenge 1 (whole class and individual)

Explore lines in nature

Using dry leaves from the area, study the structure of each leaf.

Demonstrate blind contour drawing a leaf outline, saying that you are picking a point on the object where the eye can begin its slow 'journey' around the contour (or edge) of the object, and showing how when your eye moves, your hand moves across the page (without you looking at it). Keep it fun; show the children how the drawing may not quite resemble the leaf, as this technique takes practice.

Independently, the children explore blind contour drawing of nearby leaves and other objects.

Challenge 2 (whole class and individual)

Explore and collect 'lines found in nature'

On a fresh page draw a leaf outline, then demonstrate how to draw extended lines to the edge of the paper to create widening 'zones' on the page.

The aim of this challenge is for children to find lines

from the area (such as lines in leaf structures or tree bark) and record them in the 'zones', aiming to capture the 'essence of place'.

Using a pencil, show how to create a range of marks, including dashes close together and far apart, hatching and cross-hatching, stippling (dots), curves, zig-zags, small circles and swirls, with one type of mark in each zone. Experiment with pressure to make lines darker and lighter. Review and discuss the effect of the lines.

The children then explore the area, finding and recording different lines in each 'zone' around their own leaf outlines.

Children share their findings with others, reviewing the effects that have been created. Can their designs be said to capture the 'essence' of the place? In what way, e.g. by recording lines found in the area?

Back in the classroom

Studying the colours of their original leaf, make 'colour matches' using oil pastels on the real leaf itself, before colouring the drawn leaf to replicate the original.

The children could use pen to draw over the pencil lines.

- What went well and why?
- What didn't go as well as expected?
- What could be changed?
- Who stood out and why?

PREPARATION

At the start of the session, make the children aware of poisonous or hazardous plants in the outdoor area, with a warning not to use them in the session.

Resources

- Selection of leaves and plants from the area
- Leaf and plant identification guide
- Clipboards, paper and drawing pencils
- Coloured crayons (a variety of shades of each colour)
- Watercolour boxes, water and fine-tipped brushes
- Thin marker pens

CONSIDER

Health & Safety

Assess and evaluate hazards and risks in your setting. See the health and safety chapter.

LESSON OBJECTIVES

We are exploring the use of line to recreate patterns from nature.

National Curriculum Content

- Create sketch books to record observations and use them to review and revisit ideas.
- Improve their mastery of art and design techniques, including drawing and painting with a range of materials.

ADULT ROLES

- Ask questions such as 'Can you see how... ?', encouraging justified answers, and well-structured descriptions and explanations.
- Encourage the use of art vocabulary.

WARM UP IDEAS

Explain that today children will be exploring line and colour in nature to capture the 'essence' of the outdoor area, recording it in their sketchbooks.

What do they remember about how Da Vinci and Kelly (from Progression 1) communicated meaning or information through their use of detail or expressive lines? How were the lines used? Encourage the use of art vocabulary (see the word bank on page 86).

Have they heard the expression 'A picture is worth a thousand words'? What could this mean? Discuss the communication of meaning through images, such as:

- How pictures have been used throughout history to communicate meaning (such as cave paintings and Egyptian hieroglyphics). Ask the children to share what they know.

- How there is sometimes an emotional reaction to observing an artwork, for example an 'Oh yes!', moment when the observer sees or understands the artist's ideas. Have they experienced this? What did it feel like? Did they share the moment with anyone?

- How we can learn to see the world differently or from different perspectives through the eyes of other people, such as artists, who create a representation of not only what they see, but how they feel about what they see. Do they have any examples of this?

- How art is the expression of the artist's skill and imagination, and how the artwork comes 'alive' or 'realises its purpose' when it is seen and appreciated by people who look at it (its audience) and who understand the meaning or message, or read the information in the picture. Can they think of a time when this happened to them? A simple example might be seeing information signs, but the children might have other experiences of narrative artwork.

Introductory activity

Children find a quiet place from which to sit and observe nature.

Using continuous line mark-making and blind contour drawing, the children observe and record the journey or route taken by wildlife in the area, such as a snail's pathway, the movements of a spider in its web, or a bird's flight.

What does it look like? Can they share and explain their lines to a partner?

MAIN ACTIVITIES

Line patterns in nature

Challenge 1 (in pairs or groups of four)

Explore lines and patterns in nature using leaves

Children observe key features of leaves and plants from the area, such as their shape, structure and colour. Can they identify the plants or leaves using an identification guide?

Ask pairs or groups to sort the leaves and plants by a chosen category, such as colour, intensity, shape or size. They then make a repeating pattern with the leaves and plants and share this with another pair or group. Encourage well-structured descriptions and explanations.

Challenge 2 (whole class)

Observe techniques to record line, pattern and colour

Remind the children of the contour leaf drawings (in the style of Ellsworth Kelly) from Progression 1.

Show the children how to rehearse a 'composition'. Place a selection of leaves, with some overlapping, on the sketchbook page, thinking out loud about careful placement and how an 'essence of place' might be communicated.

Ask the children how the arrangement could be developed or improved, e.g. by changing the order or orientation of the leaves.

Recreate the composition by drawing around the leaves, adding structural details (veins) to the leaf shapes.

Using watercolours (or evenly applied crayon), show how to add colour, ensuring that no two adjacent colours are the same. (The colours do not need to be the same as the leaves.)

Once dry, embolden the lines using thin marker pens. Encourage discussion about how effectively this technique captures and communicates information, such as nature's lines, colours and patterns.

Note: An alternative approach is to create a line-only composition. Use fine-tipped coloured felt tip pens to draw each leaf outline and structure lines (veins), ensuring adjacent lines are in different colours.

Challenge 3 (individual or in pairs)

Use techniques to record line and colour to make patterns from nature

Children use these techniques to make patterns from nature, exploring the area, choosing leaves or plants to create their own pattern in their sketchbook, and deciding on developments and improvements.

They add colour to their pattern, ensuring that no two adjacent colours are the same.

PLENARY

Encourage the children to explain what they have discovered. Can they identify the leaves from the drawings? Do the designs communicate information about the learning area? In what way? Can they explain why they made their choices?

Back in the classroom

Children review their paintings to assess new design ideas, such as adding fine black lines to exaggerate the leaf structures.

EVALUATION/FOLLOW ON

- What went well and why?
- What didn't go as well as expected?
- What could be changed?
- Who stood out and why?

PREPARATION

Use a plant guide to check for harmful plants and berries in the outdoor area, pointing these out for the group to avoid. If none are present in the area, you may need to find long grasses and leaves elsewhere.

For information, Claude Monet (1840–1926) was a founder of French Impressionism. The invention of tubes for oil paint meant that more colours could be used to capture changing nature and light. Photography (monochrome, sepia or black and white) also had an influence on art of the time.

Resources

- Leaf identification guides
- Selection of colour images of Monet's artwork
- Clipboards, sketchbooks or paper, and pencils
- Primary yellow and blue watercolour paints
- Fine-tipped brushes
- Water

Previous learning

This progression introduces colour tone awareness, which is reinforced in Year 5 Religious Education.

CONSIDER

Health & Safety

Assess and evaluate hazards and risks in your setting. See the health and safety chapter.

LESSON OBJECTIVES

We are exploring a 'limited palette' technique to record nature's tones and shades.

National Curriculum Content

- Create sketch books to record their observations and use them to review and revisit ideas.
- Improve their mastery of art and design techniques, including drawing and painting with a range of materials.
- Learn about great artists in history and understand the historical and cultural development of their art forms.

ADULT ROLES

- Model the activity, encouraging careful observation of colour intensity and variety and how this can be replicated using limited colours.
- Ask questions such as 'Can you see how... ?'

WARM UP IDEAS

Look around the learning area. How has it changed from the previous session and why might this be? Discuss the human (both positive and negative) impacts on the setting and the effect of seasonal changes.

Explain that today the children will be exploring lightness and darkness, colour tone and intensity. Revise the art vocabulary 'tone' and 'intensity'. Can they give examples?

Introductory activity

Collect and identify a selection of long green leaves and tall plants, such as grasses and reeds, from the area. In groups, children sort the leaves and plants by the intensity of their colour, ranging from a light tone to a dark tone.

Groups share their arrangements with other groups. Does everyone agree?

MAIN ACTIVITIES

Limiting nature's palette

Challenge 1 (whole class and in pairs or groups)

Share images of Monet's artworks, illustrating limited palett

Showing the Monet artworks, explain who Monet was and how he limited his palette to white, yellow, green, blue, red and black, choosing not to use the newly available, ready-mixed colours that resulted from the invention of the 'tube' to transport oil paint. Clarify the terms 'limited' and 'palette'.

Providing multiple copies of Monet's artwork for the class, the children identify the brush strokes used (varying from thick to thin), the use of dabs of light, and how definition is created by adding 'contour lines' (outlines). How do the artworks differ and how are they similar?

Pairs or groups talk about the work, discussing the technique and composition, use of tones and colour, what effect it has, whether it is effective and why.

Challenge 2 (whole class)

Observe how to use a limited palette of colours

Examine the leaves and plants that children sorted by tone and intensity in the introductory activity. How could these colours be recreated using a very limited palette of just blue, yellow and water?

Choose a selection of the long leaves and lay them out on the sketchbook page with some overlapping. Think out loud about the arrangement.

Ask the children how the pattern could be developed or improved, e.g. by changing the order or orientation of the leaves. Act on some of their suggestions, discussing what difference it makes to the design on the page.

Draw outlines of the leaves from observation, enlarging or taking the lines to the edge of the paper to fill the page, overlapping the outlines to experiment with the composition.

Paint the leaves from the palest to darkest colours, showing how to mix the paints with water to achieve different tones and intensities. Study the shapes and spaces between the leaves (negative shapes).

Challenge 3 (individual or in pairs)

Use a limited palette to record nature's tones and shades

Children choose leaves (or plants) to create their own leaf line drawings in their sketchbooks, deciding on careful placement and composition and then adding blue to yellow watercolour paint to match the colour of the leaves. Apply the colour from lightest to darkest, experimenting with colour intensity by adding more water or adding more blue.

PLENARY

The children discuss in groups what they have learned about colours in nature and limited palette colour-mixing. They feed back to the whole class with well-structured descriptions and explanations.

Back in the classroom

Children review their ideas, choosing whether or how the work could be improved or done differently another time. Allow time to 'free practise' the activity, e.g. at break times.

EVALUATION/FOLLOW ON

- What went well and why?
- What didn't go as well as expected?
- What could be changed?
- Who stood out and why?

PREPARATION

Check the area for hazards and remove these or make the children aware of them.

Collect large autumnal leaves, such as sycamore or chestnut leaves, and cut them into pieces, placing sets of three leaf jigsaws in separate envelopes, one envelope per group.

Resources

- Leaf identification guides
- Selection of autumnal or differently coloured leaves
- Leaf jigsaws
- Copies of *Almond Trees in Provence* (1900) by Paul Cézanne
- Clipboards, sketchbooks or paper, and pencils
- Yellow and blue watercolour paints
- Fine-tipped brushes and water

Previous learning

There are links to Year 5 science (living things).

CONSIDER

Health & Safety

Assess and evaluate hazards and risks in your setting. See the health and safety chapter.

LESSON OBJECTIVES

We are finding colours in autumnal leaves and exploring how these can be recorded using the wet-on-wet watercolour technique.

National Curriculum Content

- Create sketch books to record their observations and use them to review and revisit ideas.
- Improve their mastery of art and design techniques, including drawing and painting with a range of materials.
- Learn about great artists in history.

ADULT ROLES

- Model the activity in your own sketchbook, acknowledging difficulties and successes.
- Ask questions such as 'Can you see how… ?'
- Encourage the use of appropriate art vocabulary.

WARM UP IDEAS

Look around the area and ask whether children notice any changes in the area since the previous session. Examples may include a change in the colour of the leaves or more leaves being on the ground. Hypothesise why these changes may have occurred, asking pertinent questions and suggesting reasons for similarities and differences.

In pairs, children review and revisit ideas from previous sessions by sharing sketchbooks, discussing the lines and colour techniques they have explored, and evaluating and sharing what worked well and what they would do differently another time, using art vocabulary.

Explain that today the children will be exploring and studying the wet-on-wet watercolour technique.

Introductory activity (small groups)

Divide the class into groups and give each group an envelope containing the three jigsaw leaves. They have three minutes to put the leaves back together (reform them).

As a class, children point out the clues they used to help reform the leaves, and name them if they can. They identify and discuss the colours and how these change throughout each leaf.

Wet-on-wet autumn colours

Share images of artworks illustrating the wet-on-wet technique

Explain that Post-Impressionists such as Paul Cézanne (1839–1906) used the wet-on-wet technique for some of their paintings. Show Cézanne's tree study *Almond Trees in Provence* (1900).

Ask the children to identify how the image has been created (drawing and watercolours). Point out how the trees appear to be quickly sketched and then painted using 'flares' of colour, which give a sense of movement to capture the 'essence' of the trees and area.

Allow time for the children to study the artwork (providing multiple copies for the class), asking what they can see in the painting, identifying how the artist has used line and colour, discussing the technique and composition, and considering whether it is effective and why.

Ask the children to think about the different effects of painting on wet or dry surfaces. Explain that painting 'wet on dry' gives precise edges to shapes, whereas painting wet-on-wet produces soft edges and 'blending' as colours mix and spread into one another unpredictably.

Show the two different effects to the group, firstly by painting a leaf shape on dry paper using a loaded brush, and then paint a leaf on paper using just clean water to create the leaf shape.

Add colour by touching the water with a paint-loaded brush tip, so that the colour runs to the edges of the shape. The paint will 'bloom' across the moistened area. It may go over the edges of the leaf, but do not worry about this. Can they see the difference?

Challenge 1 (whole class)

Observe how to use the wet-on-wet technique to represent autumn leaves

1. Draw an outline of a leaf onto a piece of watercolour paper or in the sketchbook using pencil, then use the brush to 'paint' clean water inside the leaf outline.

2. Using colours mixed to match the colours of the original leaf, touch the tip of the brush to the moistened leaf shape and watch how the colour spreads and blends.

3. While the paint is still wet, draw veins onto the leaf with the tip of the brush, pressing gently to leave the veins a darker colour. Discuss the effect that this has.

4. Next, show how to make a quick sketch of a tree from direct observation, then apply wet-on-wet paint in the style of Paul Cézanne to communicate the 'feeling' of the tree and the space around it. Does the resulting painting capture the movement and 'essence' of the tree? In what way?

Challenge 2 (individual)

Use the wet-on-wet technique to record leaf tones and shades

Children experiment with the wet-on-wet technique, choosing individual leaves or whole trees as their subject. They experiment with colour-mixing and intensity by adding more water or more paint.

PLENARY

Pairs or groups discuss what they have learned about colours in nature and wet-on-wet colour-mixing. They share their ideas with the class.

Allow time to 'free practise' the activity, e.g. at break times or as a rainy-day activity outdoors on wet surfaces.

EVALUATION/FOLLOW ON

- What went well and why?
- What didn't go as well as expected?
- What could be changed?
- Who stood out and why?

PREPARATION

Use a plant guide to check for harmful plants and berries in the outdoor area, pointing these out for the group to avoid.

Make a collection of six to eight pinnate leaves, such as elder or ash.

Collect a few simple leaves with a strong outline shape, such as oak or maple.

Resources

- Copies of William Morris prints, such as *Rosehip* or *Jasmine*
- Leaf and plant identification guides
- Leaves: some pinnate and some simple (see Preparation)
- Clipboards, sketchbooks, paper and pencils
- Coloured pencil crayons or thin felt tip pens in a limited palette (similar in colour to the available leaves, e.g. brown, red and orange or dark green, light green and yellow)
- Optional: Styrofoam printing blocks, rollers and ink

Previous learning

This progression extends learning about design and placement from previous progressions.

CONSIDER

Health & Safety

Assess and evaluate hazards and risks in your setting. See the health and safety chapter.

LESSON OBJECTIVES

We are exploring pattern and spatial organisation by studying the style of William Morris, using leaves and plants.

National Curriculum Content

- Create sketch books to record their observations and use them to review and revisit ideas.
- Improve their mastery of art and design techniques, including drawing with a range of materials.
- Learn about great artists in history.

ADULT ROLES

- Ask questions such as 'Can you see how... ?'
- Look for and praise places where the pattern works well.
- Model the activity, acknowledging levels of challenge and how they can be overcome.

WARM UP IDEAS

Explain that in this session, the children will be exploring 'pattern' and 'spatial organisation' (placement) by drawing leaves and plants in a repeating pattern in the style of William Morris. Explain the new vocabulary and give examples to clarify it.

Introductory activity (whole class and pairs or groups)

Explain that William Morris (1834–1896) was an English artist and designer who became famous for creating handcrafted wallpaper and fabric designs in the mid-1860s, inspired by the natural world. Show examples of his work to the children. Encourage pairs or groups to study and discuss the images, using the following questions as a basis for discussion:

- What medium might have been used and how has it been applied? (Smooth blocks of colour show that it has been printed using a printing block.)
- How has line and pattern been used? How effective is it?
- Are the images very realistic or 'impressionistic'?
- How is the plant or tree structure highlighted or emphasised?

Ask the children to share the techniques they have identified with the class, describing how effective the techniques are and why. Can they give examples of 'spatial organisation', e.g. the use of repeated patterns or of simple rotation to balance the composition on the page?

William Morris patterning

Challenge 1 (whole class)

Identify examples of the use of pattern in work by William Morris

Point out the effects created by Morris through his use of simple plant shapes, repetition and 'flat' colours. How do his designs capture the wildness of the plants? How could his designs be recreated?

Do any plants that the children can see in the setting resemble these plants created by Morris? In which ways are they similar or different?

Arrange pinnate leaves (see preparation) on a page in the same orientation to create a repeating pattern similar to *Rosehips*.

How could this be captured in the children's sketchbooks as artwork?

Take suggestions such as:

• Drawing the leaves.

• Printing the leaves using ink or paint.

• Using technology by photographing one leaf and copying and pasting it many times (which could be done as a follow-up back in the classroom).

Challenge 2 (whole class)

Observe how to draw leaves, emphasising lines and 'spatial arrangement'

1. Model how to use a limited palette of coloured pencils or thin felt tip pens (reflecting the colours of the leaf) to draw around a simple leaf outline, such as a maple or oak leaf. Draw the veins using a few simple lines.

2. Move the leaf and draw around it again with a different colour, again drawing the veins. Then repeat with the leaf in a different position (but same orientation) until the page is covered with leaves. Discuss the effect this has.

3. On a different page, draw around one of the pinnate leaves. Discuss the challenges of using this kind of leaf and how to overcome them.

Challenge 3 (individual)

Use pattern and limited colour to record leaf shapes as a design

Children should have multiple attempts at drawing around the leaves, exploring and developing their ideas, discussing with a partner how effective the technique is and why.

They use leaf and plant identification guides to learn which leaf they used in their design, recording the name to one side of the page.

Children explain what they have noticed about the improvements in their work with subsequent attempts. Did they consider 'spatial organisation', use different colours in different positions on the page, or colour one or two examples of the leaf in completely?

Back in the classroom

Some children may be able to experiment with printing techniques, painting or inking leaves and carefully printing them onto the page, or drawing leaf designs into Styrofoam to create a printing block, which could then be printed to make a repeated pattern.

• What went well and why?

• What didn't go as well as expected?

• What could be changed?

• Who stood out and why?

PREPARATION

Cut paper into 15 cm squares.

Cut tile-sized strong card squares to be used as cutting guides.

Set aside a safe storage area for the completed clay tiles, such as large trays which can be carefully carried back indoors to dry.

Resources

- Selection of leaves with prominent veins
- Leaf identification chart
- Images of William Morris tiles inspired by plants, such as *Daisy, Primrose* or *Willow Bough*
- Air-dry modelling clay
- Rolling pins
- Guide sticks (to manage the thickness of the tiles)
- Knives, card squares and paper (such as baking paper)
- Large trays or another storage method for the tiles
- Strong card
- Clay boards or tree stumps
- Small bowls

Previous learning

This session reinforces and extends design elements explored in Progression 5.

CONSIDER

Health & Safety

Assess and evaluate hazards and risks in your setting. See the health and safety chapter.

LESSON OBJECTIVES

We are using clay to create tiles to capture the essence of place, inspired by nature.

National Curriculum Content

- Improve their mastery of art and design techniques, including sculpture with a range of materials.
- Learn about great artists in history and understand the historical and cultural development of their art forms.

ADULT ROLES

- Ask questions such as 'Can you see how... ?'
- Encourage independent rolling and pressing of the clay.
- Model the activity, acknowledging levels of challenge and how they can be overcome.

WARM UP IDEAS

Look around the area and ask whether the children notice any changes, discussing why these changes have occurred. Is there anything that they notice now that they haven't noticed before? Why is that?

Explain that in this session, the children will be using clay to create tiles or bowls in the style of William Morris, inspired by nature and aiming to capture the 'essence' of the setting.

Pairs should collect six different leaves with prominent veins that they feel represent the 'essence' of their learning area. Can they classify and group the leaves by their outlines or by the arrangements of veins on the leaves?

Introductory activity (in pairs)

Pairs place the leaves on the ground and study them. Each partner states the number of leaves they can identify.

The partner stating the highest number of leaves then names each leaf, with the other partner checking whether they are correct by using the leaf identification chart.

If they name the stated number of leaves correctly then they win. Together, they identify the other leaves using the identification guide. How can they remember these mystery leaves for next time?

Essence of place tiles

Show the children examples of plant-inspired William Morris tiles, often used to decorate fireplaces and walls in the 1870s and still popular today. What do the children think of them? Do they like them? Why? How similar are they to the designs (used for wallpaper and fabrics) from Progression 5?

Challenge 1 (whole class)

Observe how to press leaves into tiles to create nature-based designs

Explain that the children will be exploring shape, line and pattern by making tiles in the style of William Morris, capturing the 'essence of place' in clay.

1. Model how to place a ball of clay onto a square of card (see preparation) on a flat surface, such as a tree stump or clay board.

2. Place two smooth sticks either side of the clay ball, explaining that these guide sticks will ensure that the clay is rolled out evenly and has the same depth all over.

3. Model how to roll out the clay, aiming to create a tile as close to a square as possible.

4. Choose a leaf with prominent veins and place it underside-down on the clay tile, thinking out loud about the placement, e.g. in the middle or to one side, and what effect this would have on the composition.

5. Use the roller to press the leaf into the clay by gently rolling across the top of the tile.

6. Peel off the leaf and show the children the imprint, pointing out the lines, textures and shapes.

7. Using a knife and cutting guide, carefully cut the tile into a square, asking the children why it might be important that all the tiles are the same size. (For ease of fitting them together.)

8. Show how to indent initials in the side of the tile with a pencil, for identification purposes.

9. Ask how it could be improved or modified, e.g. by making it into a bowl instead?

Challenge 2 (in pairs)

Make a leaf tile

Pairs follow the above instructions, taking their tile to a storage area for safe placement to dry (check they have initialled their tiles). Provide enough time and materials for multiple attempts, allowing children to vary their designs and improve their technique.

Optional: Create a nature-inspired bowl by pressing a large leaf into the clay, then placing the clay into a small bowl (as a mould) to dry.

Discuss the challenges the children encountered and how these were overcome, and which bits of their own work (and the work of others) they are most pleased with and why. Do their designs capture the 'essence' of the outdoor learning area and if so, in what way?

Review the whole unit. What was the most memorable part and why? How have they developed as artists?

Back in the classroom

Create a tiled feature wall somewhere in the school grounds, illustrating the 'essence of place' of the outdoor learning area.

- What went well and why?
- What didn't go as well as expected?
- What could be changed?
- Who stood out and why?

Design and Technology

Cooking and nutrition

In this unit, children explore cooking and nutrition, experiencing a variety of cooking techniques in the outdoor learning area. Based on the Key Stage 2 design and technology cooking and nutrition attainment targets identified in the 2014 National Curriculum for England, this unit gives a 'taster' of how the outdoors can provide an opportunity to demonstrate and showcase not only the statutory requirements, but also current healthy eating advice from professional associations including Public Health England. Ingredients and recipes have been suggested (see www.bloomsbury.com/NC-Outdoors) but other foods can be substituted, reflecting cultural diversity or regional variations. Knowledge and skills from previous Key Stage 2 DT progressions are reinforced and extended, including exploration of functional design, manufacturing and materials, and there are links to other subjects such as RE and maths, using and applying maths learning linked to calculation, estimation and measures from the Year 5 numeracy objectives.

To support inclusive practice or to extend learning, the space, task, equipment and people (STEP) approach can be adopted throughout this unit. By changing the space, task, equipment or people, the activity can be made more challenging or easier to understand, enabling all pupils to take part in the activity, as explained in the assessment chapter. In the context of design technology, this could mean providing a well-defined learning space, positioning pupils away from potential distractions, considering whether the task needs to be simplified by breaking it down into component parts or extending it by making it more challenging, using smaller or lightweight equipment in order to make the task more accessible, working independently on a specified task, or working in small groups, with a buddy or with an adult as appropriate.

The role of the adult is to lead the sessions safely whilst providing direct support and reassurance as appropriate.

Additional health and safety for this unit should include consideration of outdoor food preparation practices, adherence to Food Standards Agency guidelines (including allergies) and religious diet considerations.

You may wish to record the activities using a camera.

Natural connections

- Awareness of human impact on the natural environment
- Understanding of seasonality of ingredients
- Awareness of the environmental impact of food transportation.

Health and wellbeing

- Physical activity
- Being creative and evaluative
- Thinking about others and how to design with purpose
- Safety management
- Appreciation of the value of eating together.

Word bank

Design

- function
- purpose
- safety
- efficiency
- ergonomic
- functional
- aesthetic
- heat transference
- technical knowledge

Food preparation

- hygiene
- bacteria
- knife safety
- press
- peel
- spread
- grate
- combine
- portion
- drain
- measure
- chop
- dice
- slice
- mix
- stir

Summary overview

Progression	Curriculum content	Learning experiences/activities
Lesson 1	This unit progressively builds on: Investigate and analyse a range of existing products. Generate, develop, model and communicate their ideas through discussion. Select from and use a wider range of tools and equipment to perform practical tasks.	Children explore a range of ways of cooking outdoors, including using direct heat, roasting, grilling, boiling, frying and baking, and consider safety aspects of outdoor cooking. They evaluate and investigate products, looking at materials, functional properties, components and moving parts, who the target users are and whether the products are innovative, sharing findings with other groups.
Lesson 2	Evaluate their ideas and products against their own design criteria and consider the views of others to improve their work. **Cooking and nutrition**	Children explore cooking using direct heat. They use and apply their knowledge of food hygiene and nutrition. They help light a group fire and observe how to make a quesadilla. In groups, they design, prepare and cook (with adult supervision) their own quesadilla. They evaluate their product.
Lesson 3	Understand and apply the principles of a healthy and varied diet. Prepare and cook a variety of predominantly savoury dishes using a range of cooking techniques. Understand seasonality, and know where and how a variety of ingredients are grown, reared, caught and processed.	Children explore cooking using hot water. They revise hygiene and safe practice, and study the design of a storm kettle. They sample drinks made using the kettle, before watching a demonstration of how to use hot water to cook. Suggestions include couscous, boiled eggs, gnocchi, pasta and poached pears, with options for non-cooked products. In groups, they design and prepare their own ingredients and cook these as demonstrated.
Lesson 4		Children cook using direct heat. They revise health and safety and hygiene key points, before watching a demonstration of how to cook on direct heat. Suggestions include crumpets, toast, vegetable kebabs, garlic bread, cinnamon apples, oranges with chocolate, and vegetable or banana fritters. They identify food groups. They are introduced to the Great Campfire Cook Off, which they will need to research and plan for before the next sessions.
Lesson 5		Children practise for the Great Campfire Cook Off, demonstrating their knowledge and understanding of food safety and fire safety. They rehearse their plan for Progression 6, taking photographs of the process and product. They plan and design a menu card, which will be given to the judges next session, describing their product (with illustration or photograph). They evaluate and make changes as necessary.
Lesson 6		Children take part in the Great Campfire Cook Off. They impress the judges with their knowledge of food hygiene, nutrition and cooking skills. Back in the classroom, they collate their recipes to make a recipe book for the outdoors.

PREPARATION

If possible, source as many tools for cooking outside as you are able to: this may involve a call-out to staff and parents or a class visit to a local outdoors shop. It is also possible to use pictures. For images, see www.ukfinefoods. co.uk/outdoor-cooking.

Prepare an area for food preparation (including hand-washing).

Optional: prepare a worksheet to use as a prompt for Challenge 2.

Resources

- A variety of cooking tools or images of them
- Additional adult support for fire-lighting
- Fire-lighting equipment, materials and fuel
- Water to extinguish the fires
- Heat-resistant gloves

CONSIDER

Health & Safety

Assess and evaluate hazards and risks in your setting. See the health and safety chapter.

LESSON OBJECTIVES

We are investigating and analysing a range of existing products used for cooking in the outdoors.

National Curriculum Content

- Investigate and analyse a range of existing products.

ADULT ROLES

- Support activities by encouraging analytical observation and open questioning.
- Ensure safe practice around the fire.

WARM UP IDEAS

Introduce the purpose of the next six sessions: to explore cooking techniques and nutrition; and to plan and cook food for the rest of the group on a stove or fire top.

Ask the children what experience they have of cooking at home or in the outdoors and share their stories and experiences:

- What went well and what didn't go so well?
- What made it memorable?
- What cooking equipment have they used and do they know about?

Ask the children for ideas about how to stay safe when cooking in general, and when cooking around a fire in particular. These could include:

- Ensuring that there is a safety space around the fire.
- Ensuring that hair is tied back.
- Adopting a safe stance.
- Using heatproof gloves where necessary.
- Limiting the number of people around the fire at one time.
- Making sure water is available for hand-washing, treating burns or putting the fire out.

MAIN ACTIVITIES

Outdoor cooking resources

Introduce and explore safety aspects of different means of cooking in the outdoors

What methods of cooking are the children familiar with and how might these be different outside? Examples could include using direct heat (fire) or portable stoves, roasting (on skewers or a spit), grilling (on a barbeque), boiling, frying (in a pan) or baking (in the fire).

Challenge 1 (in pairs or groups of four)

Evaluate and investigate products

With the range of cooking tools arranged within easy reach and available for all to see and explore, talk the children through the available items, asking whether they can see how they might be used.

Consider and discuss:

- What has influenced the design?
- What design criteria might have been specified to produce the product?
- What are the functional aspects of the product, such as its weight or size?
- Is it fit for purpose?
- Who is it aimed at?
- Are there any safety features or special safety considerations to think about during its use, such as how the fire is contained or controlled?
- What method of cooking is it used for?

Examples of different products could include:

- an established fire pit
- a free-standing fire pit
- storm kettle
- portable stoves, such as camping gas cookers
- gas or charcoal barbeques
- a tripod for 'over the fire' cooking
- pans made of different metals
- cooking utensils.

Challenge 2 (in pairs or groups of four)

Evaluate and investigate products

Provide a 'focus question' worksheet if required.

In pairs or groups, the children choose one of the products. They draw and label the product, showing:

- what materials it is made out of
- its functional properties
- its key components
- any moving parts and their purpose
- what they like about the product and why.

The children then find another group or pair who have investigated a different product. They compare the two products.

PLENARY

If time allows, use one of the methods to cook something that can be shared with the group, such as heating water for a drink or cooking banana fritters (see www.bloomsbury.com/NC-Outdoors).

Encourage the children to explain what they have been doing in the session and state what they have found out about outdoor cooking methods.

Back in the classroom

Children research recipes suitable for future outdoor cookery experiences.

EVALUATION/FOLLOW ON

- What went well and why?
- What didn't go as well as expected?
- What could be changed?

PREPARATION

Identify the area to be used as a fire-lighting area, such as a cleared area of ground, surrounding this with well-defined markers such as large branches or tree stump seats to create the safety zone.

Sticks for fuel may need to be pre-collected and dried.

Prepare an area for food preparation (including hand-washing).

Prepare the ingredients.

Resources

- Fire-lighting equipment, materials and fuel
- Water to extinguish the fires
- Heat-resistant gloves
- Cooking utensils
- Ingredients (see recipes), food preparation equipment, plates and cutlery
- Optional: charcoal

Previous learning

Prior teaching and exploration of aspects of food hygiene and preparation would be beneficial.

CONSIDER

Health & Safety

Assess and evaluate hazards and risks in your setting. See the health and safety chapter.

LESSON OBJECTIVES

We are exploring how to cook on direct heat (fire) and understand (and manage) the risks involved.

National Curriculum Content

- Investigate and analyse a range of existing products.
- Select from and use a wider range of tools and equipment to perform practical tasks.
- Understand and apply the principles of a healthy and varied diet.
- Prepare and cook a variety of predominantly savoury dishes using a range of cooking techniques.
- Understand seasonality, and know where and how a variety of ingredients are grown and processed.

ADULT ROLES

- Support activities by encouraging careful observation.
- Support the learning of new skills but encourage the children to develop independence, helping one another, cooperating and demonstrating safe practice.
- Ensure safe practice around the fire.

WARM UP IDEAS

Explain that today children will be exploring how to cook using the direct heat of a fire. This is the oldest-known cooking method and is traditionally used for cooking in the outdoors. They will be using and applying their knowledge of food hygiene, as well as devising and cooking a nutritionally balanced product.

Discuss with the children when we would need or want to cook on a fire, e.g. camping, at a barbeque or in a survival situation.

When cooking outside, what do we need to consider? Key points should include:

- cleanliness and cleaning
- prevention of cross-contamination
- the importance of keeping food cold
- the need to cook food thoroughly or ensure that food is steaming hot if reheated

Explain why in each case and explore how this will be done in practice, such as tying hair up, washing and drying hands, wearing an apron, checking food labels for allergens or to ensure that food is in date, using separate chopping boards (in particular for meat), washing fruit and vegetables, and keeping food covered or chilled.

Revise key safety points about cooking over direct heat, and creating a safety zone around a fire.

MAIN ACTIVITIES

Cooking over direct heat

Although it is possible to do the session as a whole-class activity, alternatively you could divide the class into groups and rotate the activities. These could include: cleaning cooking equipment; researching recipes and menu-planning; investigating food nutrition and the origins of ingredients (from labels and online research); or creating non-cooked dishes to enhance or supplement the cooked dish (e.g. guacamole or salsa).

Challenge 1 (whole class)

Model preparing the fire and cooking area

Discuss the positives and negatives of fire and the key safety points outlined in the health and safety chapter. Can the children remember the fire triangle theory from prior learning, or explain that fires need heat, fuel and oxygen?

1. Work as a group to collect materials for the fire (see page 12).
2. Prepare the fire using the materials gathered.
3. Point out the container of water near the fire circle. What is its purpose?
4. Light the fire, adding charcoal if preferred (note that charcoal gets very hot and produces a longer-lasting heat).
5. While the fire is building, explain that different woods impact on cooking. Explain that 'soft woods' such as pine wood are quite resinous and, although this makes them burn well, it makes food taste smoky. Hard wood is preferred for cooking, with some chefs even adding wood to barbeques to add flavour, such as oak and hickory.

Challenge 2 (whole class and groups of four)

Observe, prepare and cook on a fire

Note: The quesadilla is a suggestion. There are many other food items that could be cooked in this way.

1. Demonstrate how to make the quesadilla (see recipes in www.bloomsbury.com/NC-Outdoors), explaining that quesadillas originate from Mexico and use ingredients popular in Mexican cuisine, such as cheese, spices, beans, vegetables and avocados.
2. Cook the quesadillas on the fire by wrapping them in foil and placing them on a grill or in the embers for around five minutes, turning them halfway through.
3. Encourage the children to smell and taste portions of the uncooked food as the cooking demonstration progresses, naming the ingredients and discussing how a quesadilla is prepared and eaten, e.g. using hands or cutlery.
4. In groups, the children prepare their own quesadilla and, when invited to do so, cook it on the fire. Allow time for it to cool before eating.

PLENARY

Clear and clean the food preparation area. Encourage the children to explain what they have been doing in the session and share what they have found out. Would they eat the quesadilla again? How could the recipe be adapted, for example through the addition of other ingredients, and why? Did they like eating together?

EVALUATION/FOLLOW ON

- What went well and why?
- What didn't go as well as expected?
- What could be changed?
- Who stood out and why?

PREPARATION

Ensure that the fire pit area is clearly identified according to health and safety procedures.

Sticks for fuel may need to be pre-collected and dried, then redistributed in the learning area for the children to find.

Prepare an area for food preparation (including facilities for hand-washing).

Resources

- Fire-lighting equipment, materials and fuel
- Water to extinguish the fires
- Heat-resistant gloves
- Storm kettle
- Cooking utensils
- Ingredients (see the recipes in www.bloomsbury. com/NC-Outdoors), food preparation equipment, plates and cutlery

Previous learning

Prior teaching and recapping of aspects of food hygiene and preparation would be beneficial.

CONSIDER

Health & Safety

Assess and evaluate hazards and risks in your setting. See the health and safety chapter.

LESSON OBJECTIVES

We are exploring how to use hot water for cooking and understand (and manage) the risks involved.

National Curriculum Content

- Investigate and analyse a range of existing products.
- Select from and use a wider range of tools and equipment to perform practical tasks.
- Understand and apply the principles of a healthy and varied diet.
- Prepare and cook a variety of predominantly savoury dishes using a range of cooking techniques.
- Understand seasonality, and know where and how a variety of ingredients are grown and processed.

ADULT ROLES

- Support activities by encouraging careful observation.
- Support the learning of new skills but encourage the children to develop independence, helping one another, cooperating and demonstrating safe practice.
- Ensure safe practice around the fire.

WARM UP IDEAS

Explain that today children will be exploring how to cook using the heat of a fire to heat water in containers. They will be using and applying their knowledge of food hygiene, as well as devising and cooking a nutritionally balanced product.

Discuss why boiling water on a fire is useful, giving reasons such as it being used for washing, cleaning or hot drinks. Revise key hygiene points, including:

- cleanliness and cleaning
- prevention of cross-contamination
- importance of chilling
- the need to cook food thoroughly or ensure that food is steaming hot if reheated.

Explain why in each case.

Revise how this will be done in practice, such as tying long hair up, washing and drying hands, wearing an apron, checking food labels for allergens or to ensure that food is in date, using separate chopping boards (in particular for meat), washing fruit and vegetables, and keeping food covered or chilled.

Revise key safety points about cooking over fires, including making a safety zone around a fire (see the health and safety chapter).

MAIN ACTIVITIES

Cooking with hot water

Although it is possible to do the session as a whole class with additional adult support, alternatively you could divide the class into groups with some groups preparing non-cooked products, such as making fruit kebabs, combining ingredients to make raita dip or buttering bread for sandwiches.

Model preparing the storm kettle and cooking area (whole class)

Revise the positives and negatives of fire and the key safety points outlined in the health and safety chapter. Can the children remember the fire triangle theory from prior learning?

1. Show the children the storm kettle, allowing them to hold it and examine its features. Is it innovative, functional or appealing? Is it fit for purpose? Who is it aimed at?

2. Explain its innovative design and usage as described by the manufacturer. Point out key safety points (see the health and safety chapter). This type of kettle was first designed by Patrick Kelly in the 1890s in Ireland, originally for anglers to heat water for drinks on wet and windy days. Similar designs were used by the New Zealand army in World War 2.

3. Demonstrate how to safely use the storm kettle (see page 13).

4. Use the hot water to make a drink, such as hot squash or a type of 'tea', e.g. make mint, lemon, orange or ginger tea by pouring hot water over mint leaves or lemon, orange or ginger slices respectively.

Challenge 1 (whole class and groups of four)

Observe, prepare and cook on a fire

Note: The following 'menu' is a suggestion. There are many other food items that could be cooked in this way (see the recipes in www.bloomsbury.com/NC-Outdoors). Always follow health and safety guidance.

1. Show how to safely place a pan or kettle on the fire to heat water. Using a pot-holder such as a tripod could also be demonstrated.

2. Use the water to cook e.g. gnocchi, pasta, noodles or couscous. This can be added to a ready-made sauce to finish the meal.

3. Allow the children to smell and taste individual portions of the foods as appropriate during the cooking demonstration process, reinforcing the names of the ingredients, and asking whether they have tasted them before and how they were prepared. From where and how are the ingredients sourced?

4. In groups, the children then design and prepare their own ingredients and, when invited to do so, cook them as modelled. Allow time for the food to cool before eating.

5. Other activities could include preparing the additional ingredients for the couscous, combining ingredients for raita, or making sandwiches.

PLENARY

Clear and clean the food preparation area. Encourage the children to explain what they have been doing in the session and share what they have found out. Would they eat the food again? How could the recipes be adapted, for example through the addition of other ingredients, and why? Explore how it feels to be eating together.

EVALUATION/FOLLOW ON

- What went well and why?
- What didn't go as well as expected?
- What could be changed?
- Who stood out and why?

PREPARATION

Ensure that the fire pit area is clearly identified according to health and safety procedures.

Sticks for fuel may need to be pre-collected and dried, then redistributed in the learning area for the children to find.

Prepare an area for food preparation (including facilities for hand-washing).

Prepare ingredients for the cooking demonstration (children could prepare kebabs etc, in class or in groups outside).

Pre-light the fire, ensuring that it is supervised at all times.

Resources

- Fire-lighting equipment, materials and fuel
- Water to extinguish the fires
- Heatproof gloves
- Cooking utensils
- Ingredients, food preparation equipment, plates and cutlery
- Laminated copy of the NHS *Eatwell Guide*: www.nhs.uk/live-well/eat-well/the-eatwell-guide

Previous learning

Recap food hygiene and preparation.

CONSIDER

Health & Safety

Assess and evaluate hazards and risks in your setting. See the health and safety chapter.

LESSON OBJECTIVES

We are exploring how to use direct heat (fire) for cooking and understand (and manage) the risks involved.

National Curriculum Content

- Investigate and analyse a range of existing products.
- Select from and use a wide range of tools and equipment to perform practical tasks.
- Understand and apply the principles of a healthy and varied diet.
- Prepare and cook a variety of predominantly savoury dishes using a range of cooking techniques.
- Understand seasonality, and know where and how a variety of ingredients are grown and processed.

ADULT ROLES

- Support activities by encouraging careful observation.
- Support the learning of new skills but encourage the children to develop independence, helping one another, cooperating and demonstrating safe practice.
- Ensure safe practice around the fire.

WARM UP IDEAS

Explain that today children will be exploring how to cook using the direct heat of a fire. They will be using and applying their knowledge of food hygiene, as well as devising and cooking a nutritionally balanced product in order to cook food on and in the fire. Revise key hygiene points, including:

- cleanliness and cleaning
- prevention of cross-contamination
- importance of chilling
- the need to cook food thoroughly or ensure that food is steaming hot if reheated.

Explain why in each case.

Ask the children to discuss in pairs how this will be done in practice, asking them to name at least five essential practices (see the health and safety chapter).

MAIN ACTIVITIES

Cooking using direct heat

Although it is possible to do the session as a whole class activity with additional adult support, alternatively you could divide the class into groups with some groups preparing non-cooked products, including making a rainbow fruit salad, preparing a topping for the bruschetta, or cutting and preparing vegetable kebabs.

Model preparing the fire and cooking area (whole class)

If not already done, light the fire, adding charcoal if preferred, and revising health and safety rules around the fire.

Challenge 1 (whole class and groups of four)

Observe, prepare and cook on a fire

Note: The following 'menu' is a suggestion. There are many other meals that could be cooked in this way. Always follow health and safety guidance.

1. On the fire pit and using a sturdily placed grill, demonstrate (with support from selected children) how to:
    a. Toast crumpets or bruschetta with long-armed utensils.
    b. Cook vegetable kebabs on the grill, turning with long-armed tongs.
    c. Place foil-wrapped garlic bread, cinnamon apples or oranges filled with chocolate in the embers as a treat.
    d. Cook vegetable or fruit pancakes, or corn or banana fritters (see the recipes in www. bloomsbury.com/NC-Outdoors).

2. Allow the children to smell and taste individual portions of the foods as appropriate during the cooking demonstration process, reinforcing the names of the ingredients, and asking whether they have tasted them before and how they were prepared. Where and how are the ingredients sourced?

3. Discuss the nutritional information for each product, identifying the food group and the key health benefits of each. Refer to the *Eatwell Guide*.

4. Hydration can also be discussed, such as aiming to drink six to eight glasses of fluid every day and avoiding sugary drinks.

5. In groups, the children plan and prepare their own ingredients, using and applying calculation, estimation and measures from the Year 5 numeracy objectives.

6. When invited to do so, they approach and cook on the fire as modelled. Allow time for the food to cool before eating.

PLENARY

Clear and clean the food preparation area. Encourage the children to explain what they have been doing in the session and state what they have found out.

Back in the classroom

In the final week, children will take part in a 'Great Campfire Cook Off', where they will cook a nutritionally balanced dish in the outdoors, to be judged by staff and other invited judges (such as governors or parents). In preparation, children work in groups to plan and design a simple menu or product, which can be cooked in the outdoors. Choose who will work with whom so that the children can agree roles and research together back in the classroom.

EVALUATION/FOLLOW ON

- What went well and why?
- What didn't go as well as expected?
- What could be changed?
- Who stood out and why?

PREPARATION

The children research and plan their recipe(s) in groups. They take their plan to an adult for approval. They then source the ingredients they need.

The children send out invitations to 'judges', asking them to attend the Great Campfire Cook Off in Progression 6.

Note: If the research and sourcing of ingredients has not yet been carried out, then research and planning can form the basis of this progression, with cooking taking place in Progression 6.

Resources

These will vary according to what menus the groups have planned.

- Cooking facilities, ingredients and equipment as needed
- A food preparation area
- Fire-lighting and safety equipment
- Water to extinguish the fires

Previous learning

The children demonstrate their understanding of previous learning in this progression.

CONSIDER

Health & Safety

Assess and evaluate hazards and risks in your setting. See the health and safety chapter.

LESSON OBJECTIVES

We are using and applying our learning to create products to satisfy a cooking and nutrition brief in preparation for a Great Campfire Cook Off.

National Curriculum Content

- Investigate and analyse a range of existing products (prior to the session).
- Generate, develop, model and communicate their ideas through discussion.
- Select from and use a wide range of tools and equipment to perform practical tasks.
- Understand and apply the principles of a healthy and varied diet.
- Prepare and cook a variety of predominantly savoury dishes using a range of cooking techniques.
- Understand seasonality, and know where and how a variety of ingredients are grown and processed (prior to the session).

ADULT ROLES

- Support activities by encouraging careful attention to detail.
- Acknowledge difficulties and model how they can be overcome and be seen as learning opportunities, being positive about the management of the difficulty.
- Support safe food preparation and cooking.
- Ensure safety near the fire.

WARM UP IDEAS

Explain that today children will be demonstrating and applying their knowledge of food hygiene and cooking skills by practising cooking a nutritionally balanced menu or product in preparation for the Great Campfire Cook Off next week.

Encourage the children to explain to one another the key hygiene rules that will be demonstrated to the judges next week, explaining how this will be done in practice (see the previous progressions).

Ask the children to identify key safety points about cooking over direct heat, including the need to create a safety zone around a fire, so that they can ensure the safety of their guests next week (who may be unaware of safety principles).

Ask the children to share their planned menus with one another, justifying their choices of ingredients by identifying the food groups they are in and the key health benefits of each.

They will need to answer questions from the judges on this next week.

Great Campfire Cook Off practice

Challenge 1 (in groups of four)

Practising cooking the meal

Children will have decided and agreed (with approval) what they will prepare and cook, and will now work as a group to follow their planned recipes, ensuring that everyone has a task and is involved.

Note: Consider STEP - working independently, or with adult support, alongside a group on a specific product may be a helpful option for some children.

The activities will depend on the plans that the children have decided upon, but they should demonstrate and follow key food hygiene and fire safety guidelines and recommendations.

Groups need to ensure that their food preparation area is clean and ready, that they have all the ingredients and equipment they need, that everyone knows what their role is, and that the cooking methods are in place (with adult support). When this has been demonstrated, the children can start the task.

Encourage the children to take particular care in adding the additional 'finishing' details to make their menu appealing and tasty for the judges. Take photographs of the processes and products, which can be used to create menu cards for the judges.

PLENARY

Encourage the children to share their ideas and food with different groups, to evaluate their product against the cooking and nutrition brief, and to consider the views of others in order to improve their work.

Ask the children to make notes and adjustments accordingly. Are they going to change anything as a result of their practice today? If so, what and why?

Back in the classroom

How could children make their menu or product more appealing? Using computing, the group write their 'menu', adding an illustration or photograph of their product for the judges. They plan a short presentation to show their knowledge about nutrition, food hygiene and fire safety.

EVALUATION/FOLLOW ON

- What went well and why?
- What didn't go as well as expected?
- What could be changed?
- Who stood out and why?

PREPARATION

The children will have practised their product and menu in groups and had approval from adults of what they wish to prepare and cook, with appropriate ingredients sourced.

Verify the attendance of the invited judges.

A checklist of criteria for the judges could be prepared with the children.

Resources

These will vary according to the menus the groups have planned.

- A range of cooking facilities and equipment
- An equipped food preparation area
- Ingredients for the children's recipes
- Fire-lighting and safety equipment
- Water to extinguish the fires

Previous learning

In this progression, the children demonstrate their understanding of what they have learned in the previous five progressions.

CONSIDER

Health & Safety

Assess and evaluate hazards and risks in your setting. See the health and safety chapter.

LESSON OBJECTIVES

We are using and applying our learning to produce a product satisfying a 'cooking and nutrition' brief for a Great Campfire Cook Off.

National Curriculum Content

- Investigate and analyse a range of existing products (prior to the session).
- Select from and use a wider range of tools and equipment to perform practical tasks.
- Evaluate their ideas and products against their own design criteria and consider the views of others to improve their work.
- Understand and apply the principles of a healthy and varied diet.
- Prepare and cook a variety of predominantly savoury dishes using a range of cooking techniques.
- Understand seasonality, and know where and how a variety of ingredients are grown and processed (prior to the session).

ADULT ROLES

- Support activities by encouraging careful attention to detail.
- Acknowledge difficulties and model how they can be overcome and seen as learning opportunities, being positive about the management of the difficulty.
- Support safe food preparation and cooking safety.
- Ensure safety near the fire.

WARM UP IDEAS

Remind children of the brief to produce a nutritionally balanced menu or product in preparation for today's Great Campfire Cook Off. Has anyone changed or modified their plans in light of feedback from others? Explore any changes and discuss how these have impacted on their plans or resourcing.

Introduce the judges and ensure that they know the criteria for their judgements (see preparation).

Each group will share their planned menus with the judges, handing them menu cards and justifying their choices of ingredients by identifying the food groups they are in and the key health benefits of each. Children explain to the judges the key hygiene rules that will be demonstrated in the session (see the previous progressions). They will identify and point out key safety points for cooking over direct heat to the judges, including the need to create a safety zone around a fire so that they can ensure the safety of their guests. The judges ask questions where possible.

Great Campfire Cook Off

Children will have agreed and practised what they are going to prepare and cook, and now have the opportunity to work as a group to perfect their planned designs, ensuring that everyone has a task and is involved.

The activities will depend on the plans that the children have decided upon, but should clearly demonstrate and follow key food hygiene and fire safety guidelines and recommendations.

Challenge 1 (in groups of four)

Great Campfire Cook Off!

Groups need to ensure that their food preparation area is clean and ready, that they have all the ingredients and equipment they need, that everyone knows what their role is, and that the cooking methods are in place (with adult support).

When this has been demonstrated, the children can start the Great Campfire Cook Off. The judges should circulate amongst the groups, asking questions and providing support where required.

Encourage the children to take particular care in adding additional finishing details to make their menu appealing and tasty for the judges.

When each meal is completed (which may happen at different times), the judges should inspect and taste the products, making judgements on presentation as well as taste and nutritional balance.

Each group sums up their experience and product, evaluating their product against the cooking and nutrition brief. They receive feedback from other groups and the judges. The judges decide on a winner or commend all of the cooks, depending on school policy.

Back in the classroom

Use the menus to create a recipe book to raise funds for the school's outdoor learning area.

- What went well and why?
- What didn't go as well as expected?
- What could be changed?
- Who stood out and why?
- Additionally, consider:
  - Is the product the same as the original plan and if not how is it different?
  - What problems were encountered and how were these solved?
  - Which bit did they like most and why?
  - Which bit are they most proud of and why?
  - Which bit would they change next time and why?
  - How will they use their learning outside of school?
  - Are there other projects they would like to pursue?

Languages (French)

In this unit, the content of the Key Stage 2 languages attainment targets in the National Curriculum for England (2014) is used to develop the understanding and ability to communicate ideas in French, using the outdoor setting and team-building activities. The children practise the vocabulary and phrases, reinforcing and providing depth to previous learning. They revise greetings, the numbers 1 to 12, colours and the letters of the alphabet, using these to play *Le pendu*. They are introduced to the numbers 13 to 69, parts of the body for both humans and birds, and the vocabulary used to identify and describe common garden birds. They use their learning to explore the outdoor area, observing and making nests and eggs and using identification sheets to identify and record birds in a daily survey, linking to the Year 5 science programme of study, before creating a guide to birds found in the setting.

The activities offer opportunities to practise and apply oral language skills, with the expectation being that written elements will be reinforced in the classroom. The progressions can also be used to practise or to reinforce existing foreign language learning, in the context of the outdoors, with other age groups.

To support inclusive practice or to extend learning, the space, task, equipment and people (STEP) approach can be adopted throughout this unit. By changing the space, task, equipment or people, the activity can be made more challenging or easier to understand, enabling all pupils to take part in the activity, as explained in the assessment chapter. Makaton signing and mime can be used to support understanding.

The main activities offer opportunities for adult-directed whole class and group work, as well as opportunities for individual exploration and experimentation where appropriate.

You may wish to record the activities using a camera.

Natural connections

- Identifying trees, birds and other living things
- Knowledge of life cycles and reproduction cycles
- Using natural materials for creative purposes
- Caring for the environment.

Health and wellbeing

- Physical activity
- Teamwork
- Communication

- Recognising their own and others' strengths by giving and accepting feedback
- Self-regulation and independence.

Word bank

Greetings / conversation

- Bonjour!
- Salut!
- Au revoir
- Je m'appelle...
- Comment t'appelles-tu?
- Comment ça va?
- Ça va bien, merci.
- Comme ci, comme ça
- Ça ne va pas.
- Quel âge as-tu?
- J'ai neuf ans / J'ai dix ans
- Où habites-tu?
- J'habite...

Body parts

- la tête – head
- l'œil (m) / les yeux – eye / eyes
- l'oreille (f) – ear
- la bouche – mouth
- le nez – nose
- le cou – neck
- l'épaule (m) – shoulder
- la poitrine – chest
- le dos – back
- la jambe – leg
- le genou – knee
- le pied – foot
- le bec – beak
- la queue – tail
- l'aile (f) – wing
- la patte – leg / paw / hoof

Types of bird

- un oiseau – bird
- un merle – blackbird
- une alouette – lark
- un pinson – chaffinch
- une hirondelle – swallow
- un muguet – thrush
- un moineau – sparrow
- un pigeon – pigeon
- un rouge-gorge – robin
- un corbeau – crow
- un martinet – swift
- un pivert – green woodpecker
- une mouette – gull

Summary overview

Progression	Curriculum content	Learning experiences/activities
Lesson 1	In this unit, children will learn how to: Listen attentively to spoken language and show understanding by joining in and responding. Present ideas and information orally.	Using a variety of handshakes, the children revise formal and informal greetings using *bonjour, salut* and *ça va*?. They revise the numbers 1 to 12 using 'Pass the knot' and 'Step in' activities, and are introduced to the numbers 13 to 30. They apply the use of numbers by collecting and counting items to make a bird's nest and clay (or stone) eggs. They extend their learning by looking for language patterns for the numbers 40 to 69.
Lesson 2	Speak in sentences, using familiar vocabulary, phrases and basic language structures. Describe people, places, things and actions orally. Understand basic French grammar, including feminine, masculine, key features and patterns of the language and how to apply these, for instance to build sentences, and how these differ from or are similar to English.	Children revise informal greetings, shaking hands with one another and asking and saying how old they are. They practise numbers by playing 'Eliminer' and 'Compter'. They are introduced to the parts of the body using a French version of the *Heads, shoulders, knees and toes* song, and apply this by making a model person using clay, sticks, tools and square lashing.
Lesson 3		Children greet one another in French, shaking hands, revising asking and answering where they live, using 'J'habite dans... à... en... ' They then revise parts of the body, singing *Tête, épaules, genoux et pieds*. They learn the parts of the body of a bird using the song *Alouette*, before using a bird identification sheet to find out which birds are in the area.
Lesson 4		Children greet one another in French, shaking hands, revising asking and answering where they live using 'J'habite dans... à... en... ' In groups, they revise and perform *Tête, épaules, genoux et pieds* or *Alouette* to the rest of the group. They revise the alphabet in French, before using sticks to make *Le pendu* ('Hangman'), naming parts of the body. They play *Le pendu* with French bird names.
Lesson 5		Children reintroduce themselves formally in French, shaking hands with one another before verifying the spelling of their names by saying the letters in French and saying *merci*. They play a date of birth number-ordering game, practising numbers up to 31. They speed-name as many birds in English as they can and revise the French words for the birds. They learn the days of the week and use these to conduct a daily bird survey, linking to Year 5 science by experimenting with different bird food.
Lesson 6		Children reintroduce themselves in French, shaking hands with one another before telling each other which birds or how many birds they saw on particular days. They revise parts of the bird by singing *Alouette* and learn additional words for key features used by ornithologists for identification. They revise colours and learn new colours, applying these whilst describing key features of birds in sentences to a partner for them to draw, producing a guide to birds found in the setting.

PREPARATION

Prepare the cue cards using numbers and words.

Know how to tie a water knot (see www.bloomsbury.com/NC-Outdoors).

Nest-type materials may need to be sourced prior to the session.

Resources

- Cue cards with key French vocabulary, supported by pictures or photos as necessary
- 13 m length of tubular webbing
- Abandoned nest or images of birds' nests
- Nest-type materials from the area
- Stones or clay and marker pens

Previous learning

These progressions revise, reinforce and extend greetings and number learning.

CONSIDER

Health & Safety

Assess and evaluate hazards and risks in your setting. See the health and safety chapter.

LESSON OBJECTIVES

We are revising how to say our names in French, greet one another and use the numbers 1 to 12, and learning the numbers 13 to 30.

National Curriculum Content

- Listen attentively to spoken language and show understanding by joining in and responding.
- Speak in sentences, using familiar vocabulary, phrases and patterns of the language, and consider how to apply these
- Understand basic French grammar, including key features and patterns of the language, how to apply these and how these differ from or are similar to English.

ADULT ROLES

- Allow time for children to process their questions and answers. Come back to them if necessary.
- Support with mime and sign language.

WARM UP IDEAS

Explain that for the next six sessions children will be developing their understanding of French in the outdoor learning area. Today they will be learning and using numbers. Can they remember any numbers from previous learning?

Introductory activity

Using a variety of different fun handshakes, children find and shake hands with a partner and say:

- Partner A: Bonjour! Je m'appelle...(giving their own name). Comment t'appelles-tu?
- Partner B: Je m'appelle... ' (giving their own name).
- Both: Au revoir! (Both wave goodbye.)

Reintroduce *salut* as an informal 'Hi' greeting at this point.

Can the children remember how to ask someone they know well how they are? (Ça va?) Revise the possible responses:

- Ça va bien, merci.
- Comme ci, comme ça.
- Ça ne va pas.
- Pas très bien.

More numbers

Challenge 1 (whole class)

Revise numbers 1 to 12 using 'Pass the knot'

Join the ends of the 13 m webbing using a water knot (see www.bloomsbury.com/NC-Outdoors). Explain that the children are going to use the tubular webbing to make a circle and play some games.

1. The children stand in a circle holding the webbing 'overhand' over the top of the tape (rather than from below).
2. Name whoever is nearest the knot 'the keeper'.
3. Children pass the knot around the circle.
4. As the knot returns to the keeper, everyone raises the tape above their heads and then back to waist height again.
5. Repeat in the other direction, ensuring that the overhand rule is kept. Practise a few times.
6. Once the children are secure with the technique, the children count to 12 in French as they pass the knot around the circle. Can they pass the knot so that it gets back to the keeper before they run out of numbers? Repeat the counting slower and faster.

Challenge 2 (whole class)

Practise numbers 1 to 12 and learn numbers 13 to 30

Place the tubular webbing on the ground in a circle and introduce the numbers 13 to 30 using the cue cards.

1. As each number is introduced, the children 'step in' over the webbing on the ground into the circle, repeating the number before stepping out again. A more dynamic approach is for them to jump in and out, rather than stepping.
2. Point out the patterns of the language and how to use these, e.g. for 17 (ten seven), 18 (ten eight), 19 (ten nine) and following multiples of ten, e.g. *vingt-deux, vingt-trois, vingt-quatre*, etc. Point out that twenty-one is different: *vingt-et-un*. Repeat until the children feel confident with the number names.
3. Call out the numbers at random – if it's an even number, the children jump into the circle, and if it's an odd number, they stay where they are.
4. Hang the cue cards from a washing line or attach them to a tree or fence for reference.

Challenge 3 (in pairs or groups of four)

Practise and apply the numbers 1 to 30 by making a nest and eggs

Show the children an abandoned bird's nest or images of one. What is the purpose of a nest? What materials were used? Observe how it has been constructed and joined. They may be able to identify which type of bird made the nest.

1. Explain that for the final challenge they will make a bird's nest using 30 items (sticks, grasses, feathers, etc.), and make clay eggs (or use stones) to practise their numbers.
2. The groups find 30 items to make a nest, counting them in French as they find them.
3. They interweave sticks and found objects to make the nest, counting each one as the nest is made.
4. They make eggs from balls of soft clay or mud, or decorate stones from the area using marker pens and place these in the nest, counting them as they are put in.

⌐

PLENARY

Extend children's learning by giving them the words for 40, 50 and 60 and asking them to predict the language patterns, such as *quarante-et-un, quarante-deux, quarante-trois*, etc., based on their learning of 21, 22, 23, etc.

Back in the classroom

Teach the children to spell the number words they have learned in the session.

⌐

EVALUATION/FOLLOW ON

*   What went well and why?
*   What didn't go as well as expected?
*   What could be changed?
*   Who stood out and why?

PREPARATION

Prepare the cue cards to include new body parts vocabulary.

Revise the square lashing technique (see www. bloomsbury.com/NC-Outdoors).

Resources

- Cue cards with key French vocabulary, supported by pictures or photos as necessary
- Tree identification sheets
- Collection of sticks and mud (or clay) from the area
- Leaves, scraps of material, lengths of wool or string
- Optional: potato peelers or knives, hacksaws, scissors, secateurs and safety gloves

Previous learning

This session revises how to give your age in French and practises and extends vocabulary and phrases from the previous progression.

This session links to Design and Technology and Maths.

CONSIDER

Health & Safety

Assess and evaluate hazards and risks in your setting. See the health and safety chapter.

LESSON OBJECTIVES

We are practising the numbers 1 to 30 and learning the names for parts of the body.

National Curriculum Content

- Listen attentively to spoken language and show understanding by joining in and responding.
- Speak in sentences, using familiar vocabulary and phrases.

ADULT ROLES

- Allow time for children to process their questions and answers.
- Model the activities and language, reinforced with images, sign language or gestures.
- Assist with knots as necessary.

WARM UP IDEAS

Explain that today children will be introduced to the parts of the body, but first they will practise greetings and numbers. Begin by revising greetings and numbers by adding 'Quel âge as-tu?' to the warm up conversation used in the previous progression.

- Partner A: Salut! Ça va?
- Partner B: Ça va bien, merci (or comme ci, comme ça/ça ne va pas/pas très bien), et toi?
- Partner A: Ça va bien, merci (etc.). Quel âge as-tu?
- Partner B: J'ai neuf ans, et toi?
- Partner A: J'ai dix ans. Au revoir! (Find another partner.)

Introductory activity (whole class)

Make a circle with the tubular webbing and ask children to stand around the perimeter.

Play 'Eliminer' ('Eliminate')

1. One at a time, they 'jump in', counting from one to 30.
2. When the numbers 5 and 10 are said, those two children stay inside the circle.
3. Repeat until the whole class is inside the circle (eliminated).

Play 'Compter' ('Count up')

1. One at a time, the children 'step in' to count in consecutive numbers up to the number of children in the class.
2. Either go around the circle with each child saying a number in turn, or a more challenging version is for any child to 'step in' at any time, but they can only 'step in' once, and only one child can be in the circle at any one time.
3. If two or more children 'step in', then the game has to be started again.

MAIN ACTIVITIES

Body parts

Challenge 1 (whole class)

Learn the names of the parts of the body

Do the children remember the song *Heads, shoulders, knees and toes*? The class sing and act it out in English.

Introduce the new French vocabulary, showing the body parts cue cards and reinforcing the words by touching the named parts. Then sing the song in French.

Note: In the French version, it is 'feet' and not 'toes'.

Tête, épaules, genoux et pieds, genoux et pieds

Tête, épaules, genoux et pieds, genoux et pieds

J'ai des yeux, des oreilles, une bouche et un nez

Tête, épaules, genoux et pieds, genoux et pieds

Challenge 2 (individual)

Make a model person using square lashing, sticks and clay

Explain that the children will make a model of a person using sticks and clay.

Tell the children that sycamore and ash twigs are good for this activity as they have opposite branches (good for forming the legs and arms of a model person). The children find sycamore and ash trees, if possible, using identification sheets and collect suitable twigs from the ground.

Reinforcing the new body parts vocabulary, show how to create a model of a person using sticks and clay:

1. Join arms to the stick using square lashing (see www.bloomsbury.com/NC-Outdoors).
2. Create a head with eyes, ears, mouth and nose from clay.
3. Add knobbly knees and feet, using more clay or found objects.
4. Add clothing using wool, string and grasses.

Children then create their own stick person model, as shown. Encourage them to use the new body parts vocabulary as they do so.

They can use these to have conversations in French, as in the warm ups, or to tell stories to each other.

Optional tools use:

Arms and legs can also be joined by drilling a hole through the larger (body) stick to insert smaller twigs to form arms and legs.

Using knives or peelers, make patterns on the stick to add detail such as fingers or muscles.

PLENARY

Encourage the children to explain what they have learned about trees in the area and about French names for parts of the body. Sing the song again.

Back in the classroom

Photos of the children's stick people can be used as inspiration for story-writing or to record learning by adding text boxes or speech bubbles using the new vocabulary.

EVALUATION/FOLLOW ON

- What went well and why?
- What didn't go as well as expected?
- What could be changed?
- Who stood out and why?

PREPARATION

Prepare the cue cards to include new vocabulary.

Practise the *Alouette* song (see www.bloomsbury.com/NC-Outdoors).

Scatter bird seed in the learning area in the days prior to the session and on the day.

Resources

- Cue cards with key French vocabulary, supported by pictures or photos as necessary
- *Identification des oiseaux* cue cards
- *Identification des oiseaux* sheets (see the worksheet at the end of this book or www.bloomsbury.com/NC-Outdoors) or other bird identification sheets (e.g. from the Woodland Trust website)
- Pencils and clipboards
- Optional: binoculars

Previous learning

This session links to Year 5 science (living things and their habitats).

CONSIDER

Health & Safety

Assess and evaluate hazards and risks in your setting. See the health and safety chapter.

LESSON OBJECTIVES

We are learning the names of bird body parts and spotting and identifying 'les oiseaux'.

National Curriculum Content

- Listen attentively to spoken language and show understanding by joining in and responding.
- Present ideas and information orally.
- Speak in sentences, using familiar vocabulary, phrases and basic language structures.
- Understand basic French grammar, including feminine and masculine, and how this differs from or is similar to English.

ADULT ROLES

- Allow time for children to process their questions and answers.
- Model the language, reinforced with images, sign language or gestures, acknowledging the tricky parts and being positive about managing difficulties.

WARM UP IDEAS

Explain that this session is about learning the parts of a bird, learning the French names of birds and identifying birds in the area.

Children greet one another in French, with a variety of funny handshakes, adding the question 'Où habites-tu?' to the warm up conversation. Revise how to answer the question with types of accommodation, towns and countries.

- Partner A: Salut! Ça va?
- Partner B: Ça va bien, merci (or comme ci, comme ça/ça ne va pas/pas très bien), et toi?
- Partner A: Ça va bien, merci (etc.). Quel âge as-tu?
- Partner B: J'ai neuf ans, et toi?
- Partner A: J'ai dix ans. Où habites-tu?
- Partner B: J'habite dans une maison à Truro en Angleterre (they name their own town). Et toi?
- Partner A: J'habite dans un appartement à Truro en Angleterre. Au revoir! (Each child then finds a new partner.)

Introductory activity

Explain that today children will be learning a new song and using the words to identify parts of a bird.

Revise the song *Tête, épaules, genoux et pieds* (see Progression 2).

Do birds have the same body parts as people? What other words might they need? Teach them how to say wing, beak, tail and leg (of an animal).

The song we are learning today is called *Alouette*, which means 'lark', but can the children name any other birds (in English)?

MAIN ACTIVITIES

Bird-spotting

Explain that you can use a bird's beak, head, back, throat, breast, wings, tail and legs to identify it.

Challenge 1 (whole class)

Learn a French song – 'Alouette'

Children learn the parts of the body of a bird using the song *Alouette*:

> *Alouette, gentille alouette; alouette, je te plumerai.*
>
> *Je te plumerai la tête; je te plumerai la tête*
>
> *Et la tête! Et la tête! Alouette! Alouette! A-a-a-ah.*
>
> *Alouette, gentille alouette; alouette, je te plumerai.*

(Continue with other body parts: see www.bloomsbury.com/NC-Outdoors)

Note: The song is about the bird being plucked. You may wish to link this to discussion and debate about caring for nature or even about animal cruelty or bullying.

Challenge 2 (whole class)

Learn the names of common birds in French

Introduce the character Madame Oiseau and use this character to teach the children the names of birds in French.

Introduce the names of birds in French using the cue cards, asking the children to repeat the names as you show the cards.

Challenge 3 (individual)

Spot and identify birds of the region in French

Explain that the children will be exploring the outdoor area looking for *des oiseaux*.

They will need to be very quiet or they will frighten the birds away.

What could they do to attract more birds to the area? Explain that putting out food and water, keeping very still and quiet or even hiding themselves will all help.

With the *Identification des oiseaux* sheets, pencils and clipboards, the children find a quiet spot to sit quietly and still, observing birds in the area and tallying the birds they see.

Set a time limit on this activity, such as 15 minutes, or extend this as appropriate.

How many birds can they find and identify? Can they say their French names?

PLENARY

Children share the birds they have identified (in English and French), noting the key identifying features and encouraging the rest of the class to find the same birds on the identification sheet.

Explain that the birds were attracted to the area by having a source of food and water, and discuss whether this should be continued in order to attract more birds to the outdoor learning area. Debate the pros and cons of this idea.

Revise and sing *Alouette*, touching the parts of the body or miming wings, etc., adding more body parts if wished.

Back in the classroom

Children can annotate photos of the birds they found in computing sessions, adding captions, speech bubbles, etc. to record the learning.

EVALUATION/FOLLOW ON

- What went well and why?
- What didn't go as well as expected?
- What could be changed?
- Who stood out and why?

PREPARATION

Prepare cue cards for for the sounds of the alphabet in French.

Resources

- Cue cards with key French vocabulary, supported by pictures or photos as necessary

- *Identification des oiseaux* sheets (see www.bloomsbury.com/NC-Outdoors)

- Variety of small sticks and leaves from the area

- Marker pens

Previous learning

This lesson practises, reinforces and extends learning children may previously have done using the French alphabet.

CONSIDER

Health & Safety

Assess and evaluate hazards and risks in your setting. See the health and safety chapter.

LESSON OBJECTIVES

We are revising and practising the parts of the body and letters of the alphabet, and playing *Le pendu* ('Hangman').

National Curriculum Content

- Listen attentively to spoken language and show understanding by joining in and responding.

- Present ideas and information orally.

- Begin to speak in sentences, using familiar vocabulary, phrases and basic language structures.

- Begin to understand basic French grammar, including feminine, masculine, key features and patterns of the language.

ADULT ROLES

- Allow time for children to process their questions and answers. Come back to them if necessary.

- Model the language, reinforced with images, sign language or gestures.

WARM UP IDEAS

Explain that today children will revise the letters of the alphabet and names of parts of the body, and use this to play a game of *Le pendu* ('Hangman').

Begin with the warm up conversation, using a variety of funny handshakes:

- Partner A: Salut! Ça va?

- Partner B: Ça va bien, merci (or comme ci, comme ça/ça ne va pas/pas très bien), et toi?

- Partner A: Ça va bien, merci (etc.). Où habites-tu?

- Partner B: J'habite dans une arbre à Paris en France (they can make this up). Et toi?

- Partner A: J'habite dans une tente à Newquay en Angleterre. Au revoir! (Find another partner.)

Introductory activity (groups of four to eight)

In groups, the children work together to sing and perform either *Tête, épaules, genoux et pieds* or *Alouette* to the rest of the group.

Some children may prefer to watch this rather than participate. Encourage these children to think of the words in their heads as it is being performed or to join in with the actions.

MAIN ACTIVITIES

'Hangman' body parts

Revise and write the alphabet in chalk on the ground or on a fence or tree to support visual learners.

Challenge 1 (whole class)

Revise the letters of the alphabet in French

Revise the letters of the alphabet using actions.

A. Put your finger in the air as if you've just remembered something and say 'ah!'.

B. Mime swaying on a boat in a bay and say 'bay'.

C. Place your index finger at the corner of your mouth, then point it forwards. Say, 'Say'.

D. Cover your eyes with your hands, then gradually uncover your eyes and say 'day'.

E. Imagine something disgusting on the floor and say 'euh!'.

F. Mime scrunching up your face in the 'effort' to remember the sound 'eff'.

G. Flap your arms like a jay, squawking the sound 'zhay' (J and G sounds are the reverse of English).

H. Point to the ash in the fire pit, saying 'ash'.

I. Lean backwards looking scared and cry 'eeeee!' (different from English I).

J. Swagger and sway your shoulders and say 'zhee'.

K. Imagine steering a 'kaa' (steering wheel of a car).

L. Place your index finger on the palm of the other hand and say 'el'.

M. Make the shape of a letter M on your head and say 'em' (as in YMCA).

N. Place two fingers on the palm of your hand and say 'en'.

O. Open your eyes wide as if shocked and say 'oh!'.

P. Rub your index finger and thumb together to mime 'pay'.

Q. Move your head forwards and backwards like a pigeon, and 'coo'.

R. Take a deep breath of 'air'.

S. Snake both your arms and hiss 'essss'.

T. Model pouring a cup of French 'tay' (make sure it's not English tea!).

U. Put your hands on your hips and say a cheeky 'oo!'.

V. Spread one hand out to the side as if you are 'vay-ing' (weighing) something.

W. Spread both hands out to the side in a 'doobla vay' (pointing out that the W is written as two Vs).

X. Pretend to hiccup, hiccupping 'icks'.

Y. Make the letter Y by raising your arms above your head (as in YMCA) and calling 'eee greck'.

Z. Swish the letter 'zed' like Zorro's sword mark.

Repeat as necessary and allow children to practise spelling their own names in pairs.

Challenge 2 (whole class and in pairs or groups of four)

Use sticks and leaves to play *Le pendu*

Clear an area of ground and create *Le pendu* ('Hangman') using sticks, seeds and found objects, naming parts of the body – head, shoulders, legs, feet, etc. – and revising previous learning.

Take the hangman apart, placing all the pieces in a pile, and explain how to play the game.

1. Think of a French word for a bird (refer to the *Identification des oiseaux* sheets for spelling) and use sticks as dashes to represent the number of letters.

2. Ask the children to suggest letters.

3. If the word contains that letter, write the letter on a leaf and place it in the correct place. Can they identify the leaves they are writing on?

4. If it is incorrect, start to rebuild *le pendu*.

5. The aim is to get the word before *le pendu* is complete.

The children play their own versions with a partner or in a small group.

PLENARY

The children role-play and revise a formal greeting, stating their name and spelling it out to a partner:

• Partner A: Bonjour! Je m'appelle... (spell out their name in French). Comment t'appelles-tu?

• Partner B: Bonjour! Je m'appelle...

EVALUATION/FOLLOW ON

• What went well and why?

• What didn't go as well as expected?

• What could be changed?

• Who stood out and why?

PREPARATION

Prepare the cue cards to include new vocabulary – days of the week. The images on the cue cards can be those used to support SEND timetables.

Revise how to tie a water knot (see www.bloomsbury.com/NC-Outdoors).

Resources

- Cue cards with key French vocabulary, supported by pictures or photos as necessary
- 13 m length of tubular webbing
- *Identification des oiseaux* sheets (see www.bloomsbury.com/NC-Outdoors)
- Clipboards and pencils

Previous learning

This session revises and extends vocabulary and phrases from the previous progressions.

CONSIDER

Health & Safety

Assess and evaluate hazards and risks in your setting. See the health and safety chapter.

LESSON OBJECTIVES

We are learning the names of the days of the week and using these to do a daily survey of birds in the school grounds.

National Curriculum Content

- Listen attentively to spoken language and show understanding by joining in and responding.
- Present ideas and information orally.
- Speak in sentences, using familiar vocabulary, phrases and basic language structures.
- Understand basic French grammar, including feminine and masculine, and how this differs from or is similar to English.

ADULT ROLES

- Allow time for children to process their questions and answers. Come back to them if necessary.
- Model the language, reinforced with images, sign language or gestures.

WARM UP IDEAS

Explain that today children will practise the alphabet by greeting each other and spelling their names, and they will also learn the days of the week, as they will need these to do a daily survey of birds in the area.

Moving around the area, the children introduce themselves to one another in French, shaking hands and spelling out their names. As they are asking and spelling names, the assumption is that they are making first introductions, so use 'Bonjour' rather than 'Salut'.

- Partner A: Bonjour! Je m'appelle... (and spell out their name in French). Comment t'appelles-tu?
- Partner B: Bonjour! Je m'appelle... (and spell out their name in French).
- Both: Merci! Au revoir! (Find another partner.)

Introductory activity

1. In groups of six to eight, ask children to think about the French vocabulary needed for the number of their date of birth , e.g. 27 February – *vingt-sept* or 3 November – *trois*.
2. On your signal, ask the children to line up in order from the lowest to highest number, by saying their number out loud so that the rest of the group know where to stand.

MAIN ACTIVITIES

Days of the week

In pairs, the children speed-name as many birds in English as they can remember in one minute. Can they remember what the birds look like?

How many bird names can they remember in French?

Tell the children that they will be visiting the outdoor learning area every day of the week and conducting a bird survey. They will be using this back in the classroom.

Challenge 1 (whole class)

Learn the names of the days of the week

1. Join the ends of the 13 m webbing using a water knot (see www.bloomsbury.com/NC-Outdoors).
2. Ask the children to make a circle (as they did in previous progressions), holding the webbing 'overhand'.
3. Explain that they are going to use the tubular webbing to learn the days of the week using 'Jump in'.
4. Place the tubular webbing on the ground in a circle and introduce the names of the days of the week in French using the cue cards.

Note: Days of the week do not start with a capital letter in French.

- lundi (Monday)
- mardi (Tuesday)
- mercredi (Wednesday)
- jeudi (Thursday)
- vendredi (Friday)
- samedi (Saturday)
- dimanche (Sunday)

5. As each day is introduced, the children 'jump in' over the webbing on the ground and into the circle, repeating the name of the day and jumping out again.
6. Repeat until they feel confident with the new vocabulary.
7. Change the activity to calling out a day at random in French and the children 'jump in' to state its English name.
8. Do the same in reverse, calling out the English day name and the children jumping in with the French word.
9. Hang the cards from a line or pin them to a tree or fence for the children to refer to.

Challenge 2 (individual)

Conduct a daily bird survey (food experiment)

Explain that over the next few days, the children will be conducting a daily survey in the outdoor learning area to see whether *les oiseaux* appear on one day more than another.

Each day they will be coming out to the area for ten minutes with *Identification des oiseaux* sheets, pencils and clipboards, finding a quiet spot to sit quietly and record the birds they see.

Experiment with different types of bird feed, such as peanuts (beware of allergies), seeds in feeders, fruit, scraps, vegetable suet or specialist bird food, to see whether more birds – or which birds – are attracted to the area, drawing a conclusion based on their data and observations, linking to upper Key Stage 2 science.

How many and which types of birds can they find, identify and say the French names for?

PLENARY

Encourage the children to explain what they have been doing, demonstrating new learning.

Back in the classroom

Children research more about the birds they saw and compile charts to show their results.

EVALUATION/FOLLOW ON

- What went well and why?
- What didn't go as well as expected?
- What could be changed?
- Who stood out and why?

PREPARATION

Make cue cards for colours.

Resources

- Cue cards with key French vocabulary, supported by pictures or photos as necessary

- *Identification des oiseaux* sheets (see www. bloomsbury.com/NC-Outdoors)

- Paper and clipboards

- Pencils, coloured pens or crayons

- Clipboards

CONSIDER

Health & Safety

Assess and evaluate hazards and risks in your setting. See the health and safety chapter.

LESSON OBJECTIVES

We are practising all the learning from this unit by describing key characteristics of birds.

National Curriculum Content

- Listen attentively to spoken language and show understanding by joining in and responding.

- Present ideas and information orally.

- Speak in sentences, using familiar vocabulary, phrases and basic language structures.

- Describe people, places, things and actions orally.

- Understand basic French grammar, including feminine, masculine, key features and patterns of the language and how to apply these, for instance to build sentences, and how these differ from or are similar to English.

ADULT ROLES

- Allow time for children to process their questions and answers.

- Model the language, reinforced with images, sign language or gestures, acknowledging the tricky parts and being positive about managing difficulties.

WARM UP IDEAS

Tell the children that they will be using their learning to identify and describe birds in order to produce a guide to birds found in the outdoor learning area.

Children first greet one another informally in French, with a variety of funny handshakes, practising the day of the week and numbers, introducing the phrase 'J'ai vu' (I saw), e.g. 'Mardi j'ai vu... ' , to explain what birds they have seen in the area.

- Partner A: Salut! Ça va?

- Partner B: Ça va bien, merci (or comme ci, comme ça/ça ne va pas/pas très bien), et toi?

- Partner A: Ça va bien, merci (etc.).

- Partner B: Mercredi j'ai vu une hirondelle. Et toi?

- Partner A: Jeudi j'ai vu seize oiseaux. Au revoir! (Find another partner.)

Introductory activity

Explain that when children are describing birds, they will need to use the French words for parts of the body. Sing *Alouette* as a class, emphasising the body part by touching or miming and adding new words: *une gorge* (throat) and *une poitrine* (breast).

MAIN ACTIVITIES

All about 'les oiseaux'

What differences in the beak, head, back, throat, breast, wings, tail or legs might people use to identify birds, e.g. size, colour or stripes?

Challenge 1 (whole class)

Revise the vocabulary for colours

Do the children remember the 'Rainbow song'? Revise it in English.

Revise French colour vocabulary using the question: 'Quelle est cette couleur?' Use *rouge* (red), *orange* (orange), *jaune* (yellow), *vert* (green), *violet* (purple), *rose* (pink) and *bleu* (blue).

Sing the 'Rainbow song' in French:

> *Rouge et jaune et rose et vert, violet, orange et bleu*
>
> *Je connais les couleurs, toutes les couleurs, celles de l'arc-en-ciel.*

From their experience of identifying birds, what other colours do the children need to know in French, e.g. brown (*brun*) or grey (*gris*)?

Explain that it is usually the male bird that is the colourful one. Why is this?

Display the cue cards for the birds and colours on a washing line or on a tree or fence for reference.

Challenge 2 (in pairs)

Describe birds in sentences using familiar vocabulary, phrases and basic language structures in English

Using the bird identification sheets, one child describes a bird in English, identifying the colours of features such as its beak, head, back, throat, breast, wings, tail or legs, for their partner to guess which bird it is. Then they swap roles.

For example: A bird with a red breast and brown back could be a robin.

Challenge 3 (whole class and in pairs)

Describe birds in sentences using familiar vocabulary, phrases and basic language structures in French, noting key differences

Explain that in English we place the adjective before the noun (red breast) but in French the adjective follows the noun, e.g. *une poitrine rouge* (breast red), which is a key difference.

Model the whole sentence, using the picture cue cards for reference. For example:

- *Un oiseau avec une poitrine rouge et un dos brun* – A bird with a red breast and brown back. (A robin.)
- *Un oiseau avec un bec jaune et un dos noir* – A bird with a yellow beak and a black back. (A male blackbird.)

Using the bird guides, one child describes a bird in French, identifying key colours of its beak, head, back, throat, breast, wings, tail or legs for their partner to guess which bird it is. Then they swap roles.

As one child describes the bird, the other makes a drawing of it from the descriptions.

PLENARY

Share the drawings of the birds and ask the children to identify the names of the birds in English and French. Children share with a partner the key learning points from the unit that had the biggest impact on them, and which activity or learning really made them go 'Wow!' and why this is.

Back in the classroom

Children create a display showing the birds from the setting area, demonstrating their French language skills.

EVALUATION/FOLLOW ON

- What went well and why?
- What didn't go as well as expected?
- What could be changed?
- Who stood out and why?

Music

In this unit, 'dynamic musicians' are created as children tune in to the sounds of nature. Children are encouraged to investigate 'nature's orchestra' by listening to the sounds around them in outdoor soundscapes, imitating what they have heard and composing their own music inspired by the sounds of nature. The use of vocabulary linked to the dynamics of music is integral to the unit. The children will also explore sounds that can be created using natural and man-made objects. They will improvise and compose their own music using instruments made of recycled junk, forming their own junk band. They will also develop their own soundscape through the 'garden of sound'. The skill of listening runs throughout the unit as pupils listen with attention to detail and recall sounds with increasing aural memory. The children get the opportunity to perform in an outdoor musical festival, 'The Wild Side', which enables them to express and show off their musical talents.

Prior to starting this unit, you may wish to start a sound collection box in the school and encourage parents, children and the community to donate unwanted instruments and junk items.

To support inclusive practice or to extend learning, the space, task, equipment and people (STEP) approach can be adopted throughout this unit. By changing the space, task, equipment or people, the activity can be made more challenging or easier to understand, enabling all pupils to take part in the activity, as explained in the assessment chapter in this book.

You may wish to record the activities using a camera.

Natural connections

- Exploring the local environment
- Identifying and appreciating natural sounds
- Tuning into the local soundscape.

Health and wellbeing

- Listening
- Physical activity
- Teamwork
- Self-regulation and independence
- Risk management
- Creativity
- Confidence.

Word bank

Percussion
The striking of one solid object with or against another; instruments whose sound is created by striking / hitting them

Orchestra
A large group of musicians who play together

Conduct / conductor
The lead of an ensemble (group) of musicians, who gives directions using their hands or a baton (stick)

Beat
A rhythmic pulse; the speed at which a piece of music is played

Dynamics
The loudness or softness of sound

Crescendo / diminuendo
Getting louder / getting quieter

Tempo
The speed of the beat

Compose / composition
To create a piece of music / a piece of music

Soundscape
A collection of individual sounds within a given environment

Presto / lento
A rapid speed / a slow speed

Accelerando / ritardando
Speeding up / slowing down

Pulse
Steady underlying beat

Rhythm
Patterns of long and short notes or rests (intervals of silence)

Texture / timbre
How many instruments / voices, rhythms and pitches make up the overall piece/quality of sound

Summary overview

Progression	Curriculum content	Learning experiences/activities
Lesson 1	The series of progressions across Key Stage 2 music all address the following curriculum content: Play and perform in solo and ensemble contexts, using their voices and playing musical instruments with increasing accuracy, fluency, control and expression. Improvise and compose music for a range of purposes, using the interrelated dimensions of music. Listen with attention to detail and recall sounds with increasing aural memory.	**Sound clips of nature:** Children will listen to and identify sounds within an outdoor soundscape, playing the game 'Secret sound'. They will then have the opportunity to record and create their own 'sound clips' and create a sound map for the school. They will need to listen with attention to detail as they recall the sounds and identify the source.
Lesson 2		**The rhythm of sound:** Children explore the potential of the natural world to provide rhythmic and percussion sounds, then use tools to make an instrument from natural materials – a 'nature instrument'. They become 'dynamic duos' as they experiment with dynamics (loudness/softness) of sound. They create a sound trail through the discovery and description of found sounds.
Lesson 3		**Body percussion:** Children explore percussion, beat, tempo, orchestra and conducting, using body percussions to create rhythm compositions as a body percussion orchestra. With a 'musical buddy', they compose and perform a short body percussion composition reflecting the natural world. They create a 'sound slide' to overlay natural objects, words, voices, movement and body percussion.
Lesson 4		**The garden of sound:** The children take part in a musical challenge to identify a range of different sounds in the outdoor area. They then improvise and make a range of items to develop a 'garden of sound', including a stage, listening pod, sound trail and music wall.
Lesson 5		**The junk band:** Children continue to explore, improvise and compose as they develop their own musical instruments by recycling junk, and compose a musical piece performing in a junk band in the 'garden of sound'.
Lesson 6		**Music festival – 'Music on the Wild Side':** In this final session, children perform. They use the 'garden of sound' as an outdoor venue. They decide which songs they will sing, how they will use the junk band performances and how they can use other musical talent in the class to play and perform in solo and ensemble contexts. Children should be encouraged to play musical instruments they have made or instruments they are learning to play to improve their accuracy, fluency and expression in music.

PREPARATION

Prepare a recording of six to eight sounds, both from natural and artificial sources (e.g. birds or machines) for the 'Secret sounds' activity.

Make a basic map of the school grounds. Note: younger children may need to follow an exemplar map with sound points already on it prior to creating their own; create this if applicable.

Ensure that the children have access to a natural environment for this session in which they can listen to a variety of sounds.

Resources

- www.scoutresources.org.uk/ SR/songs/index.html
- 'Secret sounds' recorded on a tablet or other device
- Card or paper, permanent markers and pencils
- Maps of the school grounds, enough for one per pair
- Wooden discs
- Tablets or other recording devices, enough for one per pair

Previous learning

This session reinforces the geography progressions (using orienteering and map-work).

CONSIDER

Health & Safety

Assess and evaluate hazards and risks in your setting. See the health and safety chapter.

LESSON OBJECTIVES

We are learning to create sound clips using sounds from nature and identify sounds within our outdoor soundscape.

National Curriculum Content

- Listen with attention to detail and recall sounds with increasing aural memory.

ADULT ROLES

- Encourage a 'have a go' approach and to ask for help when it's needed.
- Model how to listen, describe and identify.

WARM UP IDEAS

Tune in

Explain to the children that through this unit they will be exploring the sounds of nature. They will have the opportunity to compose their own music and make their own instruments from natural items.

Singing school

Start this session by singing a song that the children know. This could include songs accompanied by percussion or percussive noises, e.g. *If you're happy and you know it*, or campfire songs, e.g. *She'll be coming round the mountain, You'll never get to heaven* or *London's burning*, which could be sung in rounds. See the resources section for further ideas.

Introductory activity

Talk to the children about the sounds of nature.

- What sounds can they hear in the outdoor learning area?
- What sounds could they create using natural objects?
- Ask the children to find two items in the area that they can use to make a noise.
- Share the sounds with a partner.

Secret sound

- Give the children a piece of card and a pencil and ask them to write the numbers one to eight as a vertical list. Explain that this is their secret sound answer card.
- Play the children the pre-recorded sounds (see preparation).
- Can they guess the sounds? Write each one down in turn.
- Which sounds are easy to identify? Which require further listening and analysis? Why is this?

MAIN ACTIVITIES

Sound bites of nature

Introducing the terminology of sound

Talk to the children about sounds. Clarify and define the meaning of 'sound', 'soundscape' and 'sound clip'.

- A sound is vibrations through the air, which can be heard by the ear.
- A soundscape is a collection of sounds within a given environment.
- A sound clip is a short clip from a longer sound or piece of music.

Challenge 1 (in pairs)

Creating a soundscape map using sound clips

Note: younger children may need to follow an exemplar map modelled by the teacher prior to creating their own map.

Tell the children that they will now be given the opportunity to create their own sound clip using a tablet or other recording device.

- Give the children a map of the school grounds, explaining that they will use this to mark the location of each listening spot used for their sound bite, e.g. if they record a sound clip in the corner of the football field, they will mark the location with 'sound clip' on the map, along with a number.
- Explain that they will need to identify at least six points on the map where they can record their own sound clips, first checking that it is possible to record a sound at each point.
- Give the children wooden discs. They leave one disc at each point they record a sound, giving each one a different number.
- Explain that they will need to come up with a symbol to represent the sound that has been recorded. These will be drawn on the wooden discs.
- Make sure that the children create a master answer sheet, recording which symbol has been left at which point on the map, e.g. 1 – corner of football field, bird call, bird symbol, as they will be giving their map to another pair.

- Once the children have recorded all their sound clips. Talk to the children about the sounds they have recorded. They have created their own soundscape by using a map and recording their own sounds.

Challenge 2 (in pairs)

'Go find it' sound hunt

Using a map and the recorded sound clips created by another pair, the children go and find the sounds on the sound map. They will need to identify the point on the map and then play the first sound clip to see whether they are correct. They will also need to collect the correct wooden disc from each sound point.

Once they have completed the challenge, talk to the children about their findings.

- Did they locate all the sounds from the sound map?
- What sounds did they hear?
- How many different sounds did they pick out?
- Can they name any of them?
- Compare and contrast: what sounds were similar/different? Pleasing/displeasing? How does the soundscape make them feel?

PLENARY

Talk to the children about the sounds they have heard in the session, the sound clips they have created and how they have used these to develop sound maps for the school.

EVALUATION/FOLLOW ON

- What went well today?
- Which children understood the concepts?
- Which children needed more help?
- Are there other resources you can use?
- Can the children use some of the sound clips created to develop a secret sound quiz back in the classroom?

PREPARATION

There are Italian words and abbreviations for different dynamics:

ff – *fortissimo*, very loud;

f – *forte*, loud;

mf – *mezzo forte*, quite loud;

mp – *mezzo piano*, quite quiet;

p – *piano*, quiet;

pp – *pianissimo*, very quiet.

Write the word and abbreviation on one side of the wooden discs, and the English on the other.

Make two V-shaped sticks, one to be labelled and angled as *crescendo* (<), one as *diminuendo* (>).

Resources

- Percussion sticks (or other percussion) – one per child
- Six wooden discs and two V-shaped sticks with dynamic markings
- Rope and string
- Pegs

Previous learning

Revisit and review: What is percussion? What is a beat?

Build on singing school skills (Progression 1) by mimicking a conductor's set beat and percussion skills, working as part of an ensemble.

Links to geography (rope trail).

CONSIDER

Health & Safety

Assess and evaluate hazards and risks in your setting. See the health and safety chapter.

LESSON OBJECTIVES

We explore the dynamics of sound and create a sound trail and a musical instrument from natural objects.

National Curriculum Content

- Play and perform in solo and ensemble contexts, using their voices and playing musical instruments with increasing accuracy, fluency, control and expression.
- Improvise and compose music for a range of purposes, using the interrelated dimensions of music.

ADULT ROLES

- Encourage a 'have a go' approach and asking for help.
- Model how to listen, describe and identify.

WARM UP IDEAS

Exploring dynamics in pairs to become a 'dynamics duo'

Today we will be experimenting with the loudness and softness of sound.

1. Demonstrate how to sing the dynamic signature of a wooden disc. Ask the children to repeat.
2. One child (as the 'conductor') sings a dynamic signature name at the volume level it stands for by selecting a wooden disc from the sound box. The class repeat the name at the same volume, then another child becomes the 'conductor'.
3. When the children have used their voices using a variety of the wooden discs, introduce percussion sticks or other percussion.
4. Model how the conductor taps and speaks a beat, which their partner then repeats after them. The children have a go with their partner.
5. Introduce *crescendo* and *diminuendo* dynamics symbols, getting louder and quieter. Tap the sticks a total of 10 times, counting from one to ten and tapping, gradually increasing the volume of the taps and voice for *crescendo* and gradually decreasing the volume of the taps and voice for *diminuendo*.

Then explore and vary the tempo.

Examples of instruments made from natural materials.

MAIN ACTIVITIES

The rhythm of sound

Challenge 1 (in pairs)

The sound trail

Explain that the children will now create a sound trail by discovering and describing 'found' sounds.

Working in pairs, they find natural or man-made objects, which make a sound when touched or moved.

They create a sound trail by hanging objects from a rope with pegs, then try out each other's trails.

Challenge 2 (individuals and small groups)

Make a percussion stick

Tell the children they will now have the opportunity to make a percussion stick.

- Using tools following the health and safety chapter guidance, the children gather two sticks at least 2 cm in diameter and 10–15 cm in length, or cut sticks to this length.

- Saw a series of equally spaced notches about 2 cm apart and 1 cm deep along the middle section of the stick, placing the blade of the knife halfway between two of the vertical cuts and carving down towards the base of the next vertical notch. A rubber mallet can be used to help create the notches and remove the wood.

- Repeat this process along the stick to create a series of notches.

Let the children try it out, moving the un-notched stick forwards and backwards over the notches. In groups, can they create a rhythm using the stick? Can they create soft and loud sounds, fast and slow, using the dynamics and tempo of sound?

Extension activity (individual with adult support)

Creating a clacker rhythm stick

In this challenge, children will create clacker rhythm sticks using a sharp knife, saw and a palm drill.

- Following the safe tool-use principles, the children will need to select and cut a length of bough wood, ideally from a chestnut or ash tree. This will need to be at least 3–4 cm thick and 25–30 cm long.

- Working under the supervision of an adult, measure 15 cm in from the end and make a cut by sawing one third of the way through.

- Turn the wood a half turn and make another saw cut one third of the way through, opposite the first saw cut, and place the bough length upright on a drill stump.

- Place the knife on the top of the bough, aligning it with the saw cuts one third across the diameter, then cleave the wood down to the saw cut. This will remove a section from the main bough.

- Repeat the process on the other side of the wood by turning the piece of wood 180 degrees.

- You will be left with two rectangular pieces of wood, curved on one side, which will form the moving clacker parts, and the remaining bough, the uncut part of which will become the 'handle'.

- To reassemble the bough, drill two holes through the slender part of the bough and the bottom of the two 'clacker' parts, and reattach the two clacker parts by threading string through the holes, tightening as necessary to allow them to 'clack' together when shaken.

- If time allows, the bough can be stripped of bark and shaped using whittling.

PLENARY

Talk to the children about the sound trail they have created, their understanding of the dynamics of sound and how they have made a musical instrument from natural objects. What has worked well? What do they still need to improve with their instrument?

EVALUATION/FOLLOW ON

- What went well today?
- Which children understood the concepts?
- Which children needed more help?
- Are there other resources you can use?
- Can the children develop their instrument further back in the classroom?

PREPARATION

Access to a range of natural objects to create a 'sound slide'.

Create discs for the tempo markings *accelerando* and *ritardando* in the same way as for dynamics in Progression 5.

accel. – *accelerando*, get faster;

rit. – *ritardando*, get slower.

Resources

• A range of natural objects

• Two wooden discs with tempo markings

• https://pdst.ie/sites/default/files/Exploring%20sound%20body%20percussion.pdf

Previous learning

Build on previous session's learning of dynamics by incorporating a range of soft and loud sounds in a 'musical buddies' activity. Revise tempo as the speed of the beat.

CONSIDER

Health & Safety

Assess and evaluate hazards and risks in your setting. See the health and safety chapter.

LESSON OBJECTIVES

We can explore our bodies as a musical instrument and develop body percussion.

National Curriculum Content

• Play and perform in solo and ensemble contexts, using their voices and playing musical instruments with increasing accuracy, fluency, control and expression.

• Improvise and compose music for a range of purposes, using the interrelated dimensions of music.

ADULT ROLES

• Conduct – teaching, modelling, leading group ensemble work.

• Encourage a 'have a go' approach and to ask for help when it's needed.

• Model how to listen, describe and identify.

WARM UP IDEAS

Body percussion (whole class and in pairs)

Explain to the children that in this session they are exploring a variety of body sounds using their own bodies as instruments, creating rhythm compositions as a body percussion orchestra.

1. Model the following pattern with the children:
   • One hand clap
   • One double-handed chest thump
   • Two separate thigh slaps.
2. Repeat with the children now joining in, mimicking the adult-modelled body percussion.
3. Now ask the children to work in pairs. Can one member of the pair come up with a rhythm, which is repeated by the other child? Repeat twice and then swap over.
   • Can they now tap out their names in a rhythm to add to the sequence?
   • Can they build up the composition with six sounds using MTYT (my turn, your turn)?
4. Introduce two tempo word discs: *accelerando* (speeding up) and *ritardando* (slowing down).
5. Can they include this in their body percussion sequence?
6. For further ideas, see the resources section.

MAIN ACTIVITIES

Body percussion

Children explore vibrations and sounds of their body instruments.

Challenge 1 (in pairs and whole class)

Musical buddies composition

Children work as 'musical buddies' to explore the range of their body instruments, including experimentation with body percussion sounds as part of a description of activities done in the natural world, e.g. rolling down a hill, splashing in a puddle or climbing a tree.

'Musical buddies' compose and rehearse a short sequence of body percussion sounds to perform in front of the rest of the class.

Extension activity (in pairs)

Children consider the dynamics of their composition, experimenting with the loudness and softness and the tempo (speed) of their body percussion sounds.

For further ideas on the development of body percussion, see the resources section.

Challenge 2 (in pairs)

Composition 'sound slide'

Children create a 'sound slide' to overlay natural objects, words, voice, movement and body percussion.

1. Working in pairs, the children collect natural materials/objects from the environment. They attribute a sound or sound word to each material/object.

2. Children lay their materials/objects out in a row. Each child stands on one side of the row of materials/objects, facing one another.

3. Children move in unison, sliding along the row of materials/objects, stopping at each and making the sound of the object through either body percussion or word, e.g. a piece of charcoal from the fire could be 'sizzle' (sound word), a rock could become 'stomp' (body percussion foot stomp), a stick could become 'snap' (body percussion finger click) or a length of wood or stick could become 'slide', which the children use to move along their sound slide, sounding it between each of the other materials/objects.

4. Children compose, rehearse then perform their sound slide to the rest of the class.

PLENARY

Discuss body percussion with the children. What have they learned about body percussion and how they can use their bodies to create sound in a performance? How did they use a 'sound slide' with natural objects? What did they learn about how natural objects can vibrate to create different sounds? Link to science by talking to the children about different materials producing different pitches: if an object vibrates quickly, we hear a high-pitched sound; if the same object vibrates slowly, we will hear a low-pitched sound. Sounds are made up of different kinds of sound waves.

EVALUATION/FOLLOW ON

- What went well today?
- Which children understood the concepts?
- Which children needed more help?
- Are there other resources you can use?
- Can the children develop their knowledge of sound back in the classroom?
- Can they carry out further investigations in sound?

PREPARATION

In advance of this session, set up six to ten 'sound points' in part of the outdoor area (see resources). Mark their locations on a map with a number.

These will be 'tune it in' stations. Children will visit each point to see whether they can name the sound, tune or instrument that is played by the items placed in sound boxes around the site. This sets the scene for the creation of the 'garden of sound'.

Resources

- Six to ten boxes containing musical instruments or items that make a sound
- Pictures and photographs of music walls, sound gardens and junk instruments.
- Resources for the sound garden will depend on what ideas the children have – see Challenges 1 and 2
- https://creativestarlearning. co.uk/c/art-music-outdoors

Previous learning

This reinforces listening skills from previous sessions and links to geography.

CONSIDER

Health & Safety

Assess and evaluate hazards and risks in your setting. See the health and safety chapter.

LESSON OBJECTIVES

We can work as part of a group and create a garden of sound, where a range of music dimensions can be experienced.

National Curriculum Content

- Improvise and compose music for a range of purposes, using the interrelated dimensions of music.
- Listen with attention to detail and recall sounds with increasing aural memory.

ADULT ROLES

- Support children to generate ideas

WARM UP IDEAS

Name that sound (groups of 4)

Place musical challenge stations (numbered) to 'name that sound' at varying locations in the outdoor environment, with a different sound at each point (see preparation and resources). Show the map (if being used).

Explain that at each musical challenge station there will be a box containing a sound or an item with which to make a sound.

Two of the children will create the sound and the other two children (blindfolded prior to the sound being made) will identify the sound.

They will need to record the number of the musical challenge station and write what they think the source of the sound is next to the number, e.g. it could be a musical instrument – a violin. It could be the clap of someone's hands or two saucepan lids banging together.

Introductory activity

Talk to the children about the sounds they have experienced in the outdoor area.

- Where are the best locations to create, hear and identify the sounds?
- Where is it most difficult to identify the sounds?
- If they were going to develop a 'garden of sound', where would they locate it?

MAIN ACTIVITIES

The garden of sound – it rocks!

Challenge 1 (whole class and groups of 4-6)
Creation of a garden of sound

Talk to the children about the creation of a garden of sound. This will be an area in which they can listen to and create a variety of sounds. It should include a performance area and a listening pod, where children can listen to a variety of music and sounds.

- The first thing the class will need to decide is whether there are any natural features in the environment where natural sounds can be created. Could this be a listening and composing zone?

- Look at examples of other sound areas in schools and gardens through pictures and images.

- The children then need to decide on what they are going to put into their sound garden. This could include a sound trail, a junk band area, a secret sound area, a listening pod and a stage area.

- Once the children have decided what they would like to include in the area, they will then need to be placed into working groups to develop each part of the garden of sound.

- The creation could take two or three outdoor learning sessions or it could be a simple creation completed within a session, depending on time.

Challenge 2 (groups of 4-6)
The big build

Working in small groups, children are given the opportunity to develop their part of the garden of sound. See the resources section for further ideas.

- Using the step-by-step principles for using tools, as identified in the health and safety chapter, children could develop a stage area using pallets, to be used in Progression 5 for the junk band.

- The stage could then be decorated with natural foliage.

- Musical notes could be made from willow; wooden discs decorated with different dynamic symbols could also be used to decorate the stage area.

- Other groups could develop a listening pod. This could be a shelter made with a tarpaulin or natural foliage, or willow transformed into a listening pod.

- An additional pod could be created as a composing pod.

- Show the children images of a music wall or a large xylophone and discuss how a music wall could be developed with a variety of junk items, such as pots and pans and beaters, or a large xylophone could be created using planks of wood.

- Sound boxes containing instruments or dynamics signature discs could be put in secret places.

- A 'sound trail' could be developed in order to enter the garden of sound.

Once the children have developed their part of the garden of sound, decide where each item will be placed if it was not built in location. How does the garden of sound work? Who will visit it? How will it change? Who will maintain it? Can a sound trail map be created to fully explore the garden of sound?

PLENARY

Talk to the children about how the garden of sound has been created. Has it covered all the elements of sound, such as dynamics? Are there a range of different sounds? Are there different pitches – high and low notes? Is the timbre rich? What do they still need to develop?

EVALUATION/FOLLOW ON

- What went well today?
- Which children understood the concepts?
- Which children needed more help?
- Are there other resources you can use?
- Can the children develop further sounds back in the classroom for the garden of sound?

PREPARATION

Prior to this session, show the children a clip from Stomp (see resources). This should inspire the children to think differently about junk and how it can be developed into music.

Resources

- Items of junk which could be used to make instruments, such as kitchen utensils, old containers, balloons, elastic bands, tubes or tape
- Stomp: www.youtube.com/watch?v=kdbuJkJsXt0
- www.thejunkorchestra.co.uk
- https://feltmagnet.com/crafts/Music-Instruments-for-Kids-to-Make
- Images of musical instruments made from junk
- Blindfolds
- Other resources or tools may be needed to make the children's planned junk instruments

CONSIDER

Health & Safety

Assess and evaluate hazards and risks in your setting. See the health and safety chapter.

Examples of instruments made from natural and artificial materials.

LESSON OBJECTIVES

We can create a musical composition with musical instruments made from junk and perform in a junk band.

National Curriculum Content

- Improvise and compose music for a range of purposes, using the interrelated dimensions of music.

ADULT ROLES

- Model the use of tools and how to make musical instruments from junk items
- Support the children in selecting materials and making junk instruments.

WARM UP IDEAS

Musical challenge: junk sounds and secret sounds (in pairs)

- One child will be blindfolded. The other child makes a secret sound. These can be made from voice, body percussion, natural materials/objects or using an item of junk from those previously collected.
- The child who is blindfolded has to guess what has made the sound. Each child is given three secret sound challenges and then they swap.
- Encourage the children to think about sound dynamics and how the sound can be made louder or softer. Use the wooden discs from Progression 2.
- Talk to the children about the different sounds they have created.
  - What sounds were most effective?
  - Which sounds were the easiest to guess?
  - Which sounds were harder?
  - Which sounds were more difficult to create dynamics with?

Introductory activity

Talk to the children about the clip they have seen from the musical Stomp. How have junk items been used to create musical instruments? Which instruments are simple to create and effective as instruments? Which instruments have they seen that they are most impressed by?

Ask the children to look at the junk items they have collected. Can they create a junk band as a class?

The junk band

Challenge 1 (whole class and groups of 4-6)

Exploring sounds

Give the children the opportunity to experiment with the junk items to establish what sounds can be made.

- Show the children images of musical instruments made from junk.

- Talk to the children about the different sounds that will need to be created by a band.

- There will need to be some percussion instruments that create a beat (pulse).

- Some instruments will need to create a rhythm.

- Are there any instruments that can make a tune? What do we mean by the term 'tune'?

Once the children have explored the possible sound that can be created, place the children in groups (reflecting the sections of the orchestra).

- There could be a percussion group who are making shakers, drums, tambourines or similar creations.

- Another group could be a string group, using string, elastic bands and natural items to create instruments.

- There could be a group using only natural items to make instruments.

- One group could look at sounds using different amounts of water in jam jars.

- A 'pipes group' could create bagpipe-type instruments from clean, used hosepipes, or they can be whirled around (in a large space) using the air to create sound.

- Note: a tune can be created from an A4 slide clip used on files. Hum a tune into the clip and it can be heard through the clip.

- See the resources section of this progression for further ideas on making musical instruments from junk.

Once the groups have established their roles, give them the opportunity to make their instruments, using tools if required, following the principles in the health and safety chapter.

Challenge 2 (new groups of 4-6)

Composition – the junk band

Place the children in groups, with one child from each of the junk band creation groups forming a new group, i.e. each group will have someone from the strings group, percussion group, pipes group, etc., so that they have a range of instruments to make their band.

Encourage the children to develop a music composition using all the instruments in the band.

They create a musical piece or they could include a song.

Model some examples with a group using the instruments that have been made, remembering and demonstrating the dynamics of sound and the symbols they have used in previous sessions.

Do they need a conductor for their band to support them with the dynamics of their composition?

Performance and appreciation

Give the children the opportunity to perform their musical composition to other groups. Discuss and review each composition.

PLENARY

Which instruments have worked well? Which need further improvements? Which bands were most successful? What can we learn from other groups to support us further in the development of our junk band? How would you describe today's music? What did it make you think of? How did it make you feel?

EVALUATION/FOLLOW ON

- What went well today?
- Which children understood the concepts?
- Which children needed more help?
- Are there other resources you can use?
- Can the children develop their junk band further back in the classroom?

PREPARATION

Prior to this session, the children may wish to develop posters about their music festival and invite an audience to their performance. They may wish to dress in festival style.

Select items made in previous sessions that can be used in the performance, including musical instruments and songs the children have sung.

Prepare the garden of sound with a decorated stage.

Prepare an outline programme for the performance, in discussion with the children.

Resources

Resources will depend on the children's ideas.

- Resources and instruments from previous progressions as needed
- Items to decorate the stage
- Card and writing materials for making the programme

Previous learning

Children bring together all the learning from the past sessions as they perform in a music festival.

Examples of instruments made from natural materials.

LESSON OBJECTIVES

We can plan and perform in an outdoor music festival.

National Curriculum Content

- Improvise and compose music for a range of purposes, using the interrelated dimensions of music.
- Play and perform in solo and ensemble contexts, using their voices and playing musical instruments with increasing accuracy, fluency, control and expression.

ADULT ROLES

- Support the children in reflecting on their own performance and identifying areas where they can improve.

WARM UP IDEAS

Discuss with the children the variety of musical activities they have taken part in through the progressions of this unit. What have they most enjoyed about the sessions? What have they found the most difficult? What do they still need to work on prior to the music festival?

Introductory activity (in pairs)

Give the children the opportunity to reflect on the unit.

Ask them to discuss in pairs what they would like to do in the music festival.

- What would they like to perform?
- What instruments would they like to play?
- Who would they like to work with?

Give each pair a piece of card and ask them to write down their top three performance pieces. This can then be used to support the development of a programme in the next challenge.

CONSIDER

Health & Safety

Assess and evaluate hazards and risks in your setting. See the health and safety chapter.

Music festival – 'Music on the Wild Side'

Final rehearsal and performance of 'Music on the Wild Side' for performance as a musical ensemble.

Challenge 1 (individual, in pairs or groups of 4-6)
Planning the performance

In this challenge, children will need to decide on their performance and work as a solo, duet or small group to rehearse their performance.

In deciding what items will be in the performance, they will need to consider the following:

- What songs are they going to sing and where will this performance be located?
- How will they use the sound trail they have developed?
- At what point will the stage be used?
- Who will perform a body percussion piece of music?
- Which junk bands will perform?
- Can anyone play a musical instrument that could be used as part of the performance?
- Will the performance follow a theme or type of music?
- Are there a range of performances, including percussion, dynamics, part or whole orchestra and a conductor?

Once the programme for the music festival has been agreed, give the children the opportunity to rehearse their performances.

Talk to the children about what they are doing well, what they need to improve and how to prepare for the performance. What do they need to remember? What equipment do they need?

Challenge 2 (whole class)
Performance and appreciation

Give the children the opportunity to perform to an invited audience. This could be a class from the school or a local community group.

- Children could prepare posters and invitations in advance of the session.
- Refreshments that have been made by the children could be served.

Ensure that the children get the opportunity to appreciate the performances of their peers.

PLENARY

What part of the performance did the children most enjoy? Which parts do they think they performed well? Which parts could be improved? If they were to perform again, what would they change and why?

EVALUATION/FOLLOW ON

- What went well?
- Which children understood the concepts?
- Which children needed more help?
- Are there other resources you can use?
- Can the children develop their music further with the use of the junk band and the garden of sound?
- Can these areas be used to develop further curriculum links?
- Can the children write a review of the festival?
- Are there further opportunities to take part in music festivals in the local community?

Religious Education

This unit aims to support your local authority Standing Advisory Council on Religious Education (SACRE) syllabus in the context of outdoor learning, since although it is a statutory 'basic curriculum' subject, Religious Education is not included in the 2014 National Curriculum for England. This unit includes the non-statutory recommendations of the Religious Education Council of England and Wales (REC), 'A curriculum framework for religious education in England' (2013), published following the REC review to promote equity with the national curriculum subjects aiming to ensure that pupils:

A: Know about and understand a range of religions.

B: Express ideas and insights about the nature, significance and impact of religions.

C: Gain and deploy the skills needed to engage seriously with religions.

These are referenced as A, B and C in the attainment target aims within this unit.

In this unit, children explore some of the 'big' questions posed by religion, such as 'How did the world begin?' and 'How did life start on Earth?' They explore their own environment and relate their own setting to beliefs about creation and ideas of stewardship. They create documentaries and take part in a court case to explore damage and risks to the environment, including ethical discussions. They explore how our unique and colourful world is celebrated in the Hindu faith by the creation of Kolam designs. They explore the role of food and harvest in different religions and cook food on the fire.

To support inclusive practice or to extend learning, the space, task, equipment and people (STEP) approach can be adopted throughout this unit. By changing the space, task, equipment or people, the activity can be made more challenging or easier to understand, enabling all pupils to take part in the activity, as explained in the assessment chapter in this book.

The children will be expected to work as a whole class directed by the teacher, together in small groups, with support from adults and independently. The role of the adult is to lead the experiential learning safely, to model and support the activities, but also to allow time and space for the children to reflect on possible answers, to gather evidence, knowledge and understanding and to draw conclusions or rethink initial ideas.

You may wish to record the activities using a camera.

Natural connections

- Expressing wonder
- Celebrating nature.

Health and wellbeing

- Reflective practice
- Physical activity
- Expressing feelings, beliefs and opinions
- A sense of responsibility and stewardship
- Respecting viewpoints and cultural differences.

Word bank

Religious terms

- Christian
- Jewish
- Genesis
- Qu'ran
- Muslim
- Allah
- Buddhist
- Rangoli/Kolam
- Hindu
- Onam
- Christmas
- Lent
- Easter
- Shrove Tuesday
- Ramadan
- Eid
- Diwali
- Rosh Hashanah
- Hanukkah
- halal
- Mithai
- Kosher
- Yom Kippur
- Sukkot
- Passover
- Creator

Other

- designer
- universe
- power
- cycle
- uniqueness
- diverse
- ecosystem
- interaction
- abundant
- undernourished
- nutrients
- decomposition
- remedial
- conservation
- contravening
- prosecute
- detective
- accused
- stewardship
- repellent
- adjournment
- sustenance
- harvest
- damper bread

Summary overview

Progression	Curriculum content	Learning experiences/activities
Lesson 1	All the lessons in this unit address the following attainment targets: A: Appreciate and appraise the nature, significance and impact of different ways of life and ways of expressing meaning. B: Express with increasing discernment their personal reflections and critical responses to questions and teachings about identity, diversity, meaning and value, including ethical issues. C: Articulate beliefs, values and commitments clearly in order to explain why they may be important in their own and other people's lives.	Children consider scientific and religious accounts of the creation of the Earth. They debate 'How did life begin?' from a variety of worldviews and viewpoints. They consider a quote by Brian Cox and how this applies to their setting by exploring the learning area with 'fresh eyes', using the 'Spotters' activity. They explore in detail the patterns and colours found in nature and use cameras to record these and make a mini wildlife documentary describing the uniqueness of the setting.
Lesson 2		Children continue to consider the Earth's ecosystem and identify key needs for life. They explore the learning area looking for these key features. They plan and make a TV broadcast, reporting on and highlighting any successful aspects of the setting, or any damage or risks to the local ecosystems that have arisen through neglect or a lack of care or stewardship.
Lesson 3		Children consider how beliefs impact on ethical issues by exploring damage or harm in the local ecosystem. They use the 'Spotters' activity to explore the area, looking for the effects of pests on plants. They become 'nature detectives', gathering evidence to be used to 'prosecute' a suggested offender. The evidence is used 'in court', where it is opposed by a defence case. Both sides are supported by researched facts about the role of insects in the ecosystem, the impact of the use of pesticides and the discussion of how a person's beliefs impacts on their viewpoint.
Lesson 4		Children explore how to celebrate 'our unique and colourful world'. They study satellite photographs of the Earth, such as those by Bernhard Edmaier. They go on a colour hunt, identifying nature's colours and explaining why seasonal changes occur. They learn about the Onam festival and create colourful patterns, reflecting on how celebrations using colour can explain identity, diversity, meanings and values.
Lesson 5		Children focus on sustenance and how food is celebrated and used to express beliefs, including ethical beliefs, by different faiths. Beforehand, the children may have researched the relationship between food and religion, and how ethical beliefs can impact on diet. They prepare and cook food on fires, to be shared with the whole class at the end of the session.
Lesson 6		Children explore religious celebrations of the harvest. They explore the local area looking for nature's harvest of seeds and fruits, or observe and taste a selection provided by the teacher. They learn about the origins of harvest bread and cook damper bread on their own fires. They reflect on how celebrations using food can explain identity, diversity, meanings and values.

PREPARATION

Source a selection of creation stories to share with the class.

Write the Brian Cox quotation at the top of page 145 onto card or a wooden board, which can be left in situ.

Source clips from a wildlife documentary.

Optional: cut cards enough for one per pupil into the shape of an artist's palette and add two rows of double-sided tape to one side.

Resources

- Brian Cox quote (see the Main Activities section)
- Magnifying glasses
- Selection of found objects to share, such as leaves, feathers, eggshells, seedpods, etc.
- Optional: artist palettes with double-sided tape attached
- Devices with the ability to record video: as many as possible, up to one per pair

Previous learning

This unit links to the Year 5 art progressions.

Watch clips from a wildlife documentary beforehand to inspire their own documentary-making, and read creation stories in class.

CONSIDER

Health & Safety

Assess and evaluate hazards and risks in your setting. See the health and safety chapter.

LESSON OBJECTIVES

We are learning how to address and answer 'big' questions, such as the creation of the earth.

Attainment targets

A: Appreciate and appraise the nature, significance and impact of different ways of life and ways of expressing meaning.

B: Express with increasing discernment their personal reflections and critical responses to questions and teachings about identity, diversity, meaning and value, including ethical issues.

C: Articulate beliefs, values and commitments clearly in order to explain why they may be important in their own and other people's lives.

ADULT ROLES

- Allow time for children to process the questions, to reflect, gather information, clarify or verify using partner talk, and to draw conclusions, before asking them to give justified answers.

WARM UP IDEAS

Explain that for the next six sessions children will be exploring how the outdoors can provide questions and answers about our beliefs, and how this helps us consider the bigger questions in religious education.

Introductory activity (whole class and in pairs)

Begin by explaining that many religions include stories about how the universe was created.

Ask the children to share with a partner their views and stories about how they think the world started, then feed back to the whole class. Is there a right answer or is that what makes it a big question?

Encourage debate, including around worldviews (both religious and non-religious) and scientific perspectives (see your local SACRE for statutory content). Include a variety of explanations and creation stories, for example:

- The book of Genesis, a text used in both Judaism and Christianity, contains a story about how God created the world in six days. Some Jews and Christians believe this, while others see it as figurative and instead use the science of the Big Bang and evolution to explain creation.
- The Qu'ran explains that Allah created the universe. Some Muslims believe this is compatible with scientific explanations, while others reject the Big Bang and evolutionary theories.
- Most Buddhists believe that the world follows a cycle of decay, death and rebirth.
- Most humanists and atheists accept scientific explanations of creation.

MAIN ACTIVITIES

Creation

Introduce the next big question by sharing and discussing a non-religious quote:

'Why is the Earth a living oasis amid, as far as anyone can tell, a forbidding expanse of nothing? What is special about our pale blue anomaly of a world that makes it home to life?' (Brian Cox, *Wonders of Life*, 2013)

Challenge 1 (in pairs)

Spotters

Explain that children will be celebrating the uniqueness of their own outdoor area, in order to start to appreciate the diverse and unique nature of the Earth. They will observe the area through 'fresh eyes', as if it has just been created and is very new. Explain that the word 'genesis' means a 'start' or 'origin'.

1. Pairs walk around the outdoor learning area as if they are seeing it for the first time. They carefully explore until something catches their attention. This could be something big or small, a flash of colour, the shape of a group of plants or trees, something creating a new smell, a drip of sap, sunlight shining through a transparent leaf, a face-like shape in the bark of the tree, etc.
2. The 'spotter' says 'I can see something!'
3. Their partner asks 'What can you see?'
4. The spotter describes, in great detail, what they are looking at, giving the context too, e.g. 'I can see a split in a tree. In the split I can see golden sap oozing from under the bark like syrup.'
5. Their partner asks 'How does it make you feel? How do you think it got here?'
6. The spotter tries to explain how it made them feel when they spotted it. What has caused their reaction to seeing it? How is it making them feel now and why? They share their ideas about the 'genesis' of things.
7. Pairs continue to explore the area, taking it in turns to spot new or different things that catch their eye,

describing and explaining how they make them feel.

8. Make a collection of found objects to share with the class. A more structured version of this could be to have a 'scavenger hunt' list of items for the children to collect. Optional: these could be collected on the 'artists' palettes'.

Challenge 2 (in pairs)

Explore patterns and colours of nature

Pairs examine the found objects in minute detail, such as the structure of leaves, patterns on eggshells, the hidden colours in feathers, the delicate fibres in wool, the textures of seedpods and plants, etc. The purpose of this activity is to describe and celebrate in words the uniqueness of each item.

The children can take photographs of the items or draw them in their sketchbooks.

Challenge 3 (in pairs or groups of four)

Celebrate the uniqueness of the outdoor area

Using their own photographs, or using video recording, the children work in pairs or groups to develop a mini-documentary celebrating the uniqueness of their natural learning area.

They describe what can be seen using words of awe and wonder, as if the discovery was a new one, from a freshly created Earth.

PLENARY

Raise the question of our role as 'stewards', with a responsibility to treat the Earth with care and respect. What does religion teach us about our responsibilities to the Earth? For example, the Bible says that God put people in the Garden of Eden to take care of it; Buddhists try not to harm any living thing. Discuss how people feel responsible for the Earth outside of religion, e.g. caring for the environment is an important principle for many atheists.

Back in the classroom

Photos can be used to support artwork or reports. Videos can be edited using computing and form part of an assembly or interactive display.

EVALUATION/FOLLOW ON

- What went well and why?
- What didn't go as well as expected?
- What could be changed?
- Who stood out and why?

PREPARATION

Resources

- Devices with the ability to record video: as many as possible, up to one per pair
- Whiteboards (or paper and clipboards) and pens

Previous learning

Reflect on the activities from Progression 1 and the follow-up work that was done in the classroom.

CONSIDER

Health & Safety

Assess and evaluate hazards and risks in your setting. See the health and safety chapter.

LESSON OBJECTIVES

We are considering beliefs and the big questions they raise in relation to our stewardship of Earth's unique ecosystem.

Attainment targets

A: Appreciate and appraise the nature, significance and impact of different ways of life and ways of expressing meaning.

B: Express with increasing discernment their personal reflections and critical responses to questions and teachings about identity, diversity, meaning and value, including ethical issues.

C: Articulate beliefs, values and commitments clearly in order to explain why they may be important in their own and other people's lives.

ADULT ROLES

- Encourage the children to see the relevance and importance of the questions that are being asked and how they relate to them.
- Allow time for children to process the questions, reflect, gather information, clarify or verify using partner talk, and to draw conclusions, before asking them to give justified answers.

WARM UP IDEAS

Explain that today children will continue to explore the unique nature of the Earth's ecosystem, pointing out that an ecosystem can be as large as an ocean or as small as a muddy puddle. Everything in an ecosystem works together in balance, such as the plants, animals and weather interacting with one another.

Ask the children to come up with a list, itemising the minimum basic needs of all living things, agreeing on sunlight (as a source of energy and heat), water (the medium in which living cells work and as a habitat for some living things), food (nutrients for energy), temperature (not too hot or too cold) and air (oxygen and carbon dioxide), the purpose being to identify the unique qualities of Earth.

Did they know that the Earth is the only planet in our solar system where water is found in all three states: solid, liquid (it is the only planet where water is found in a liquid state) and gas?

Introductory activity

1. In pairs, the children explore the outdoor learning area, looking for any changes in the things they 'spotted' from the previous session and discussing possible reasons for these changes.
2. Look for evidence of the 'essentials for life' in the outdoor learning area, such as evidence of water from recent rainfall (pointing out that in a puddle they might find all sorts of living things that depend on the rainwater), the sunlight, and just the right temperature and nutrients for life to maintain an ecosystem.
3. Look for the effect of too much or a lack of water on plants, or for evidence of food for animals, birds and insects, linking to prior learning if possible.
4. Pairs report back to the class.

Beliefs and stewardship

As discussed in Progression 1, the principle that humans should care for the planet and protect the environment and wildlife is shared across many religions as well as people who are not religious.

Challenge 1 (groups of four)

Exploring the ecosystem

Groups explore the area again, this time looking for clues of lack of plant growth, litter, damage near the edges of paths, lack of care, death or destruction.

- Is there evidence that some creatures and plants are finding it challenging or hard to live?
- Is there abundant plant, bird and insect life? If not, why not?
- Are there areas where no plants are growing? Why might this be so, e.g. a lack of water or sunlight, or wear and tear from footfall?
- Are any plants looking undernourished, or broken/damaged?

Groups take photographs of the evidence and return to share their findings with the class.

Point out that although decomposition and decay are often seen as signs of death and as a 'negative', the decay of living things actually plays an essential part in the natural ecosystem. Every living thing dies and decomposition is nature's way of dealing with this in a way that recycles nutrients from one living thing to another, lower down the ecosystem. How is this reflected in the findings of the children?

Challenge 2 (groups of four)

Highlight the problems (or celebrate the good points) of the area

Groups plan a television-style broadcast, reporting on any successful aspects of the setting, or any damage or risks to the local ecosystems that have arisen through neglect or a lack of care or stewardship.

- How will it be produced?
- What key messages will be conveyed?
- What questions will be asked and to whom? Who will be chosen to ask or answer these questions?
- Will it link to a national or world picture?
- What remedial conservation work could be highlighted or put in place, such as the creation of an 'eco' or nature area, or replanting to attract insects and birds?
- What rules could be publicised to support the ecosystem of the school grounds?
- Which photographs will be used to 'zoom in' on, to support the text or script?

Each group produces a plan and a loose script on the whiteboards so that everyone knows what they are expected to do.

Challenge 3 (groups of four)

Practise 'takes' for the TV news broadcast

Groups start to record the documentary/broadcast, rehearsing and filming, reviewing, retaking and filming again. Some children could film the filming, to record the learning process for assembly, assessment or record of work.

PLENARY

Spend some time reviewing and sharing some of the draft broadcasts. Take comments on the pros and cons of what has been created from the 'producers' themselves. What top tips can they share?

Back in the classroom

Groups edit their films indoors during computing sessions.

EVALUATION/FOLLOW ON

- What went well and why?
- What didn't go as well as expected?
- What could be changed?
- Who stood out and why?

PREPARATION

Find a suitable area in the school grounds that provides evidence of pest damage, e.g. the growing area. Alternatively, provide damaged or partially eaten fruits and plants for the children to observe.

Resources

- Selection of pest-damaged fruits and plants from the area or sourced elsewhere
- Paper, clipboards and pencils
- Camera(s)

Previous learning

This extends any prior knowledge the children may have around expressing feelings and beliefs.

There are also links to art progressions.

CONSIDER

Health & Safety

Assess and evaluate hazards and risks in your setting. See the health and safety chapter.

LESSON OBJECTIVES

We are exploring how a person's beliefs impact on ethical issues, using a court case to make points for and against a viewpoint.

Attainment targets

A: Appreciate and appraise the nature, significance and impact of different ways of life and ways of expressing meaning.

B: Express with increasing discernment their personal reflections and critical responses to questions and teachings about identity, diversity, meaning and value, including ethical issues.

C: Articulate beliefs, values and commitments clearly in order to explain why they may be important in their own and other people's lives.

ADULT ROLES

- Allow time for children to process the questions, to reflect, gather information, clarify or verify using partner talk, and to draw conclusions, before asking them to give justified answers.
- Provide prompts to develop powerful imagery, extended sentences and adverbial phrases.

WARM UP IDEAS

Explain that children will be exploring how a person's viewpoints and beliefs affect how they approach perceived problems. Revise the point that many people believe that we have a responsibility to care for the Earth, regardless of their religious or non-religious beliefs. But how is this applied in the school setting? What is or is not being done to protect the local ecosystem from harm and threats?

Introductory activity

Use the 'Spotters' activity from Progression 1.

1. Pairs walk around the outdoor learning area, looking for changes since their last visit and checking for any evidence of the effects of pests or damage.

2. They explore carefully until something catches their attention. This could be evidence of snail damage, holes in fruits and leaves, spots on leaves or changes in the colour and texture of leaves, or nut cases or egg shells that have broken open.

3. The spotter says 'I can see something!'

4. Their partner asks 'What can you see?'

5. The spotter describes what they are looking at.

6. Their partner asks 'How do you think it happened? How does it make you feel?'

7. The spotter tries to explain how they feel about what they have found, e.g. perhaps asking whether a snail eating the fruit is a positive or a negative thing.

8. Pairs continue to explore the area, taking it in turns to spot new or different evidence of pests, describing it and explaining how it makes them feel.

9. Pairs make a collection of objects or take photographs to share with the class.

Ethics and beliefs

Challenge 1 (whole class)

Identify and describe our feelings

In order to provide the opportunity to express their feelings or beliefs, encourage the children to reflect on how they felt during the introductory activity. How did the evidence of damage/pests make them feel? Ask the children to name and identify some feelings that they may have experienced during the introductory activity. Can they classify them in some way? Were they 'big feelings' or 'small feelings'? Were they 'hot' or 'cold' feelings, etc.?

Challenge 2 (groups of four)

Gather evidence to present a case for lack of stewardship

Working in different roles within groups, the children become 'nature police detectives', gathering evidence and proof of perceived damage to the local area caused by living creatures, which will be used in court to 'prosecute' a suggested offender.

1. Groups plan a 'court scene', with detectives gathering and providing evidence to enable a case to be brought against someone or something 'accused' of damaging or causing harm to the outdoor area, contravening religious beliefs or neglecting stewardship responsibilities.

2. The prosecution evidence will depend on the findings from the 'Spotters' activity, but could include damage through neglect or a lack of care or stewardship, or even insect damage, such as snails, and slugs eating fruit or plants in the growing area.

3. There also needs to be a 'defence' case, with supporting evidence and facts.

   - What questions will be asked and to whom? Who will ask or answer these questions?

   - What rules or measures could be introduced to prevent repeat offending, e.g. in the case

of animal damage, the provision of special accessible nutritional areas whilst protecting other valuable fruits and vegetables using netting, etc.?

   - Would it be right to use pesticides? The defence could argue the case against this on the grounds of pesticides' impact on the ecosystem, or this could lead to research into the use of natural repellents, such as hot pepper, onion, mint, soap or beer.

   - What key messages will be conveyed? Is there going to be an outcome or an agreement?

   - Which photographs will be used to support each side? Or will there be a courtroom artist recording the event, linking to art?

   - Produce a plan and a loose script on the whiteboards so that everyone knows what they are expected to do.

In order to provide a knowledge-based argument, this challenge could be supported by in-depth research on the role of snails, slugs, ants or other perceived 'pests', together with other insects seen as having 'positive' effects, such as pollinators, etc., in the ecosystem. It could also include an investigation into farming practices, including the use of pesticides and the inadvertent impact that this is having on nature's processes, such as the decline in the number of the bees, effect on climate change, etc. This could be done in the classroom using computers or on the move with tablets, in order to compile evidence dossiers for the prosecution or defence.

Challenge 3 (groups of four)

Act out the court scene

Following the gathering of research and information, groups act out the court scenes. As the court process takes place, further questions may be raised, leading to an 'adjournment' whilst further information is gathered in order to support the argument.

Spend some time reviewing and sharing some of the arguments and counter-arguments raised and the impact of 'pests' in the ecosystem. Raise the possibility that we humans may be 'pests'. Ask groups to explain their beliefs, values and commitments. How easy or hard is it to communicate beliefs and ideas?

Make links to having strong beliefs and living by shared values.

Back in the classroom

The groups could compile a dossier of the court case for display or research different religions' viewpoints and beliefs around looking after the Earth.

- What went well and why?
- What didn't go as well as expected?
- What could be changed?

PREPARATION

Resources

- Colour shade cards (available online)
- Materials of your choice for pattern-making, such as chalks or water-based paints
- Selection of images of Kolam patterns
- Colourful images of the Earth from space

Previous learning

This offers the opportunity to practise maths (symmetry).

CONSIDER

Health & Safety

Assess and evaluate hazards and risks in your setting. See the health and safety chapter.

LESSON OBJECTIVES

We are learning how colour is celebrated in religion.

Attainment targets

A: Appreciate and appraise the nature, significance and impact of different ways of life and ways of expressing meaning.

B: Express with increasing discernment their personal reflections and critical responses to questions and teachings about identity, diversity, meaning and value, including ethical issues.

C: Articulate beliefs, values and commitments clearly in order to explain why they may be important in their own and other people's lives.

ADULT ROLES

- Model the activity, acknowledging challenges and sharing possible solutions.
- Allow time for children to process the questions, reflect, gather information, clarify or verify using partner talk, and to draw conclusions, before asking them to give justified answers.

WARM UP IDEAS

Explain that in this session children will be exploring viewpoints and beliefs relating to the stewardship of, in the words of Brian Cox, 'our unique and colourful world' (*Forces of Nature*, 2016), asking the children to discuss with a partner what this might possibly mean. Why is our planet called the 'blue planet'? (Link to Progressions 1 and 2.) What is unique about our world? Why might colour be considered special and what do the colours represent scientifically? The science link between light and colour is covered in the National Curriculum at Year 6, but could be briefly explained here.

Show the children aerial images or photographs taken by satellite of the Earth, such as those by Bernhard Edmaier, asking the children to explain to a partner how the photographs make them feel.

Introductory activity

What colours can the children see around them? Discuss how this will vary according to the seasons and consider what causes the colour changes, i.e. changes in the length of daylight, changes in temperature, etc.

Pairs explore the colours they see around them in the outdoor learning area, matching these colours to the colour shade cards, or simply matching them to the clothing, eye and hair colours of a partner.

Pairs share their findings and describe what they have found to the rest of the class. How do they feel about finding such a range of colours, and scientifically what do the colours mean? Emotionally or symbolically, what could their findings represent?

MAIN ACTIVITIES

Colour and Hindu beliefs

Ask the children what they can remember about how colour is used by religions to communicate beliefs. What does this tell us about identity and diversity?

What do the children already know about Hindu beliefs and customs?

Explain that in the autumn, Hindus celebrate the end of one season and the start of the next with a festival. The Onam festival, also known as the festival of 'rain flowers', celebrates the end of the monsoon season and welcomes the harvest season. The festival is filled with colour, including carnival floats and decorated elephants taking part in street parades, and the creation of colourful artworks called Kolam (known as Rangoli in the north of India), which are geometric, colourful designs and patterns drawn on the ground.

In line with the Hindu belief in generosity, the designs were originally drawn in rice flour or grains so that they could provide food for ants, birds or other small creatures. Nowadays, coloured sand, ground-up chalk, pasta, flower petals, leaves and Rangoli powder are also used.

Share some images of Kolam designs, linking to maths and other religions to describe and discuss the use of symmetry and symbolism (often relating to plants, animals and birds).

Challenge 1 (whole class and in pairs or groups of four)

Create your own celebration of nature

Explain that the children will now have the chance to create their own artwork to celebrate nature, using materials of their choice, such as chalk, water-based paints and / or natural objects. Discuss how they could use symbols, e.g. using plants and animals to express beliefs such as celebrating the uniqueness of life on Earth. This could link to maths by demonstrating how symmetry can be created with a mirror line(s) crossing two or four quadrants, or link to art using stencils to repeat elements of patterns.

1. Give the children a few ideas of materials and designs they could use.

2. Pairs or groups discuss and plan their artwork, including how they will use symbols.
3. They then make their own artwork. Suggest that they discuss during the process if their design needs to change.

Alternatives include decorating a pebble or small stone with a pattern using marker pens, or creating a large flag or banner symbolising the group's belief or celebrating the beauty or uniqueness of plants in the area. Another suggestion is to create a design to plant seeds or real flowers in the growing area in the style often used by local councils in public areas, grouping plants together to create symmetrical and colourful designs.

PLENARY

How easy is it to express or celebrate a belief or a feeling such as gratitude, so that others can understand? Children share personal reflections with a partner, or in small groups, on how celebrations using colour can explain identity, diversity, meanings and values.

In the spring, in line with your local SACRE guidance, consider another Hindu celebration called Holi, which celebrates fertility, colour, love and the triumph of good over evil. It marks the arrival of spring and is known as the festival of colour, where coloured pigments are thrown into the air.

Consider and compare the words of Christian hymns and songs about the celebration of colour, such as 'Who put the colours in the rainbow?', and question whether these effectively communicate the unique place of colour in our world.

Back in the classroom

Use photos of example Kolam / Rangoli images in computing, adding speech bubbles and caption boxes to explain the purpose of the patterns.

EVALUATION/FOLLOW ON

- What went well and why?
- What didn't go as well as expected?
- What could be changed?
- Who stood out and why?

PREPARATION

Groups of children research the relationship between food and religion and bring their findings to the session (see main activities).

Resources

- Fact sheets (food and religions)
- Cooking ingredients and equipment (see Challenge 1)
- Fire-lighting kit (see the health and safety chapter)
- Additional adults as required
- Water to extinguish the fire

CONSIDER

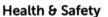

Health & Safety

Assess and evaluate hazards and risks in your setting. See the health and safety chapter.

LESSON OBJECTIVES

We are learning how food can be used to express faith identity and values, including ethical issues.

Attainment targets

A: Appreciate and appraise the nature, significance and impact of different ways of life and ways of expressing meaning.

B: Express with increasing discernment their personal reflections and critical responses to questions and teachings about identity, diversity, meaning and value, including ethical issues.

C: Articulate beliefs, values and commitments clearly in order to explain why they may be important in their own and other people's lives.

ADULT ROLES

- Allow time for children to process the questions, reflect, gather information, clarify or verify using partner talk, and to draw conclusions, before asking them to give justified answers.
- Model the activity, acknowledging challenges and sharing possible solutions.
- Ensure everyone's safety during the cooking process.

WARM UP IDEAS

Explain that children will continue to consider the unique nature of Earth's ecosystem and how it impacts on religious beliefs. Revise the minimum basic needs of all living things, i.e. sunlight, water, food, temperature and air. Explain that today children will focus on the need for food and nutrients and how this is celebrated in faith beliefs.

Introductory activity

Explain that as well as providing essential sustenance, food – or the process of eating – often demonstrates different beliefs and worldviews, providing a sense of cultural identity and impacting on diet, e.g. by people taking a moral stance on the killing of living things for food, by making people feel like they are welcomed or 'belong', or by using food for celebrations.

What celebrations do the children know of where food, or a lack of food, is important? E.g. birthday parties, Christmas, Lent, Easter, Shrove Tuesday, Ramadan, Eid, Diwali, Rosh Hashanah and Hanukkah?

Ask for personal accounts from the children, since religious faiths and experiences will vary according to each setting, providing an opportunity to explore and share knowledge and promote understanding.

Faith and food

Before the session, the children may have researched the relationship between food and religion, and how ethical beliefs can impact on diet. Use this information or present each group with fact sheets about food and religion. The facts could include:

- Many Buddhists try to avoid intentionally killing, or harming any living thing, and for this reason many are vegetarians.

- Muslims try to only eat meat if it is halal, which translates from Arabic as 'permitted'. They do not eat pork. During the month-long fast of Ramadan (when the Qu'ran was first revealed to Muhammed), most Muslims do not eat during daylight hours. Eid (the breaking of the fast) might feature celebration foods such as spicy dishes and sweet food and drinks such as date-filled pastries and honeyed milk.

- Hindus are often vegetarian, being reluctant to kill any living creature. During Diwali (the celebration of new beginnings), also known as the festival of lights, special foods are eaten, including special sweets (Mithai) and vegetarian curries.

- Some Jews do not eat shellfish, or eat meat and dairy at the same time. They do not eat pork and only eat kosher meat, which, like Muslim halal meat, has been killed in a specific way. They have 'fast days' and celebrations, including Rosh Hashanah (birthday of the universe), Yom Kippur (a day of atonement), Sukkot (a harvest celebration) and Passover (celebrating liberation of Jews from slavery in Egypt).

- Some Christians believe bread represents the body of Jesus Christ and wine represents his blood. Some Christians therefore have a small portion of each during church services.

Challenge 1 (whole class and groups of four to six)

How can we celebrate using food?

In this challenge, children will prepare pancakes and think about how different religions can influence culture or traditions in a country.

Ingredients: ½ cup of flour; 1 teaspoon of baking powder; 2 eggs; 2/3 cup of milk; cooking oil; maple syrup, honey, or another topping.

Recipe: Mix the dry ingredients in a bowl, then make a well in the centre and pour in the milk and eggs. Mix or whisk until the batter is smooth. Cook the pancakes on a lightly oiled frying pan over the fire.

The children should cook outdoors in a food-preparation area. See the health and safety chapter for details on how to safely light, maintain and extinguish fires, in accordance with your setting's policies and procedures. Make sure you have the right child/adult ratio for this activity and follow the Food Standards Agency's guidelines.

After making the pancakes, ask the children if anyone knows how pancakes are linked to Christianity. Explain that 'Pancake Day', or Shrove Tuesday is the day before the start of Lent – the 40 days leading up to Easter. Lent was traditionally a time of fasting, so Shrove Tuesday was an opportunity for people to use up eggs and fats before starting to fast. Pancakes are a good way to use up these ingredients.

Explain that nowadays pancakes are not especially linked to Christianity and they can be made by anyone at any time of year. Can the children think of any other examples of foods which have a link to a religious tradition or festival but that can be eaten by anyone at any time? Can anyone give an example using another religion where certain foods are associated with fasting? For example, dates eaten by Muslims before breaking a fast during Ramadan.

PLENARY

Share the food that has been produced and reflect on how celebrations using food can explain identity, diversity, meanings and values.

EVALUATION/FOLLOW ON

- What went well and why?
- What didn't go as well as expected?
- What could be changed?
- Who stood out and why?

PREPARATION

Resources

- Seeds and nuts identification sheet, available to download from the Woodland Trust's website
- Enough of the ingredients and equipment listed in Challenge 1 as needed for your class
- Fire-lighting kit (see the health and safety chapter)
- Water to extinguish the fire
- Pictures of a wheat sheaf or wheat heads
- Additional adults as required
- Camera

CONSIDER

Health & Safety

Assess and evaluate hazards and risks in your setting. See the health and safety chapter.

LESSON OBJECTIVES

We are learning how religious celebrations of harvest express meaning and gratitude.

Attainment targets

A: Appreciate and appraise the nature, significance and impact of different ways of life and ways of expressing meaning.

B: Express with increasing discernment their personal reflections and critical responses to questions and teachings about identity, diversity, meaning and value, including ethical issues.

C: Articulate beliefs, values and commitments clearly in order to explain why they may be important in their own and other people's lives.

ADULT ROLES

- Allow time for children to process the questions, to reflect, gather information, clarify or verify using partner talk, and to draw conclusions, before asking them to give justified answers.
- Model the activity, acknowledging challenges and sharing possible solutions.
- Ensure everyone's safety during the cooking process.

WARM UP IDEAS

Explain that children will continue to consider the unique nature of Earth's ecosystem and how the celebration of harvest expresses meaning and gratitude in many religions.

Explain that many cultures or religions have celebrations around the end of the harvest. Ask the children what experiences they have had of harvest celebrations, if any. Mention examples such as the Jewish festival of Sukkot or the fact that many Christians in Britain celebrate harvest festival.

Explain that a harvest does not have to mean the crops grown on a farm. Do any of the children go foraging for blackberries, elderberries, raspberries, wild strawberries or hazel or beechnuts, or pick fruit and flowers to use for cooking?

Introductory activity (whole class and groups of five to six)

Explain that they will be hunting for seeds and fruits in the learning area.

1. Hand out the nuts and seeds identification sheet and ask the children to identify the different plants, looking for familiar and unfamiliar items.
2. Using the guide, ask pairs to find or identify as many examples as they can in the learning area and school setting, telling them not to pick (harvest) the seeds and berries.
3. Emphasise that not all berries are edible, e.g. holly berries.

Alternatively, provide a selection of these items for the children to sample.

Harvest meanings

Show the pictures of a wheat sheaf / grains to demonstrate the origin of wheat flour.

In England up until the split from the Catholic Church in 1532, loaves of bread made from the recently harvested crop were given to the local church. This was used during services as communion bread.

This is sometimes still remembered by creating a harvest wheat sheaf, which is dough formed to look like a sheaf of wheat. This often forms the centrepiece of a harvest display.

Challenge 1 (whole class, groups of five to six)

Cook damper bread on fires

Explain that the children will be making their own versions of a harvest wheat sheaf using damper bread and cooking this on the campfire. The purpose will be to reflect the value of expressing gratitude for the harvest.

Model the activity below before the children light their own fires, mix their own damper bread dough and cook it on the fire.

Light and maintain the fires as recommended in the health and safety chapter of this book.

For each group of five to six children, provide:

- A bowl and spoon
- 250 g self-raising flour
- 100 ml water
- 40 g caster sugar
- Chocolate spread or jam
- A foil-covered stick or stick with bark removed.

1. Mix the flour and sugar in a bowl.
2. Gradually add the water, mixing after each addition, kneading the mixture into a soft dough.
3. Divide the dough into five or six equal-sized pieces (one for each child).
4. Create long, thin 'sausages' of the dough by rolling it between your hands.
5. Wrap it in a spiral around the stick.
6. Hold the stick over the heat, turning it regularly and checking for burning.
7. After about ten minutes, it should become light brown and hard to the touch.
8. The bread can be eaten on the stick, spreading it with syrup, honey, butter, jam or chocolate spread. Alternatively, slide the damper bread off the stick and fill the centre with chocolate spread or jam.

For a savoury version, substitute the sugar for a pinch of salt, and add some grated cheese or a touch of butter, garlic and herbs.

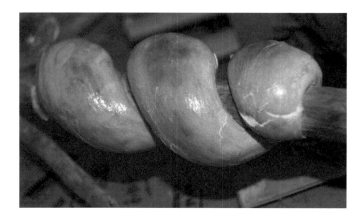

PLENARY

Reflect on how celebrations using food can explain identity, diversity, meanings and values. How do they reflect gratitude?

Children devise careful explanations of what they have been doing and why they have been doing this in the sessions, and share these with a partner or in small groups.

EVALUATION/FOLLOW ON

- What went well and why?
- What didn't go as well as expected?
- What could be changed?
- Who stood out and why?

Key resources for Year 5 progressions

Cox, B. & Cohen, A. (2016) *Forces of Nature*. London: Harper Collins.

Cox, B. &Cohen, A. (2013) *Wonders of Life*. London: Harper Collins.

Food – a fact of life (FFL) Available online at: https://www.foodafactoflife.org.uk/.

Grindley, S. (2001) *Peter's Place*. London: Andersen Press Ltd.

Public Health England (PHE) (2015) Food teaching in primary schools: a framework of knowledge and skills. Available online at: https://www.nutrition.org.uk/attachments/article/869/Food%20teaching%20in%20primary%20schools.pdf.

Public Health England (PHE) (2016) The Eatwell Guide. Available online at: https://assets.publishing.service.gov.uk/government/uploads/system/uploads/attachment_data/file/742750/Eatwell_Guide_booklet_2018v4.pdf.

Bibliography

Araneda, D., Guzmán, M.A. & Nussbaum, M. (2019) The national curriculum vs. the ideal curriculum: acknowledging student learning interests, *Oxford Review of Education*, 45 (3), 333-349.

Aronsson, J., Waite, S. & Tighe Clark, M. (2015) Measuring the impact of outdoor learning on the physical activity of school age children: The use of accelerometry. *Education and Health*, 33 (3). Available online at: http://sheu.org.uk/sheux/EH/eh333ja.pdf.

Atjonen, P. (2014) Teachers' views of their assessment practice. *The Curriculum Journal*, 25 (2), 238-259.

Ball, D., Gill, T. & Spiegal, B. (2008) Managing Risk in Play Provision: Implementation guide. Nottingham, England: National Children's Bureau and Play England. Available online at: http://www.playengland.org.uk/media/172644/managing-risk-in-play-provision.pdf

Bølling, M., Otte, C., Elsborg, P., Nielson, G. & Bentsen, P. (2018) The association between education outside the classroom and students' school motivation: Results from a one-school-year quasi-experiment. *International Journal of Educational Research*. 89, 22-35.

Bourn, D., Hunt, F., Blum, N. & Lawson, H. (2016) Primary education for global learning and sustainability. Report for Cambridge Primary Review. Available online at: https://cprtrust.org.uk/wp-content/uploads/2016/02/Bourn-report-160217-final.pdf.

British Orienteering (no date) Tri-O: Orienteering made easy. Available online at: www.britishorienteering.org.uk/images/uploaded/downloads/schools_tri_o_resources.pdf.

Cain, J. & Smith, T. (2007) *The Revised and Expanded Book of Raccoon Circles*. Dubuque, Iowa: Kendall Hunt publishing.

Cornell, J. (1999) *Sharing Nature with Children*. Nevada City: Dawn Publications.

Cornwall Agreed Syllabus for Religious Education (2014). Available online at: https://www.cornwall.gov.uk/media/9227047/Agreed-syllabus-2014.pdf.

Danks, F. & Schofield, J. (2010) *Make it Wild!: 101 Things to Make and Do Outdoors*. London: Frances Lincoln Publishers Ltd.

Department for Children, Schools and Families (DCSF) (2010) Religious education in English schools: Non-statutory guidance. Available online at: https://assets.publishing.service.gov.uk/government/uploads/system/uploads/attachment_data/file/190260/DCSF-00114-2010.pdf.

Department for Education (DfE) (2014) National Curriculum in England: Framework for Key Stages 1 to 4. Available online at: www.gov.uk/government/collections/national-curriculum.

Department for Education (DfE) (2018a) Health and safety: responsibilities and duties for schools. Available online at: https://www.gov.uk/government/publications/health-and-safety-advice-for-schools/responsibilities-and-duties-for-schools.

Department for Education (DfE) (2018b) Mental health and behaviour in schools. Available online at: https://assets.publishing.service.gov.uk/government/uploads/system/uploads/attachment_data/file/755135/Mental_health_and_behaviour_in_schools__.pdf.

Department for Environment, Food and Rural Affairs (DEFRA) (2018) A Green Future: Our 25 Year Plan to Improve the Environment. Available online at: https://assets.publishing.service.gov.uk/government/uploads/system/uploads/attachment_data/file/693158/25-year-environment-plan.pdf.

Department of Health and Social Care (DHSC) (2018) Prevention is better than cure: Our vision to help you live well for longer. Available online at: https://assets.publishing.service.gov.uk/government/uploads/system/uploads/attachment_data/file/753688/Prevention_is_better_than_cure_5-11.pdf.

Dweck, C. (2007) *Mindset: The new psychology of success*. New York: Ballantine Books.

Educational Endowment Foundation (2018) Metacognition and Self-regulated Learning. Available online at: https://educationendowmentfoundation.org.uk/tools/guidance-reports/metacognition-and-self-regulated-learning.

Edwards-Jones, A., Waite, S. & Passy, R. (2018) Falling into LINE: School strategies for overcoming challenges associated with learning in natural environments (LINE), *Education 3–13*, 46 (1), 49–63.

Garrick, R. (2009) *Playing Outdoors in the Early Years*. London: Continuum.

Gill, T. (2016) Balancing Benefits and Risks in Outdoor Learning and Play. Available online at: https://outdoorclassroomday.org.uk/wp-content/uploads/sites/2/2016/06/160606_PROJECTDIRT_ECD_BOOK7_A4-1.pdf.

Green, M. & Somerville, M. (2015) Sustainability education: Researching practice in primary schools, *Environmental Education Research*, 21 (6), 832–845.

Hammett, E. (2016) Fulfilling the first aid requirements in schools. *British Journal of School Nursing*, 11 (7), 1–4. Available online at: https://firstaidforlife.org.uk/wp-content/uploads/2017/03/BJSN-Schools-First-Aid-Sept-2016-2.pdf

Hawe, E. & Parr, J. (2014). Assessment for Learning in the writing classroom: an incomplete realisation. *The Curriculum Journal*, 25 (2), 210–237.

Health and Safety Executive (HSE) (2018) How do the Health and Safety (First-Aid) Regulations 1981 relate to first-aid provision in schools? Available online at: www.hse.gov.uk/firstaid

Ho, S. (2014) The purposes outdoor education does, could and should serve in Singapore. *Journal of Adventure Education and Outdoor Learning*, 14 (2), 153–171.

Hopper, R. (2017) Special educational needs and disability and learning outside the classroom. In: Waite, S. (ed.) *Children Learning Outside the Classroom: From Birth to Eleven (2nd edition)*. London: SAGE, pp. 118–130.

Hunt, A., Stewart, D., Richardson, M., Hinds J., Bragg, R., White, M. & Burt, J. (2017) Monitor of Engagement with the Natural Environment: developing a method to measure nature connection across the English population (adults and children). Natural England Commissioned Reports, Number 233. York: Natural England.

Institute for Outdoor Learning (2018) Teaching outdoors. Available online at: www.outdoor-learning.org/Good-Practice/Develop-your-Organisation/Outdoor-Learning-in-Schools/Teaching-Outdoors.

Lambert, D. (2014) *Taking Maths Outdoors with Raccoon Circles*. Available from Taking Maths Outdoors Facebook page.

Council for Learning Outside the Classroom (CLOtC) (2018) Get ready – managing risk. Available online at: www.lotc.org.uk/plan-deliver-lotc/planning-lotc-experiences/get-ready-managing-risk.

Malone, K. & Waite, S. (2016) Student Outcomes and Natural Schooling: Pathways from Evidence to Impact Report 2016. Available online at: https://www.plymouth.ac.uk/uploads/production/document/path/6/6811/Student_outcomes_and__natural_schooling_pathways_to_impact_2016.pdf.

Maynard, T., Waters, J. & Clement, J. (2013). Moving outdoors: further explorations of 'child- initiated' learning in the outdoor environment. Education 3–13, 41 (3), 282–299.

Morgan, A. & Waite, S. (2017) Nestling into the world: The importance of place and mutuality in the early years. In: V. Huggins and D. Evans (eds.), *Early Childhood Education and Care for Sustainability*, TACTYC series. Abingdon: Routledge, pp. 51–66.

National Health Service (England) (2018) New mental health support in schools and colleges and faster access to NHS care. Available online at: https://www.england.nhs.uk/mental-health/cyp/trailblazers/.

Natural England (2013) Learning together: Schools and the natural environment sector. Available online at: publications.naturalengland.org.uk/file/4781669567430656.

Ofsted (2013) Religious Education: realising the potential. Available online at: https://assets.publishing.service.gov.uk/government/uploads/system/uploads/attachment_data/file/413157/Religious_education_-_realising_the_potential.pdf.

Ofsted (2018) An investigation into how to assess the quality of education through curriculum intent, implementation and impact: Phase 3 findings of curriculum research. Available online at: https://assets.publishing.service.gov.uk/government/uploads/system/uploads/attachment_data/file/766252/How_to_assess_intent_and_implementation_of_curriculum_191218.pdf.

OnePoll (2018) Survey for Decathlon. Available online at: www.dailymail.co.uk/sciencetech/article-5985661/Average-child-spends-just-7-hours-WEEK-outside-twice-playing-video-games.html.

Opie, M., Ansell, K. & Goto, E. (2017) Technology and its role outside the classroom. In: Waite, S. (ed.) *Children Learning Outside the Classroom: From birth to eleven. (2nd edition).* London: SAGE, pp. 106–117.

Outdoor and Woodland Learning Scotland (2017) Tool Use guidance. Available online at: https://www.owlscotland.org/resources/resource-library/tool-use-guidance.

Paniagua, A. & Istance, D. (2018) Teachers as Designers of Learning Environments: The Importance of Innovative Pedagogies. Paris: Educational Research and Innovation, OECD Publishing. Available online at: https://doi.org/10.1787/9789264085374-en.

Porter, H. (2018) *Educating Outside: Curriculum-linked outdoor learning ideas for primary teachers.* London: Bloomsbury.

Public Health England (2014a) Improving access to green spaces. Health Equity Briefing 8. London: PHE.

Public Health England (2014b) The link between pupil health and wellbeing and attainment. A briefing for head teachers, governors and staff in education settings. London: PHE.

Religious Education Council of England and Wales (REC) (2013) A Curriculum Framework for Religious Education in England. Available online at: https://www.religiouseducationcouncil.org.uk/wp-content/uploads/2017/09/RE_Review_Summary.pdf.

Robb, M., Mew, V. & Richardson, A. (2015) *Learning with Nature.* Cambridge: Green Books.

Robertson, J. (2014) *Dirty Teaching: A Beginner's Guide to Learning Outdoors.* Carmarthen: Independent Thinking Press.

Rowe, S. & Humphries, S. (2012) *The Coombes Approach: Learning through an Experiential and Outdoor Curriculum.* London: Continuum.

Schofield, J. & Danks, F. (2009) *Go Wild!* London: Frances Lincoln Publishers Ltd.

Schofield, J. & Danks, F. (2012) *The Stick Book.* London: Frances Lincoln Publishers Ltd.

Training and Development Agency for Schools (TDA) (2009) Including children with SEN and/or disabilities in primary physical education. Available online at: https://dera.ioe.ac.uk/13804/1/physicaleducationpe.pdf.

Tuke-Hastings, T., Shireen, N., Gupta, S. & Knight, J. (2011) *Cool Camping Cookbook.* Berlin: Haffmans and Tolkemitt.

Waite, S. (2010) Losing our way? The downward path for outdoor learning for children aged 2–11 years. *Journal of Adventure Education and Outdoor Learning*, 10 (2), 111–126.

Waite (2013) 'Knowing your place in the world': how place and culture support and obstruct educational aims. *Cambridge Journal of Education*, 43 (4), 413-434.

Waite, S., Davis, B. & Brown, K. (2006) *Five Stories of Outdoor Learning from Settings for 2–11 year olds in Devon.* Plymouth: University of Plymouth.

Waite, S., Passy, R., Gilchrist, M., Hunt, A. & Blackwell, I. (2016) Natural Connections Demonstration Project 2012–2016: Final report. Natural England Commissioned report NECR215. Available online at: http://publications.naturalengland.org.uk/publication/6636651036540928.

Waite, S., Passy, R. & Gilchrist, M. (2014) Getting it off PAT: researching the use of urban nature in schools. In: E. Backman, B. Humberstone & C. Loynes (2014) *Urban nature: inclusive learning through youth work and school work.* European Outdoor Education Network, Stockholm: Recito Forlag, pp. 35-49.

Waite, S., Rutter, O., Fowle, A. & Edwards-Jones, A. (2017) Diverse aims, challenges and opportunities for assessing outdoor learning: a critical examination of three cases from practice. *Education 3-13: International Journal of Primary, Elementary and Early Years Education*, 45 (1), 51–67.

Waite, S., Wickett, K. & Huggins, V. (2014) Risky outdoor play: Embracing uncertainty in pursuit of learning. In: T. Maynard and J. Waters (eds.) *Exploring Outdoor Play in the Early Years.* London: Open University Press, pp. 71–85.

Weiner, B. (1986). *An Attributional Theory of Motivation and Emotion.* New York: Springer-Verlag.

Wild Tribe Outdoor Learning programme (2019) Available online at: https://www.arena-schools.co.uk/wild-tribe.

Wood, C., Bragg, R. & Pretty, J. (2016) The benefits of green exercise for children. In: J. Barton, R. Bragg, C. Wood & J. Pretty (eds.) *Green Exercise: Linking Nature, Health and Well-being.* London: Routledge, pp. 46–52.

Woodland Trust Scotland (no date) Outdoor learning pack. Available online at: https://www.woodlandtrust.org.uk/media/43645/outdoor-learning-resource-pack.pdf.

Wright, N., Waite, S., Graham, L., Aronsson, J. & Waite, R. (2016) *Creating Happy and Healthy Schools through Outdoor Learning.* Plymouth: University of Plymouth. Hard copies available on request or online at: www.plymouth.ac.uk/research/peninsula-research-in-outdoor-learning/resources.

York Consulting (2015) Final evaluation of Learning Away: full report. Available online at: https://www.phf.org.uk/publications/learning-away-final-evaluation-full-report/. See also: https://learningaway.org.uk.

Bird identification sheet – Identification des oiseaux

Add your own images below	Français	English	Tally
	Le merle	Blackbird	
	Le pinson	Chaffinch	
	L'hirondelle (f)	Swallow	
	Le muguet	Thrush	
	Le moineau	Sparrow	
	Le pigeon	Pigeon	
	Le rouge-gorge	Robin	
	Le corbeau	Crow	
	Le martinet	Swift	
	Le pivert	Woodpecker	
	La mouette	Seagull	